URBAN DEVELOPMENT AND CIVIL SOCIETY

Urban development and Civil society

The Role of Communities in Sustainable Cities

Edited by

Michael Carley,
Paul Jenkins and
Harry Smith

Earthscan Publications Ltd, London and Sterling, VA

First published in the UK and USA in 2001 by
Earthscan Publications Ltd

ISBN: 1 85383 717 2 paperback
        1 85383 718 0 hardback

Typesetting by PCS Mapping & DTP, Newcastle upon Tyne
Printed and bound by Creative Print and Design Wales
Cover design by Susanne Harris

For a full list of publications please contact:
Earthscan Publications Ltd
120 Pentonville Road
London, N1 9JN, UK
Tel: +44 (0)20 7278 0433
Fax: +44 (0)20 7278 1142
Email: earthinfo@earthscan.co.uk
http://www.earthscan.co.uk

22883 Quicksilver Drive, Sterling, VA 20166–2012, USA

Earthscan is an editorially independent subsidiary of Kogan Page Ltd and publishes in
association with WWF-UK and the International Institute for Environment and
Development

A catalogue record for this book is available from the British Library

Library of Congress Cataloging-in-Publication Data

Urban development and civil society : the role of communities in sustainable
cities / edited by Michael Carley, Paul Jenkins, and Harry Smith.
        p. cm.
    Includes bibliographical references and index.
    ISBN 1-85383-718-0 (hardcover) — ISBN 1-85383-717-2 (pbk.)
        1. Community development, Urban. 2. City planning—Citizen participation.
    3. Sustainable development. I. Carley, Michael. II. Jenkins, Paul, 1953- III. Smith,
Harry, 1963-

HT166 .U726 2001
307.1'416—dc21   00-067276

This book is printed on elemental chlorine-free paper

CONTENTS

PART 1 INTRODUCTION: THE CHALLENGE OF A SUSTAINABLE URBAN FUTURE – THE ROLE OF INSTITUTIONS

PART 2 CASE STUDIES: LESSONS FROM INTERNATIONAL EXPERIENCE IN KEY URBAN DEVELOPMENT ISSUES

PART 3 ANALYSIS AND CONCLUSIONS: STRENGTHENING THE CHANGING ROLE OF CIVIL SOCIETY

ACRONYMS AND ABBREVIATIONS

AMDU	Mozambican Association for Urban Development
ANC	African National Congress
BIT	Building Information and Training
BLISS	Bagong Lipunan Improvement of Sites and Services
BPD	People's Development Bank
CAHAC	Cape Areas Housing Action Committee
CAST	Civic Associations of the Southern Transvaal
CAYCO	Cape Youth Congress
CBD	central business district
CBO	community-based organization
CCP	Chinese Communist Party
CCTV	closed circuit television
CEHS	Centre for Environment and Human Settlements (Edinburgh)
COPAN	National Patriotic Committee
COSATU	Council of South African Trade Unions
CPSA	Communist Party of South Africa
Danida	Danish International Development Assistance
DCU	Construction and Urbanization Directorate
DILG	Department of Interior and Local Government
DNH	National Housing Directorate
EIA	environmental impact assessment
EPDP	Environment Protection Department Punjab
ETPI	Environmental Technology Programme for Industry
FCV	Costa Rican Housing Front
FDV	Democratic Housing Front
FNV	National Housing Front
FPCCI	Federation of Pakistani Chambers of Commerce and Industry
FRELIMO	Mozambique Liberation Front
FRHS	Forum of Researchers on Human Settlements
FUTS	Faisalabad Urban Transport Society
GD	Grupos Dinamizadores
GDP	gross domestic product
GNP	gross national product
GUHRM	Maputo Regional Housing and Urbanization Department
HDI	Human Development Index
IIED	International Institute for Environment and Development

IMF	International Monetary Fund
IRA	internal revenue allotment
ISO	International Organization for Standardization
IT	information technology
LDCs	less developed countries
LTS	Lahore Transport System
MIDEPLAN	Ministry of National Planning and Economic Policy
MMDA	Metro Manila Development Authority
MVE	Motor Vehicle Examiner
N-AERUS	Network-Association of European Researchers on Urbanization in the South
NAFTA	North American Free Trade Agreement
NGO	non-governmental organization
NIC	newly industrializing country
NIE	new institutional economics
NSO	National Statistics Office
OECD	Organization for Economic Cooperation and Development
PAC	Pan-African Congress
PACD	Presidential Assistant on Community Development
PLN	National Liberation Party
PRC	People's Republic of China
PROFAC	Community Self-management Strengthening Project
RDP	Reconstruction and Development Programme
RTA	Regional Transport Authority
SACP	South African Communist Party
SANCO	South African National Civic Organization
SAP	Structural Adjustment Programme
SPARC	Society for Promotion of Area Resource Centres
UDF	United Democratic Front
UK	United Kingdom
UET	University of Engineering and Technology (Lahore)
UNCHS	United Nations Centre for Human Settlements
UNDP	United Nations Development Programme
US	United States of America
USAID	United States Agency for International Development
WCCA	Western Cape Civics Association
WCHDA	Western Cape Hostel Dwellers Association
WECUSA	Western Cape United Squatters Association
WHO	World Health Organization
WTO	World Trade Organization

LIST OF FIGURES, TABLES AND BOXES

FIGURES

TABLES

BOXES

PREFACE

This book arose from the collective desire of the authors to link the broad range of their community development work and empirical research around the world to major urban development issues. This is undertaken by focusing on appropriate institutions for sustainable urban development, and the need for community self-development as an integral part of the role of civil society within this.

Much of the early literature on urban sustainability focused on environmental issues, but was followed by a growing understanding that social and economic sustainability are just as important and, indeed, may be a precondition for environmental health. In the book this broader view of sustainable development has been set within the context of changing political and socioeconomic developments and perspectives at global, national and local levels.

The book aims to contribute to sustainable development in cities by stressing that appropriate institutions – in the widest sense – are essential to sustainability, as are the human networks that enable mediation of environmental, social, economic and political forces. By combining an analytical framework for understanding institutional development and the vital role of civil society with vibrant case studies from around the world, the book promotes wider understanding of the means for participation and negotiation that are the basis for sustainable urban development. The book is aimed at the interested reader of urban and sustainability issues; practitioners in urban development and city management worldwide, whether government officials, professional practitioners or activists; and teachers and students of urban policy and development.

All of the country-specific case studies are based on recent fieldwork and research undertaken by staff and graduate students associated with the Centre for Environment and Human Settlements (CEHS) in Edinburgh.[1] The authors include the Centre's researchers and colleagues in the countries where they have worked, details being given below. Most of these projects are ongoing, so the book both documents 'work in progress' and is a kind of status report of the field activities of the CEHS. These activities, both in research and teaching, are continually evolving and, for up-to-date information, the reader is invited to visit the CEHS website at http://www.eca.ac.uk/planning/cehs.htm.

The book consists of three sections:

- a thematic introduction in the first two chapters, which sets the book and the case studies within the broader context of global urban development and sustainability issues, as well as introducing the analytical framework of the institutional approach;
- the country-specific experience, based on eight case studies in seven different countries across the world, each with a different sectoral focus; and
- conclusions in the final two chapters, which apply the analytical framework in the first section to the various case studies, and draw broad conclusions concerning the role of civil society in sustainable urban development, and the forward tasks necessary to bring this about.

The wide-ranging research on urban areas documented here brings geographical and sectoral diversity to the book, with reports on urban development initiatives in a range of countries from Africa and Asia to South America and Europe, and from the least to the most developed countries. The focus of the community development activities reports vary from aspects of housing delivery such as land access, to aspects of planning, such as transport and industrial planning.

There is therefore a diversity in the country-specific experience, which is drawn together through a focus on common themes of the institutional relations between state, economy and civil society in each experience. In many of the cities and countries, major political and socio-economic transitions are underway. This is related to the changing economic role of urban areas within a global economy, and diminishing political power of nation states in the face of globalization and a roll-back in the functions of the state vis-à-vis the market. This situation poses new opportunities and challenges for civil society.

The book thus allows a broad application of the institutional approach mentioned above, but in no way does it pretend to provide a definitive guide to best practice. While the editors believe much can be learnt from the experience of others, they understand that the political, economic and cultural context within which each experience develops is a crucial conditioning factor. In some cases the lessons learned tend to be more negative than positive, but what is important is establishing a framework for analysis that will foster better understanding of the important role of civil society in urban development, and how to achieve it.

Michael Carley   **Paul Jenkins**   **Harry Smith**
Honorary Professor   Director   Research Associate

Centre for Environment and Human Settlements
Edinburgh, Scotland
June 2000

ABOUT THE AUTHORS

Dr Ghulam Abbas Anjum is a faculty member of the City and Regional Planning Department, University of Engineering and Technology (UET), Lahore, Pakistan. He took his doctorate through CEHS and has recently served as an advisor to the Government of Pakistan.

Mrs Josefa Rizalina Bautista is a former vice-president of the Development Academy of the Philippines. She is now an independent consultant.

Professor Michael Carley is involved in a wide range of research on cities and sustainable development. His most recent book is *Sharing the World: Sustainable Living and Global Equity in the 21st Century.*

Professor Cliff Hague is Professor within the School of Planning and Housing and linked to the CEHS. He is active in planning research in the UK and Eastern Europe, and president of the Commonwealth Association of Planners.

Dr Rizwan Hameed is also a faculty member of the City and Regional Planning Department of the UET, Lahore. He recently completed his doctorate in industrial planning through CEHS.

Dr Paul Jenkins is Director of CEHS, where he teaches as well as undertakes a range of research and professional planning and housing work in the developing world, with a particular focus on development in southern Africa.

Dr Jeremy Raemaekers is a teacher and researcher within CEHS and the School of Planning and Housing. His research interests range from social anthropology to issues of environmental sustainability.

John Russell is a part-time teacher and researcher within CEHS and the School of Planning and Housing, and an independent consultant on transport issues worldwide.

Dr Harry Smith recently completed his doctorate through CEHS, focusing on housing in Costa Rica. After working as a research associate at CEHS, he is currently Central Development Officer at Community Self-Build Scotland.

Ralph Throp is undertaking his doctorate in planning in China through CEHS and works as a Housing Planning Officer for the Scottish Highlands and Islands at the national agency, Scottish Homes.

José Manuel Valverde is a lecturer in urban sociology at the Sociology Department of the Universidad de Costa Rica.

GLOSSARY

Barangay	neighbourhood, the lowest spatial unit of Filipino local government
Barangay tanods	community guards
Barong-barong	a makeshift house built of salvaged materials
Bairro	Portuguese term for neighbourhood
Barrio	Spanish term for neighbourhood
Danwei	work units
Datu	village leader
Da yuan	informally built walled compound
Hukou	household registration
Katchi abadi	unauthorized housing development
Lupon Tagapayapa	pacification committees
Pangkat Tagapagkasundo	conciliation body
Punong Barangay	barangay captain
Sangguniang Bayan	municipal assemblies
Si he yuan	courtyard house

Part 1

Introduction: The Challenge of a Sustainable Urban Future – the Role of Institutions

1 TOP-DOWN AND BOTTOM-UP: THE CHALLENGE OF CITIES IN THE NEW CENTURY

Michael Carley

With more than 70 per cent of the world's population destined to live in urban areas by the middle of the 21st century, the high quality governance of cities is essential to the sustainability of the planet, and to the economic prospects and quality of life of the majority of its residents. Because of their popularity as places to live and work, cities around the world are under a variety of pressures including rapid population growth; requirements to meet basic needs, such as for decent housing and clean water; an explosion in traffic congestion and rapid expansion of the city into surrounding agricultural land and pollution of every sort. Overall, there is a pressing need for effectiveness and democratic participation in the management of complex and unwieldy urban systems.

In turn, the quality of cities has a profound effect on national development patterns. This is true in terms of encouraging rural–urban population flows, or vice versa in developed countries, and in attracting international inward investment into urban areas by footloose capital. It is also the case in the allowing of unserviced, unhealthy shanty towns as the only choice of residence for the poor, while for richer residents, there is a self-defeating suburban sprawl as they attempt to reap the economic benefits of city life while escaping the negative social and environmental aspects of polluted and sometimes dangerous inner cities. To attempt to do so, development spreads further and further into the surrounding countryside, bringing traffic congestion and air pollution in its wake.

In terms of governance, in recent years across the world the monolithic role of the state in guiding urban development has been challenged by increasing emphasis on replacing public intervention with market-driven approaches, or attempting to combine the two. At best, three key sectors combine in urban development partnerships – state/local government, market/economy/business and civil society/communities/households – in a positive, mutually reinforcing manner. At worst, state and market ignore both long-term strategic needs for urban planning and management, and the needs of the growing numbers of urban poor, marginalized in disadvantaged communities, thus excluding an important sector of civil society from decision-making processes. Polarization between rich and poor creates conditions for future social and ecological upheaval in cities already beset with problems and challenges to their beneficial governance.

This book argues that the long-term strategic needs of the city for sustainable development and economic prosperity cannot be separated from the need to involve citizens at all levels of society in innovative ways of fashioning and participating in urban development processes. It makes the point that sustainable urban development is a political process, which involves both strategic objectives and enhanced democratic participation. It suggests practical ways to achieve this, by presenting eight case studies of the participation of civil society in urban development in countries as diverse as Costa Rica, the Philippines, Pakistan, Mozambique, Britain and others. It investigates these case studies by putting forward, in the next chapter and a concluding chapter, an analytical framework that suggests how state, market and civil society can combine forces to achieve the necessary objectives of urban development in this new century.

THE OBJECTIVES OF DEVELOPMENT

Most broadly, these development objectives were outlined in a speech by the President of South Africa, Thabo Mbeki (2000), in a speech in Havana entitled 'The North does not have all the answers':

* the permanent elimination of poverty;
* sustained improvement in living standards;
* enhancement of human dignity;
* protection of the environment; and
* respect for culture and social cohesion.

In this speech, President Mbeki spoke of the need for 'a strong spirit of communal, human solidarity' as opposed to 'the atomization of the family and the individual, driven by the entrenchment of the capitalist system'. This notion of solidarity gives a broad sense of the meaning of civil society, the opposite of a tendency to what has been termed the 'excessive individualism' of consumer societies (Carley and Christie, 2000).

But it is not enough to extol the virtues of democratic participation in general – people invariably want to participate in something tangible, in improving their lives and having the satisfaction of self-development, and the confidence it engenders. We will note below that capitalism, although more resilient than the failed socialist experiment, is itself failing in monumental ways, from a billion people living in poverty to a planet heating up its own atmosphere at an alarming rate (Carley and Spapens, 1998). Unless the 70 per cent of the world's population living in cities are enlisted actively and practically in sustainable development processes, this situation is only likely to worsen.

The challenges are complicated by a number of factors. First, we all know that the consumer lifestyle emerging all over the world, however attractive it may be, is unsustainable because it is taking us past critical thresholds in the planet's ability to absorb pollution, and in the use of scarce resources. But the real problem is that the seductiveness of consumption makes it difficult to take a critical but constructive view on the workings of the market economy and the international agencies, such as the World Trade Organization (WTO), that condition its operation. The market economy as currently constituted is necessary, but not sufficient, for quality of life. One task of civil society at a global and local level ought to be to question the direction of capitalist development, to improve the prospects for daily life within capitalist systems, but also for civil society to protect itself through community development, so that the very factors of solidarity described by President Mbeki are not lost in the rush of the newly-industrializing countries to consumerism. A more balanced approach is required. There is a growing interest in the role of consumption in a sustainable world (Robins and Roberts, 1998).

The remainder of this introductory chapter suggests some broad challenges of urban management that need to be addressed. These include urban population growth; the challenge of poverty and basic needs; the need for eco-innovation; the problem of traffic, pollution and urban sprawl; and the challenges of democratic participation.

THE CHALLENGES OF URBAN DEVELOPMENT

Urban population growth and the occupation of land

While world population has increased fivefold in the past 200 years, the number of people living in urban areas has become 25 times higher in the same period. The implications of this process of global urbanization are outlined by Carley and Christie (2000):

> *'Within a few years, half the world's population will be living in cities, and during the twenty-first century urbanisation around the globe will tend toward the 75 per cent levels of urbanisation prevalent in industrialised countries. This implies a virtual reversal of the current ratio of urban to rural population in many developing countries.'*

Urbanization in the 21st century is taking place particularly in the developing world. The proportion of the population in cities in Latin America rose from 41 per cent in 1950 to 73 per cent by 1995 and in Africa over the period since 1975 from 25 to 35 per cent. By 2015 nearly half the population of Africa and Asia will be urban. The growth of megacities is one indicator of this urbanization process: Mexico City at around 25 million people, São Paulo at 23 million, and both Mumbai and Shanghai at around 14 or 15 million are obvious examples. But urbanization is also occurring in smaller cities and in the countryside. For example, there are already 13 cities in Asia with more than

ten million inhabitants, and China has no fewer than 32 cities with populations over one million.

In some hitherto rural areas, such as the island of Java in Indonesia,
population density is growing to urban levels even outside the main megacity.
These urbanized regions are characterized by an intense mixture of land use
with industrial estates, cottage industry, agriculture and suburban development and other uses existing side by side, all linked by an intense movement
of population dependent on cheap transport, such as motorcycles, buses and
trucks. McGee (1992) argues that this is a new form of urbanization that
challenges traditional notions of urban transition.

It should not be assumed, however, that the implications of population
growth in cities need be negative: urban regions and megacities are often the
sites of remarkable adaptations and ingenuity in making high-density urban
living tolerable for even the poorest citizens. Cities can contribute to sustainable development by virtue of their concentration of people and services,
making efficiency gains in energy and materials use particularly valuable and
feasible because of the scale of their consumption. Finding innovative and
transferable innovations in urban management will be crucial to environmental quality and public health in the new century.

The challenge of poverty and basic needs

The movement from the countryside to urban areas constitutes one of the
great mass migrations in world history. Rural poverty is forcing many people,
especially the unskilled and the landless, to seek employment in the larger
cities. Lack of successful land reform, the extremes of rural poverty, the hope
and often the reality of better chances for work and income in the city, and
improved transport, encourage this movement.

But although city life is attractive and, for many, preferable to rural life,
conditions of life can be difficult. For example, India's big cities are growing by
around two million people per decade. Nearly half of Mumbai's population
live in slums, in dwellings made of tin, bits of wood or old sacks, often adjoin-
ing a main road or railway track. About one million residents live on the streets.
The strains on human services and physical infrastructure are severe, and air
and water pollution, waste disposal problems and health problems are
endemic. Mumbai's population will grow to around 18 million, still smaller
than Mexico City and São Paulo among the megacities of the South.

Overall on the planet, around a billion people – a fifth of the world's
population – are affected by poverty, malnourishment, and ill health caused by
lack of access to clean water. The consumption rate of the poorest fifth of the
world's population has remained virtually unchanged since the Second World
War, while the resource consumption of the richest fifth has increased four to
sevenfold. Low income households are reliant on a diminishing resource base
to meet basic needs as pollution added to watercourses in dense urban areas
outstrips attempts to address the problem.

Even in a static situation, the poverty of a fifth of the world's population is
a fundamental challenge to sustainability. But the gap between rich and poor

is growing, and this could heighten social tensions in cities. When the needs for day-to-day survival press so heavily, it is not surprising if vital, long-term environmental concerns receive scant attention from the poor or their political leaders. Countries and cities will increasingly see access to resources, particularly fresh water, as a matter of vital concern.

The challenge of eco-innovation

Because of their sheer scale and complexity, the problems of managing big cities and urban regions will be increasingly severe. In cities, the very fact of higher levels of economic activity means that people tend to consume more resources per capita and to produce more waste than their counterparts in rural areas. Many cities are now finding it very difficult to find anywhere to deposit the daily outpouring of rubbish, so a real need is not just for recycling but for a dematerialization of daily life (Carley and Spapens, 1998). Later, a case study in the Philippines describes a number of cases of community innovation in materials recycling.

Overall, the need for reducing global warming and global environmental degradation means it is essential to reduce daily contributions to pollution loads before problems become intractable. Unfortunately, the usual approach to managing the human–environment interaction is 'too little, too late' – economic growth means the volumes of pollution, and numbers of pollutants, increase faster than our ability to manage their cumulative impacts.

A key challenge therefore to urban sustainability is eco-innovation. For cities and towns, this has real implications for town planning: moving away from suburban patterns of development back towards dense, mixed use urban neighbourhoods with 'win–win' social and environmental effects: reduced materials consumption and increased recycling, closer linkage between jobs and residence, more use of public transport, walking and cycling, lower levels of car ownership and use, more support for local retailers as opposed to out-of-town shopping malls, and so on. However, many aspects of the urban lifestyle suggested by these objectives represent the opposite of current definitions of modernity.

Future requirements for eco-innovation will be more challenging still, requiring major reductions in the material and energy intensity of daily living, while at the same time tackling poverty and town planning issues and without any loss of current quality of life. Consumers in the developed world will need to reduce their current 80 per cent share of world wide resource consumption – to allow development in the South within the Earth's carrying capacity (Carley and Spapens, 1998). This means questioning an understanding of the quality of life based on the consumption of more and more goods, and valuing public goods such as education and public transport, and social spaces such as parks. The opposite side of this coin is that where urban public services are poor, people will be forced to compensate for the lack of these with inefficient private consumption.

Although ecological innovation sounds a grand, global objective, it can only be politically and socially feasible if it is the result of a mass movement, beginning in the household and the neighbourhood. This book charts many examples of innovative community development at this level, and examines the need to expand networks to other levels of action.

South, North and the ecological backpack

The balance and direction of effort in sustainable urban management between cities North and South depends in part on existing patterns of consumption of the world's finite resources, including the 'sink capacity' of the atmosphere to absorb CO_2 emissions. For example, it is worth noting that the average British urban resident consumes 14 times as much energy-intensive aluminium every year as the average Argentinean, while the average American consumes 45 times as much energy each year as the average Indian.

This 'ecological backpack' of Northern consumption patterns is large indeed. With these facts in mind, many people are noting that, beginning from an assessment of materials consumption and CO_2 emissions, many neighbourhoods and cities of the developing world currently live in a far more sustainable manner than their Northern counterparts.

This suggests two things. First, that the North may have as much to learn from the South about patterns of sustainable urban development as the South from the North. Second, a key question for cities in the developing world is whether they can adapt their own patterns of urban development rather than simply aspiring to prevailing Northern models. This requires that they define a style of urban living which is environmentally benign and yet socially acceptable to their residents. This is a difficult challenge when the Northern patterns of urban living, discussed in the next section, are accepted, and pushed by a globalizing media, as the *sine qua non* of the modern lifestyle.

Finally, to add insult to injury, the North, by having used up much of the planet's limited sink capacity, for example, to absorb CO_2 emissions, is foreclosing development opportunities for the South. In parallel, there is an unequal distribution of the benefits of urban industrialism compared to the costs. Most benefits accrue to the wealthy nations, which are overconsuming the planet's resources while costs are borne by people and countries which don't share the benefits.

This historical, ecological inequality means that it is difficult to convince China, India, Brazil and other newly industrializing countries (NICs) that they should adopt what are frequently perceived as Northern environmental values – or at least not without economic compensation for ecological debt, when these values also degrade opportunities for economic progress and the alleviation of endemic poverty. This issue was skirted around at the 1997 Kyoto climate change summit and will continue to bedevil negotiations on greenhouse gas emissions until North and South are linked in an equitable consumption framework.

At a global level, what is required for all countries is equal access to the world's resources, perhaps aggregated nationally on a per capita basis as proposed by Carley and Spapens (1998), but also equal responsibility for their management. This equity principle also means a lower resource use per capita than current levels in developed countries, and the opportunity for a rise in consumption of resources to a sustainable level for developing countries – to give a balanced pattern by the middle of the 21st century.

The imbalance also means, as we noted with regard to cities, that current Western development models of the 20th century, which condition so much of our thinking and are imbued in the message of the global media, in fact fail to provide realistic policy guidance for the 21st century. Finally, the imbalance also occurs within societies, with a by-product of the current economic model being, for example, high levels of unemployment in the European social democratic model, or high levels of working families in poverty, as in the American 'winner take all' model. Clearly while this 'social exclusion' persists, cities cannot achieve sustainability.

The challenge of mobility and urban form

The explosive growth of motor vehicle traffic in the past 30 years, and the spread of low density suburban settlement patterns, represent major challenges to urban governance. Urban sprawl diminishes the scarce rural land resource and can generate a range of negative impacts which will constrain development well into the next century. In the absence of strong land use planning, people and businesses enter into a vicious cycle of attempting to escape congestion by relocating to the urban fringe, such as is already the norm in Bangkok and Mexico City.

In conditions of rapid economic growth, higher incomes allow people to switch to personal vehicles. This increases congestion, rapidly diminishing the advantages of road-based public transport, like the bus, which becomes less cost effective and less efficient. This discriminates against less well off, non car-owning households, whose daily commuting journeys become longer, reaching many hours in each direction. This in turn causes more people to switch personal vehicles as soon as they can afford to, thus contributing to the vicious cycle of congestion and pollution.

As automobility grows, households tend to make three times as many trips when they acquire a car than when they relied on public transport or other modes. This generates congestion that deters sustainable modes such as cycling and walking. Indeed, often the official response to congestion is to favour the car over other modes. In Shanghai, city officials have recently announced plans to reduce the three million cyclists by two thirds, to allow more room for automobiles. Already bicycles and bicycle rickshaws are banned in central Jakarta and New Delhi as 'old fashioned'.

Once a suburbanized land use pattern is established, it is almost impossible to revert to a more sustainable pattern of concentrated, nodal density, and even rail-based transport becomes less effective because destinations are spread over the landscape. As urban life penetrates into the countryside, pressure grows for yet more road building.

A related problem is the economic and social cost of congestion, which wastes billions of dollars annually in the city-region – monies which could be devoted to private and public investment for development. Finally, there are severe implications for air quality and global warming. Many city-regions in developing countries suffer air pollution at levels harmful to health. These levels are often difficult to tackle, however, because auomobility and suburbanization are politically sensitive in many countries. Options for managing the situation must not be only technically, but also politically, feasible.

A few fortunate cities such as Singapore, Hong Kong and Curitiba in Brazil have strong urban policy systems and have exerted tight control over land use planning, the location of housing and employment, transport integration and control of the motor car. The advantages, in terms of overall energy efficiency of the urban form, are well documented (Newman and Kenworthy, 1989). These are the exceptions, all based on dominant state models. Many cities in developing countries, however, tend to an American style model of weak urban policy in land use and control of the private vehicle. These reflect broader social and historical attitudes to:

- the role of government in mediating between private property rights and the public good, reflected in the land use planning system (weak zoning versus strategic development control); and
- the balance between public and private transport, reflected in the transport policy framework and explicit or de facto inclusion of the externalities of transport within cost-benefit criteria.

Even in the context of weak urban policy, however, it can be hypothesized that there are many options for exerting subtle policy control at the conjunction of transport and land use to move towards a beneficial management regime. Later a case study looks at an approach to the management of public transport in Lahore, involving an innovative linkage between civil society and the state.

THE CHALLENGE OF DEMOCRATIC PARTICIPATION

All of the issues described above fall within the objectives of sustainable development, which is defined by Carley and Christie (2000) as:

> '*A continuing process of mediation among social, economic and environmental needs which results in positive socio-economic change that does not undermine the ecological and social systems upon which communities and society are dependent. Its successful implementation requires integrated policy, planning, and social learning processes; its political viability depends on the full support of the people it affects through their governments, their social institutions, and their private activities.*'

In suggesting this definition, and in citing what they describe as 'an immense literature', Carley and Christie propose that the 'truly political nature' of sustainable development must be recognized and that the political process of development must always precede the outcome. With this in mind, three fundamental tasks can be identified:

1   Strategic and philosophical reflection: on the future course of industrial-
     ism as a form of social organization for the fulfilment of human needs; the
     extent to which 'market friendly' policies can result in sustainable devel-
     opment; whether high economic growth, no growth or some middle
     option is the more viable in environmental and social terms; and the need
     for greater equity on a world scale and for self-determination.
2   Research and development to generate new knowledge and appropriate
     technologies, especially in sustainable energy, agriculture, transport and
     low or even zero emissions and low-energy manufacturing.
3   The development of institutional, regulatory and human networking
     capacity for managing sustainable development, at scales from the global
     to the local. This is not only about the implementation of policies for
     promoting sustainable development, but also about the pursuit of new
     knowledge and skills for both human self-development and urban and
     environmental management (Goldblatt, 1996).

The three types of response each contribute to the successful realization of the
others. This book focuses directly on the third type. The process underpinning
human networking is described by Carley and Christie (2000):

•   active participation in conditions of equality, based on teamwork;
•   a process of mutual, non-hierarchical learning-by-doing or action learning,
     intended to develop new perceptions, new skills and confidence;
•   horizontal integration between sectors of human interest such as agricul-
     ture, health, transport and housing, and vertical integration between policy
     making groups, including big business, and community levels; and
•   collective self-development and self-management.

Turning to the means of human networking, one thing is clear from the
perspective of the new century: government working on its own will never
resolve the problems and challenges of sustainable development outlined
above. Partnership is required – government working with business, the
research community and civil society at all levels.

     In addition to being responsive to the pressing, immediate demands of
urban management, which often appears a condition of short-term crisis,
policies and programmes must be sufficiently flexible to meet intergenerational needs, preserving vital resources for future generations. But taking such
a long-term perspective can be very difficult when the horizons of politicians
around the world are seldom more than five years hence. And yet sustainable
development demands both better governance and a long-range perspective.
One role for civil society, at the level of the nation, whether it be the trade
union movements, churches collectively, voluntary or service organizations, or
groups committed to Agenda 21, must be to encourage more visionary thinking and policy commitment on the part of politicians, national and urban.

     The strategic challenges to sustainable urban living described above have a
second thing in common: without broad-based, democratic participation,
reaching right down to the neighbourhood level, they are unlikely to be

resolved. In some cases this is because individuals have to change their behaviour in a positive fashion, which is difficult to do as an individual household unless the positive behaviour is socially rewarding; in others, because politicians will not have the courage to take the necessary steps without a large, even vociferous, constituency behind them. Finally, many aspects of the enormous task of managing big cities must be broken down into manageable portions, that is, neighbourhoods.

On the positive side, there is growing recognition in urban institutional management that top-down approaches, whether led by the public or private sector, will always be weak compared to stronger, more sustainable, development initiatives that combine bottom-up community involvement with integrated and guided development approaches at the city and regional level. These innovative approaches to urban development can also marry state intervention and market discipline to social ends.

Looking to best practice in disadvantaged communities in cities around the world, from the shanty towns of Africa, Asia and Latin America to the inner city estates of Britain, France or the US, much valuable energy is going into positive programmes of community self-development. This is an essential process, for people need to analyse their own problems and fashion their own solutions, for development to be effective. People are, of course, the key to the solution rather than the 'problem'. Most chapters in this book describe innovation in self-development, but also the many substantial constraints that need to be overcome to institutionalize self-development in systems of urban governance.

A chain of sustainable development

Recent research which examined participation in 'nested' urban development partnerships in city-regions found that, in addition to horizontal integration of government with civil society and business, vertical integration of action and policy between the levels of neighbourhood, city, urban region and nation is also a prerequisite to sustainable development (Carley and Kirk, 1998). This 'chain' of initiative and partnership is only as strong as its weakest link.

It is also the case that while some aspects of large, complex cities are best managed at the strategic, citywide or city-regional level, many other aspects of urban development are more effectively devolved to the local, neighbourhood level. This driving down of functions to the appropriate spatial and social level for management is sometimes called subsidiarity. A key to improved integration is to link regional, citywide and local initiatives in a systematic development framework, recognizing that guidance and decisions at the level of the region can have profound impacts on the viability of community development initiatives.

Failures of vertical integration are compounded by a frequent economic and cultural gap between a policy-making elite and the reality of life at the neighbourhood level, a reality which is often characterized by the drive for basic survival. The fine distinctions of policy and law are not applicable and government control structures are weak or non-existent.

The overall trend to globalization, in so far as it further links senior urban policy makers with each other, but not with their citizenry, reinforces top-down perspectives, but the interests of the many millions of modest income urban residents may be better served by bottom-up, community-based approaches. Of course, vertical linkage of problems requires both top-down and bottom-up approaches. Unless there is both coordination and subsidiarity (pushing decisions down to the lowest level of governance possible subject to achieving their aim) throughout the institutional system, inefficiency and lack of effectiveness are likely to be the order of the day. Finally, a gulf between the public and private sectors, and civil society, indicated by different organizational cultures and different objectives, can also heighten this constraint in policy systems and in participation.

Within this vertical chain, larger institutions invariably have the advantage by having access to power, information and resources. To balance this, self-development by communities, and empowerment of those communities by higher levels of government, are essential to the development of the whole city. If social polarization means some communities are grossly disadvantaged in terms of the basic needs of human life, or in access to a measure of control over the development process, the city as a whole cannot achieve the kind of modern, sustainable development required in the next century.

At the citywide level, there are many effective partnerships between local government and business. Top-down funding regimes empower institutional or corporate stakeholders who are represented by paid professionals, skilled at the often closed, exclusive system of urban politics meetings. More challenging is genuine involvement with communities.

Participatory tools, such as 'participatory urban appraisal' and many others, are valuable, particularly for initiating participation processes, for neighbourhood design initiatives and for local confidence building (Mitlin and Thompson, 1994). But they cannot be expected to be representative or democratic, nor do they allow communities to influence mainstream programmes or important strategic issues, like the location of a new highway. In many cities, lip service to communities means a patchwork quilt of statutory and informal consultation, described as 'chaotic' by Carley and Kirk (1998).

In spite of growing commitment to community participation, there is concern among many local people that too much is superficial and token, consisting of 'consultation, when all the real decisions have already been taken' (Carley and Kirk, 1998). The following are some concerns about participation identified by recent research (Carley and Kirk, 1998):

- representatives of powerful institutional stakeholders are paternalistic to community members;
- a need to overcome cynicism about participation, which pervades communities which have had community development initiatives undermined again and again;
- a need to involve the community at the beginning of the process in establishing development priorities; and particularly to address economic deprivation;

- the need to foster community capacity building in a formal and committed manner;
- community control of consultation processes – as opposed to the 'doling out' of information to the community in bits and pieces in one tedious public meeting after another;
- the need to reconcile the role of elected politicians with that of community representatives; and
- the multiplicity of policy units and administrative boundaries in the city which makes understanding of the holistic task of community development difficult if not impossible, and appears an administrative convenience based on tradition rather than on service to the community.

To address this broad range of issues simultaneously implies rethinking participation processes and a strengthening of longer-term organizational mechanisms for community involvement as full, rather than token, partners in regeneration. Overall, there may need to be better opportunities for citizen participation in local democracy, and reviews of local service priorities and decentralized delivery, as well as enabled self-management initiatives, such as community development trusts. Statutory planning processes in different countries may offer potential for regular participation, as yet almost wholly untapped.

In summary, therefore, cities cannot be managed without active partnership between business, local government and civil society at both neighbourhood and citywide level to bring about effective social and economic change. If decision making is not devolved as much as possible to the neighbourhood level, it is unlikely that the centre can exert effective control. Top-down solutions very often fail because they are out of touch with the reality of life on the ground. There is now increasing recognition that what is required is not top-down or bottom-up approaches on their own, but a coherent development programme that welds the two in mutually reinforcing ways.

At the city and the neighbourhood level, the research suggests that one of the most powerful ways of linking citywide strategy and local action is by seeing urban development as an opportunity for mutual learning among key stakeholders. For example, in British cities such as Birmingham and Manchester, senior local government officers and politicians are directly involved in neighbourhood initiatives, thus fostering the learning environment necessary to inform city strategy, as well as expressing commitment to action in the neighbourhood.

Finally, policy and planning processes, if they are open, participative and encompass the technical and professional requirements of governance within a broader 'layperson-friendly' consideration of quality-of-life issues, can also be processes of mutual learning which link top-down and bottom-up.

OUTLINE OF THIS BOOK

This book sets out the parameters of such frameworks for local development at the neighbourhood or community level within the context of the development of the city and the urban region. It also suggests that, although the development challenge can vary enormously from place to place, there are also strong commonalities in the formal and informal organizational aspects of development. This means that there is real potential for mutual learning and inspiration between cities and countries. However, there are often limitations on developments of mutual benefit between the state, market and civil society – from political constraints, or resource or institutional deficiencies. Even when resources are available, these are not always used efficiently. When resources are few and institutions weak, problems are more marked, but successes are even more significant.

The case studies presented here range from South to North, East to West. All are marked by a measure of innovation. These cases include urban shelter and community self-management projects in Mozambique, Costa Rica and China; institutionalization of community management in the government structure of the Philippines; shifting relationships between government and civil society in housing provision in South Africa and England; and new, innovative roles for civil society and business in the management of public transport and industrial pollution in Pakistan.

The book also reviews key issues identified in the literature of community development and participation and that of urban organizational analysis and public administration as background to the case studies. A final section draws out the common themes from the case studies, including the lessons of good practice. The two concluding chapters also review the experience illustrated by the case studies in the light of an analytical structure proposed in Chapter 2. The following questions are answered:

- What can be learnt from the case studies about how civil society can become more effective in promoting self-development and interacting with state and market in mutually beneficial ways?
- How can key issues affecting wider urban society be understood within this framework of analysis?
- How can socially and environmentally responsive urban development be achieved in a global context of weakening states and growing market forces?

The case studies and analytical chapters presented in this book examine these questions, to which we will return in Part 3.

2 THE STATE, THE MARKET AND COMMUNITY: AN ANALYTICAL FRAMEWORK FOR COMMUNITY SELF-DEVELOPMENT

Paul Jenkins and Harry Smith

INTRODUCTION

As indicated in Chapter 1, urban areas are developing rapidly and will continue to do so for the foreseeable future. The sustainability of urban development is the theme with which this book is concerned – and this includes political, social and economic sustainability as well as environmental sustainability. A principal premise of the book is that, while socially and environmentally sustainable urban development visions are absolutely necessary, realistic political, economic and institutional mechanisms to achieve these are of equal importance.

The book thus focuses on the relevant roles for the major actors in urban development – the state, the market and civil society – and how these have different interests that need balancing. In particular, it investigates the institutional bases for a more active role of civil society in relation to the state and the market, arguing that this is crucial to achieving social and environmental balance. This is essential because in the last instance it is social institutions that underpin political legitimacy, and the organizational forms of relationships that permit spaces for negotiation between different actors and different levels. Finally, it examines the need for balance between global and local perspectives, and the need for mechanisms that permit greater integration of these. These key themes are briefly expanded on below.

Key themes and wider traditions of thought

The state, the market and civil society

A first key theme that underpins the book's approach is that of the need to explicitly distinguish between the various interests of the state, the market and society. It is argued that sustainable urban solutions entail mechanisms that allow mutually acceptable equilibria to be established within these three major sectors. This therefore can not depend on associations between only two of these – such as the state and the market, with society taking a passive role. How institutions (ie both mental models and organizational forms) do or do not permit space for negotiation to achieve this form of equilibrium and the consequences in different forms in urban areas in different parts of the world is examined throughout the book. As such, the book is located within a tradition of political economy analysis.

Institutions

The second key theme that the book examines, which weaves together these conceptual areas, and indeed the geographical areas studied, is that of institutions. This book uses the term 'institutions' in two ways – firstly, meaning the 'mental models' that underpin the very structure of society, economics and politics; and secondly, as the 'organizational forms' that express relationships between those in, and of relevance to, urban space. Examples of the former use would be the concept of legitimacy of forms of governance and of attitudes to property rights. Examples of the second would be the actual institutional organizations that exist to allow linkages within society and between society and the state or the private sector, both vertically (eg trade unions, lobby groups, non-governmental organizations (NGOs)) and horizontally (eg kinship systems and religious organizations). In this, the book locates itself within a growing literature and research paradigm that can generally be termed 'institutionalism'.

Local action within a global context

Finally, a third major theme examined in the book is the relationship between local and global. 'Think global, act local' is a catch phrase that sums this up, but indeed in many situations the mechanisms or impetus to implement this are not in place. We live in an increasingly globally integrated environment – ecologically, economically and even politically. Some would argue that in fact it is just a global minority who are benefiting from this. Thus, a view on how local communities can act more appropriately within a global world-view, and global forces adjust to local needs – and how this can be expressed in appropriate mental models and organizational forms – is absolutely necessary for society in the current world order. In this sense, the book also locates itself within the widening debate on globalization, and its counterparts of regionalization and localization.

Community self-development in a global context

The book argues that while the appropriate roles for the state and the market, and mechanisms for negotiation between these for mutual benefit (at a global and/or local scale) are of great importance, in the last analysis the most important factor has to be the way these serve communities – again both at the global and local level. Communities in this conception are not just seen as geographically based, but also as interest-based groupings in society. The institutional forms within society are what we mean by the term 'civil society'. In the increasingly plural and dense human societies in which we live – especially in urban areas – the capacity of the state to represent all community interests is limited and hence needs increasingly to be balanced by direct community action. While in no way seeking to reduce the responsibility of the state, or the market, in serving society, the book argues for a strong role for community self-develop-ment. That is, development that is both socially determined and oriented – and not 'self-help' as 'self improvement', in the Victorian sense of the term. It is not suggested that this then entails the withdrawal of the state or market, but that there is a need for society to guide the activity of the state, and for the market to be held socially accountable, in conjunction with increased latitude for community self-development. The key to balancing community interests and self-development is the form in which institutions within civil society interact with the state and the market – predominantly the former.

What does it mean to talk of 'community self-development' in a global context? Information technology has permitted the Western dominated 'market' economic system to penetrate more widely and deeply across the world than ever before, and this raises major questions of the appropriate role of the state – whether nation-states, or local state forms. The global economic system in many ways is becoming less responsive to social needs and pressures as expressed through existing political forms and there is a marked absence of appropriate supranational and international organizational forms which could begin to re-establish this equilibrium. That is, there are no effective forms of world government institutions that would permit control of global economic forces and more equitable redistribution at a global level. As the President of the European Commission, Romano Prodi, recently put it in an interview:

> *'The theme of 2000 is really this: how to sew together again an institutional fabric which gives to politics the instruments of government at the level of global economics. That is the deepest significance of the Third Way... that as economic relationships are intensifying under our very eyes, there is a lack of a similar deepening of a common politics, which we must address.'*
> (Lloyd, 2000)

However, it is not just at the global level that disequilibria are felt (although this is arguably the most evident), but increasingly nation states and local states see their role as competing within the global market-place and disequilibria are created within the local societies that they purport to serve. Urban areas are thus the meeting place of both global forces (cultural, economic and polit-ical) and local forces. How is it possible to 'think global' and 'act local' at the same time? To be sustainable, this book argues that mechanisms to create adequate equilibria at both the global and local level – and between these levels – are needed. It argues that, within the various political, economic and social situations that exist in urban areas worldwide, certain key issues need to be the basis for negotiation on how these mechanisms can be created, mainly:

- the need to realize the importance of all three major sectors (state, market and civil society);
- the need to accept that each has the right to negotiate mutual benefit; and
- the need to realize that this requires adequate space for negotiation.

Addressing these issues entails an understanding of the 'mental models' that underpin the legitimacy of the state and the market in each situation; and activism in developing and strengthening appropriate roles for each sector through appropriate organizational forms.

Given the relative strength of states and the market, it is often civil society, or its role and space for negotiation, that most needs strengthening as a basis for achieving socially acceptable forms of balance between the main sectors. Within civil society, communities – ie geographical and interest groups – are perhaps the strongest potential actors. However, this book argues that there is no one simple answer as to how communities (local or global) should guide the activities of the state or demand accountability from the market in terms of sustainability. Rather there is a range of resources and constraints and some simple concepts that permit the creation of an appropriate 'framework'. What is needed is a framework that permits global as well as local mental models and their implications to be rooted in societies worldwide; that permits these societies to develop appropriate forms of governance that respect the local and the global; and that permits both society and its forms of governance to guide and develop economic activities that support socially determined objectives, both locally and globally.

It is the intention of this book to investigate the institutional basis for such sustainability within the realm of the 'urban' in a wide range of situations. As urban space becomes ever more important to society, this is crucial to global sustainability. Through this the book hopes to draw attention to the fundamental need for appropriate mental models and organizational forms as a means towards more global sustainability. The book focuses on planning and housing issues across the world, drawing from a wide range of activities within these. The inclusion of case studies from the 'developed', 'transitional' and 'developing' world is deliberate. The authors stress that, while the roles, mechanisms and activities that are appropriate (as well as the resources available) to achieve more sustainable urban areas differ immensely across these categories, the framework that can promote community self-development can be seen to be applicable in all situations.

AN ANALYTICAL FRAMEWORK

Application to the key themes

The state, the market and society

After a period of increasingly strong state roles in most aspects of life from the late 19th century to the mid-1970s in most parts of the world, there has been an equally pervasive but much swifter period of state withdrawal, fired by the rise of neoliberal approaches in what was known as the 'First World', and the collapse of state-based 'real socialism' in the 'Second World', both having direct (and negative) effects on the 'Third World'. Indeed, the postwar break-up of the 19th century Western empires was based on the construction of a host of new nation-states that in many cases bore little relation to pre-existing social formations, leading to immediate tensions in some places, and to a more widespread weakening of these nation-states during the 1990s. Thus, the withdrawal of the state is taking place both in the sense of its lessening administrative and managerial role in old established states, and in terms of its questioning as a political entity in newer states.

While in the last few decades the state has faced shrinkage or outright opposition, especially at the national level, markets have expanded their role in production. Markets themselves have undergone profound transformations, thus affecting their relations with both state and civil society. Fordism – which linked mass production to mass consumption – has been followed, though not replaced, by post-Fordism or, in Harvey's (1990) words, 'flexible capital accumulation', which is characterized by more flexible labour processes and markets, geographical mobility and rapid shifts in consumption practices. In relation to the latter, there has been a shift from the consumption of goods to the consumption of services, a trend that is attractive for capital investors because of its concomitant lowering of capital turnover time. In this climate, the production of long-term physical goods such as housing and infrastructure becomes less attractive to the market.

Given the diminishing role of government, it is civil society that appears to be taking up the slack in providing these goods that states are increasingly unable to deliver and markets are increasingly uninterested in providing. In the words of Friedmann and Douglass (1998), 'there are historical moments when [civil society] asserts itself massively in the public sphere. The current era is one such moment'. Indeed, this is apparent not only in the actual processes taking place both in 'developed' and 'developing' countries, but also in the burgeoning literature on civil society. In political science it is being related to the consolidation of democracy, in planning to the emergence of 'empowering' and 'collaborative' approaches (see below), in housing to community-based housing processes and so on. This acknowledgement of civil society in theory and, to a lesser extent, in policy making, is linked to the reappraisal of social interaction and the role of this within political and economic systems.

Institutional analysis
This reappraisal of social interaction and its role has been expressed in the 'new institutional economics' (NIE), which attempted to add social and political dimensions to economics, including development economics, in terms of neoclassical rational choice theory.[1] NIE offered the resolution of puzzles in neoclassical theory such as the role of the firm, as opposed to the rational individual, and as such, has an important role in modern economic theoretical development – all the more influential as this challenged orthodox economic policy of the 1990s, with its dominant role of the 'market'. However, the new

institutional focus did not imply a return to state intervention in markets, but stemmed from the position that other factors need to be taken into account – such as traditions, habits, ideas and ideologies.[2]

The application of institutionalism in various disciplines takes this position further into institutions of all kinds, and in turn, has given rise to a 'new political economy', which has higher sensitivity to political factors than the purer economic viewpoint of the NIE adherents. As Colin Leys indicates: '...the central idea of the new institutionalism or new political economy is that what makes for an efficient economy is a set of institutions that permit individuals to benefit personally from doing what will also serve the (material) interests of society as a whole... This reasoning can be applied to taxation, the organization of central and local government, education, banking, marketing – in effect, to any social arrangement' (Leys, 1996).

The study of institutions as mental models elucidates the assumptions these are based on, thus helping to identify inappropriate policies and the way forward for more responsive decision making. It has increasingly been recognized that mental models are embedded in the prevailing forms of reasoning, which are not limited to scientific and instrumental reason – the forms on which modern Western societies have built their model of development. In these societies, mental models such as, for example, property rights, the public interest and representative democracy have underpinned processes in urban development in ways that have fluctuated throughout time. Thus, although property rights have remained unquestioned in capitalist developed countries throughout this century, the exercise of these rights was bounded to some extent during the postwar years, when public interest became a strong mental model underpinning much policy making, including the consolidation of the welfare state in some countries. However, the resurgence of neoliberal thought strengthened the hegemony of private property rights again in the 1980s and 1990s.

Besides the waxing and waning of Western mental models, however, a far greater impact on urban development in non-Western parts of the world can be ascribed to the introduction and consolidation of new mental models, whether through 'home-grown' evolution or through imposition from outside. Thus, to continue with the example of property rights, in the Western 'developed' world the idea of private property rights as a commodity developed in parallel with industrialization and urbanization, feeding back into and strengthening these two latter processes. In many 'developing' countries, however, this mental model was introduced by the colonizing powers replacing, for example, existing communal land stewardship models, without creating an indigenous economic basis for development and hence also urban investment. Stewardship is precisely the objective of what is currently being reconstructed on the basis of another new, pervasive and highly influential mental model – sustainable development.

Mental models cannot become operational without organizations, just as organizations need to be underpinned by mental models. With the growth of the nation-state and its increasing links with the economy, organizational forms that have dominated in the past 60 years or so in the First, Second and Third Worlds have all stressed the importance of the state, although there were fundamental divergences between the model of relationship in the First and Second Worlds. The Third World tended to copy aspects of these organizational forms, but without the basis of either economic control or even a shared conception of the nation and hence this continually proved problematic. The changing basis for economic interaction worldwide and linked changes in political orthodoxy have led to changing roles and the restructuring of organizations with the rise of non-state and non-market organizations substituting for the state in various ways. This represents a danger as states become less responsive to their social bases, but also an opportunity as the dominance of, often imposed, state organizational forms is challenged.

The need for new organizational forms and new relationships between these is no clearer than in urban areas worldwide – albeit expressed in very different ways in differing political, economic, social and cultural contexts. Examples of new organizational forms in 'developed' societies are partnerships in urban development, which tend to bring together local state and market actors, leaving out civil society to a large extent. In the post-Socialist 'transitional' countries, while civil society proved an important element in the promotion of the transition, the swing from overwhelming state control has often led to an exaggerated reliance on the 'market', with questioning of the role of civil society in controlling this. In 'developing' countries, where the state and market were never firmly rooted, being to a great extent imposed from outside or by an internal elite with external backing, both political and economic transitions have opened challenging new opportunities for civil society's involvement in organizational relationships with the state.[3]

This book examines the development of alternative institutional models in various countries, with differing state–market–society contexts, all of which are responding to the changing situation through defining new roles and relationships, mainly between civil society and the state. In most cases these are emerging based on different mental models to the 'Western norm'. The book argues that, whereas these local actions are not all successes, and those that are may not be replicable in any simple way, they represent examples of the challenge and opportunity for a sustainable basis for urban development in the current and future global context.

Local action within a global context

The link between local and global has been evidenced primarily in the increasing awareness of the interconnection of ecological processes at these two levels. The detrimental effects human activities can have on the environment, with subsequent impacts on humans themselves or not, are now widely recognized, and an international agenda to respond to these has been developed in the various world conferences and summits during the 1990s. One of the outcomes of these meetings, Agenda 21, clearly articulates this local–global approach through its general formulation at the Earth Summit in Rio in 1992, and its specific implementation and development at the local level through regional and local authorities. The agenda of sustainable development, however, is not devoid of strong economic and political implications, with different interests – and therefore different conceptions of sustainable development – competing not only among but also within nations. The concern from the ecological point of view with the complex interaction between global and local processes is just as relevant to the areas of economics and politics, where global processes are increasingly affecting local processes, be it through inclusion or exclusion.

Indeed, in terms of economics the current age is characterized by global-ization. Castells defines the new global economy as distinct from the world economy, which has existed at least since the 16th century, in that the former has the 'capacity to work as a unit in real time on a planetary scale' (Castells, 1996). This is possible through new information and communication technolo-gies. Although global markets do not reach everywhere because of, for instance, government protection afforded in some major economies to certain segments of their economy, Castells argues that the dominant segments and firms, the strategic cores of all economies, are connected to the world market, although this is a trend that is not yet fully realized. The global economy, however, directly concerns only segments of economic structures, countries and regions, thus simultaneously excluding a great part of the world population.

Some analysts of globalization note that nation-states still count; with government regulation and policies affecting the form the global economy takes. Indeed, in the face of increased international competition, initiatives have arisen to create stronger political and economic units based on the model of the nation-state. The clearest example of this is the European Union, where the aim is to establish a supranational state, that is political union. This European process is already having a strong impact on the spatial develop-ment of its territory, in terms of both urban and rural development. Similar processes of integration are being attempted in other parts of the world, some limited to the elimination of trade barriers as, for example with the North American Free Trade Agreement (NAFTA), others with political union as their long term aim (eg Central America). However, as has been stated, there is no prospect of a form of government evolving that would encompass the whole of the global economy and hold economic agents accountable.

Rather than encouraging union at a global level, the rise of the global economy has been accompanied by the consolidation of three major regional areas of influence: North America, the European Union and the Asian Pacific Region. Some authors argue that trade is concentrating between and within these blocks, while other regions are being marginalized. In these marginal-ized areas countries and regions compete to attract capital, human skills and technology, and therefore a regionalized, global economy can be talked about. In parallel with this process, widespread decentralization is taking place, with city governments taking on more entrepreneurial roles and competing with each other for investment, both from the regional blocks that have formed (eg European Union structural funds) and from transnational capital. Caught in between these two linked but opposite trends, 'traditional' nation-states are shedding competencies.

Castells (1996) considers regionalization as a systemic attribute of the global economy, because states are the expression of societies rather than of economies. He considers the interaction between historically rooted political institutions and increasingly globalized economic agents to be crucial. Castells identifies technological capacity; access to a large, integrated, affluent market; and the differential between production costs at the production site and prices at the market of destination as factors that affect competitiveness. This puts developing countries at a disadvantage. Therefore, although the centre–periphery conception is regarded by some as too simplistic, it is still the case that a group of countries corresponding roughly to the Organization for Economic Cooperation and Development (OECD) concentrates an overwhelming proportion of technological capacity, capital, markets and industrial production. Patterns of domination created by previous forms of dependency thus have been reinforced. This is reflected not only in economic terms, but also in environmental and political terms, as was strongly reflected in the conflicts between 'North' and 'South' at the Rio, Kyoto and Seattle summits.

These trends linking ecological, economic and political aspects are strongly affecting urban development. Urbanization continues through both rural–urban migration and (increasingly) natural growth. This is strongest in developing countries, where local authorities, firms and society have little control over production linked to global markets, and informal economies are increasingly providing means for economic survival, a phenomenon that is becoming more widespread in 'developed' societies also. In addition, a new development is megacities, which Castells identifies as the new spatial form in our informational age. Megacities have emerged as nodes within the global economy, not necessarily all being dominant centres although they do link huge segments of the population to this economy. According to Castells, a distinctive feature of these megacities is that they are 'globally connected and locally disconnected, physically and socially' (Castells, 1996). The growing rift between segments of society that are an integrated part of the global economy and those that are not is therefore clearly evident in the forms urban development is adopting, with the growth of informality in all sectors.

An example of the application of the analytical framework: the development of 'communicative' approaches in planning

As an example of the changing mental models and organizational forms, and how this impinges on the roles of the major agents in urban development, this section briefly reviews the evolution of approaches to urban planning, drawing mainly on the United Kingdom (UK) experience, although with global relevance.

An example of the influence of this book's themes is the evolution of planning, which developed three broad paradigms during the 20th century (see Table 2.1). The first of these paradigms was that based on a 'command and control' approach that relied on the production of 'blueprints', or 'master plans' for development activities. This approach was design-based and relied on the application of an instrumental rationality by experts and officials working for what was perceived as a unitary public interest. Land use zoning was one of the instruments developed through this approach, which is still well established in Europe and America, and urban form one of its main concerns.

Table 2.1 *Paradigms of planning*

	Nature of planning	Planning techniques	Predominance in planning	Division of power	Assumed nature of relations	Philosophy
First paradigm	Fixed vision of future ('blueprint')	Master plans, zoning	State planners	Government	Common consensus exists	Rationalism
Second paradigm	Flexible vision and specific action	Structure plans, action plans, special development areas	Public–private partnerships	Government with private sector	Common consensus has to be created	Rationalism
Third paradigm	No fixed vision	Above techniques with participatory planning	Negotiation forums	Government private sector and civil society	Conflict needs negotiation	Relativism

The 'command and control' approach was critiqued in the 1960s for, among other things, its lack of regard for the actual processes of development and, in consequence, of planning itself. There was a shift in British planning from a design-based approach to one based on the formulation of policy frameworks. Planning theory focused on processes of rational decision making, drawing on public policy theory from the US. The heightened awareness of 'planning as a process' raised, in addition, questions about participation in this process. Legislation was passed in the UK which institutionalized some kind of public participation in planning, based on formal consultation and public enquiries. Thus, planning began to be perceived as a process of conflict mediation where the role of the 'experts' became one of advocacy. Healey (1995) notes that this development led to the decline in government support for planning because 'the range of interests finding the opportunity for voice within the system challenged the capacity of the political-administrative nexus to keep control of both processes and agendas during the 1980s'.

Precisely the recognition of this range of interests and of how they interact has been one of the factors giving rise to what is here referred to as the 'third paradigm' in planning, based on 'interdiscursive policy formulation'. This approach to planning has various strands, the key elements of which are summarized by Healey (1997). These involve a recognition of the social construction of mental models and knowledge, and of the various forms reasoning can take; and a recognition of the diversity of interests and expectations on the one hand, and of the fact these are the result of social contexts on the other. Therefore, planning policies need to draw upon and spread this range of interests and 'knowledges', and must do so through collaborative consensus building rather than competitive interest bargaining, thus embedding planning practice in its social context. This planning paradigm is currently still in development in planning theory in the US and Europe, and evidence of its practice is still thin on the ground; however, there has been an upsurge of interest and experience of community-based planning in recent years.

In this evolution of planning paradigms, a shift in the roles of the state, the market and civil society is clearly visible. In the blueprint approach the state took a leading role, establishing what the future of urban areas and new towns was to be in physical terms. When planning shifted towards policy frameworks with public participation, the latter provided an opportunity for interest groups to have a say. These, in theory, included all sectors of society, but it was powerful interest groups within the market that had the greatest lobbying power in policy making as well as greater resources in public inquiries. Thus, although provision was made on paper for the participation of civil society, the process was still led by the state and heavily influenced by the market. Market influence grew with the decline of planning in the UK in the 1980s. The third paradigm, however, proposes a new way of combining views from all sectors – state, market and civil society – in an ongoing consensus-seeking dialogue.

During the process of paradigm shift described above there have been institutional changes, although these have been more evident in the sense of institutions as organizations rather than as mental models. An example of a mental model that has remained unaltered throughout is that of private property, which underpins many of the assumptions and policy formulations in planning. On the other hand, the welfare state as a mental model has become weakened during the last two decades of the 20th century, thus impinging on the decreasing role of the state. In terms of organization, the first paradigm was epitomized by the new town corporations created by the state, while the second paradigm involved organizational innovations such as consultation procedures organized by planning authorities, but also fast-track planning to facilitate market activity. The third paradigm could be characterized by negotiation and partnership as the organizational principle, although normative planning theory currently advocates broad strategy making arenas involving all stakeholders rather than the predominant trend in practice of, more limited, state–market partnerships.

In addition, these changes in planning approaches have increasingly reflected global–local linkages, especially, but not only, in economic terms. Blueprint planning was prevalent at a time of rapid economic growth when economic planning by the state was considered to hold the solution to market failures that could result in depressions such as that of the 1930s. Worldwide decline of certain economic activities had a strong impact mainly on manufacturing localities in the older industrialized countries, thus bringing about regeneration initiatives and highlighting the need for public participation in these badly hit areas. Globalization, with its increasing separation between formal sources of livelihood and place, first made necessary city marketing on a partnership basis, and is increasing the need for consensual platforms that might create non-exclusionary strategies in the face of international competition among cities for footloose transnational capital.

This short review illustrates the changing roles of state–market–civil society in planning in the 'developed' world – especially in the UK. However, parallels exist in transitional and developing countries, and it is these that the book predominantly illustrates.

THE COUNTRY-SPECIFIC EXPERIENCE

As noted in the Preface, the country-specific experience has been selected from work undertaken by staff and students in the Centre for Environment and Human Settlements, and is presented within the context of the analytical framework outlined in the previous section. It is not the intention of the authors and their international collaborators to necessarily present 'best practice', as the simplistic replicability of mechanisms from one political, economic, social and cultural context to another is not possible. However, lessons can be learned both from analysis of country-specific experience and from the wider comparison of these 'local actions' in the global context. While the authors begin this analysis in their case studies, especially with reference to the changing relationships between state, market and civil society, Chapter 11 expands this analysis across the case studies.

In Chapter 3 Paul Jenkins reviews the experience of communities in involvement in state- (and international agency-) led urban shelter projects since independence in Mozambique – one of the poorest and aid-dependent countries in the world. This review is set within a historical and analytical context that outlines the processes which have led to the fragmentation of traditional civil society in Mozambique, yet the repression of 'modern' forms of civil society during most of the past century. The chapter draws on other analytical work that has stressed the need to relate to forms of civil society which are 'horizontal' (intra-social) rather than 'vertical' (state–society) and which underpin urban life for a majority in peripheral urban areas such as much of Maputo, the capital. It suggests that mechanisms need to be developed that build on the existing strengths of the horizontal forms of civil society as a basis for adequate access to land and housing opportunities – especially given the weak nature of the state and embryonic nature of any market response in the sector, and the actual weak 'vertical' forms of civil society.

In Chapter 4 Rizwan Hameed and Jeremy Raemaekers look at the weak capacity of the state to regulate land use and industrial pollution in Lahore, the resulting negative environmental situations, and the reaction from communities. They suggest that communities can have an influence on industries in terms of their pollution, but that what is needed is a better relationship between communities and the state; more scope for industrial self-regulation (such as can be promoted by globalization); as well as more effective regulatory powers of the state over industry. The chapter thus highlights some of the negative effects of global industrial sourcing, although it also shows that this global sourcing might at the same time be part of the institutional answer. Above all it stresses the need to institutionalize environmental controls in the broad sense – ie both organizationally and culturally.

In Chapter 5 John Russell and Ghulam Abbas Anjum look at a successful innovation in urban management – that of delegation of regulatory functions for public transport from the state to an NGO. In Faisalabad a local NGO has been formed, with indirect state involvement and implicit permission from the provincial Punjab government, which has been able to provide a better regulated and more consumer oriented form of public transport. The mechanism for decision making at 'arms length' from the state and constructive engagement with the community have been key elements of the success. The model is now being adapted elsewhere in Pakistan, but there are issues of transferability and sustainability, and the chapter examines the key elements necessary to permit such replication. The case study exemplifies the need for flexible local innovation in institutions and illustrates the scope for wider roles for non-state organizations in what has generally been seen as the exclusive scope of the state to date.

In Chapter 6 Ralph Throp examines the current economic transition in China, with a general introduction to the previous forms of urban development, but with a strong and detailed focus on the changing situation though a case study of a 'floating population' village. This quite unique form of urban development has appeared in more recent years in older urban centres in China, and is based both on traditions developed in the main socialist phase of urban development and more rural settlement traditions. The links between a new form of community-based enterprise and urban management and wider economic forces are strong and have, to date, survived various attempts by the state to dismantle these areas. Whether the resulting form of civil society is benign or sustainable in a wider way as well as the future of this form of development is questioned. The author argues that scope does exist, however, for its broader incorporation into mainstream urban development.

In Chapter 7 Michael Carley and Josefa Rizalina Bautista describe innovations in organization that have developed at sub-municipal and supra-municipal level in Metropolitan Manila, arguing that these permit a more sustainable form of local accountability while permitting wider strategic issues to be addressed. The chapter describes the local level barangays, detailing some of their activities, as well as the strategic Metro Manila Development Authority (MMDA). It reviews the potential for this arrangement, indicating some of the difficulties, which partly lie in the political balance between local and metropolitan levels of governance, and partly in the prevailing attitudes to, and legal basis for, land use control. Overall, the chapter stresses the need for vertical as well as horizontal integration of activity to render urban management sustainable, arguing that top-down strategic planning needs to be integrated with bottom-up community self-development and that organizational forms that permit this are essential.

In Chapter 8 Harry Smith and José Manuel Valverde investigate the experience of community-based organizations in Costa Rica in negotiating with the state for housing benefits/solutions, based on a case study in a part of the capital, Rincón Grande de Pavas. The chapter illustrates the complexities of the state–civil society nexus in sustainable urban development. Whereas civil society is historically quite free and relatively organized in Costa Rica, the co-option of community-based organization in housing delivery under various political regimes is widespread and has tended to severely diminish any lasting effect of this level of organization. The authors relate this experience to wider forces of economic and political change worldwide, arguing that economic globalization is forcing the state to relate to civil society in new, and often not conducive ways.

In Chapter 9 Paul Jenkins analyses the relationship between the state and civil society in housing supply in South Africa, from a historical and contemporary point of view, focusing on urban social movements. The chapter recounts both the birth and consolidation of urban social movements around housing issues, and their demise after the negotiated settlement for a democratic state in recent years. In doing this it illustrates the difficult relationship between organizations in civil society and the state, as well as between those organizations within civil society of a more social or political orientation. The author analytically reviews possible future directions for the 'civic movement' in South Africa within this context, with reference to alternative regime transition in other parts of the world.

In Chapter 10 Cliff Hague reviews the effect of globalization and related economic restructuring (especially employment) on housing provision in Salford as typical of areas of the UK previously dominated by the manufacturing industry. The chapter's main thrust is that these broad economic changes have social and cultural effects which together impact on the previous conceptions of housing delivery as being managed by a public–private partnership – ie through state involvement in the market – to one where the state is subsumed into the market. The reasons for this are related to changing roles of government (under neoliberalism) as well as to the effect of the changing market as quantitative demand drops rapidly, while qualitative demand rises.

Chapters 11 and 12 draw conclusions based on the case studies and draw on the themes and analytical framework introduced in Chapters 1 and 2. In Chapter 11 Paul Jenkins reviews the case studies on a country basis, focusing on the relative roles of the state, market and civil society in urban development, and how organizational forms and mental models promote or constrain the greater legitimacy of the state and greater responsiveness of civil society within this context. Despite the enormous geographic, social, economic and political differences, similar themes of the weakening of the state and dominance of market forces are apparent. This both constrains state–civil society relations and fosters activity within civil society. The chapter then investigates the role of new social movements in urban development as a key organizational mechanism through which communities can contribute in powerful ways at levels beyond the local, arguing that this could provide the way to more effectively linking 'local' to 'global'.

In Chapter 12 Michael Carley and Harry Smith revisit the themes outlined in Chapter 1, reiterating the importance of creating a more sustainable basis for urban development across the globe. The authors examine some of the key constraints to this, especially the mental models of individual consumerism and the tendency of market mechanisms under weak state regulation. The chapter stresses the need for managed economic growth and the mobilization of human creativity, rather than the marginalization of this. The chapter also reviews the arguments in the book concerning civil society and social decision making, the linkages needed to relate 'local' to 'global' and the new mental models this will require. It draws on recent experience in the UK of bottom-up innovation and local governance, as well as pointing to the wealth of participatory techniques that can support this approach. Building on the recommendations of Chapter 11, the authors suggest the important role action networks can play in linking community initiatives horizontally and creating vertical linkages through new social movements, permitting new mental models to flourish that guide the activity of the state and hold the market socially accountable, which is essential for the creation of sustainable urban development.

PART 2

CASE STUDIES: LESSONS FROM INTERNATIONAL EXPERIENCE IN KEY URBAN DEVELOPMENT ISSUES

3 THE ROLE OF CIVIL SOCIETY IN SHELTER AT THE PERIPHERY: THE EXPERIENCE OF PERI-URBAN COMMUNITIES IN MAPUTO, MOZAMBIQUE

Paul Jenkins

INTRODUCTION

Overview

Mozambique has one of the world's weakest economies, on the world's poorest continent. During the last 30 years it has been governed by a fascist colonial power, a Marxist-oriented regime, and latterly an aid-dominated free-market elite. However, while to a great extent forcibly imposed, the state has remained extremely weak. The poor majority in Mozambique thus represent what can be termed the 'periphery of the periphery' in both political and economic terms. What has happened in shelter for the growing urban population under the conditions of extremely weak state and market influences in Maputo has, however, relevance for other situations where the role of civil society in land and housing may not be so obvious, given stronger state or market systems. It is argued here that better partnerships between state and market are not enough on their own, and that partnerships between civil society and the state and/or the market are essential to create sustainable urban areas.

Land and housing for the urban poor in Mozambique have never been a state priority, nor has the formal market provided for these. As a result, the vast majority live in informal housing, and this tendency has grown in recent years. At various times the state has attempted to facilitate access to land and housing for the urban poor, and at times there has been commodification of informal access – in other words this has become based on payment as opposed to social or state allocation. In general, however, the majority of the urban population get access to land and housing through informal mechanisms, although they are not well understood. Recent research has shown that these mechanisms are complex, many involving forms of reciprocity and social (ie non-state) redistribution.[1] In the light of continuing structural constraints for widening formal access – whether state or market led – it is therefore suggested that there should be a wider role for civil society in land and housing for the urban poor based on this reality.

How this is achieved depends to a great extent on the nature of civil society. The definition of civil society as predominantly modern and vertical may well not be appropriate in circumstances such as in Mozambique, where a century of repression has weakened indigenous organizational structures, whether political, social or cultural. In this situation it is argued that the horizontal and/or traditional structures (or modified versions of these) of civil society are more important to date than the vertical structures of modern forms. This chapter therefore looks at how an approach to land and housing that recognizes the important role of civil society might be developed in the Mozambican situation, with reference to peri-urban areas in the capital Maputo. The chapter explores the above themes by investigating the involvement of low-income communities in shelter projects developed by the state and international agencies after independence in Maputo. The case studies have been selected to illustrate central government, local government and international agency initiatives. They are in close proximity and in similar low-income communities.[2]

THE STATE, THE MARKET AND SOCIETY IN MOZAMBIQUE

Brief historical development

Mozambique has had foreign intervention since the 9th century AD when Persian (later Arabic) traders sailed down the East African coastline. This intervention was predominantly economic, with limited politico-military engagement until a millennium later, at the end of the 19th century. The relatively stable relationships between large internal indigenous kingdoms and with the external foreign coastal traders was upset with the arrival of the first Portuguese navigators in the middle of the 16th century. The Portuguese initially only used Mozambique as a staging post for their trade with India, but in time they competed with the traders and their allied coastal settlements for alliances with the internal kingdoms. The eventual decline of these led to a change from gold to ivory trading (early 18th century) and later still to slave trade (mid-18th to mid-19th century). The international demand for slaves from the 'New World' in the early 19th century had a catastrophic effect on the indigenous societies in the centre and north of the country, as whole areas were depopulated with smaller weaker clans being devastated or absorbed by stronger political units. This paralleled broad social changes in the south of the country where new strong indigenous states were also formed by the effect of the Mfecane – or Zulu uprising – in the early 19th century.

These indigenous states were more powerful than the local Portuguese presence, and Portugal in fact had little interest or capacity to dominate the Mozambican territory. Thus only with the threat of large areas of potential trade being annexed by the British in the colonial 'Scramble for Africa' at the end of the 19th century, was military conquest implemented. This led, however, to an economic vacuum which was only resolved by leasing the greater part of the territory to foreign capital with effective ruling powers. The leasing companies consolidated colonial rule but implemented a backward form of capitalism based on plantation economies with forced labour. This in turn brought about economic changes in the structure of the indigenous societies, as radical as those that military and political conquest had effected on indigenous governance structures. The result was widespread labour dislocation – either forced (in plantations) or voluntary (through migrant labour, mainly to South Africa).

Portugal initially developed its colonial interests to benefit the metropolitan mercantile elite through agricultural exports and services provision, with high levels of immigration from the metropole to absorb surplus rural population. The outcome in the 1960s was a relatively underdeveloped economy with enormous deficits in human resource development for the indigenous population, and an institutionalized form of segregation underpinned by widespread repression. This repression was increased with the emergence of liberation movements in the 1960s, although in parallel some forms of economic modernization were promoted, including the opening to foreign economic investment and limited state provision of services for the indigenous urban population. This was all too little, too late, however, and the struggle for liberation (in Mozambique as elsewhere against Portuguese rule) led to growing disenchantment in Portugal with the costs of colonization becoming one of the forces leading to an abrupt change of political regime – the 'Revolution of the Carnations' in April 1974.

The Mozambique Liberation Front (FRELIMO) led the new post-independent government in Mozambique into a radical change of development direction – a Marxist orientation, with strong expressions of self-reliance and non-alignment. While achieving strong initial backing from the population who had suffered decades of harsh colonial underdevelopment, the new political regime was not able to consolidate either its economic position (due to both external and internal factors – see Abrahamsson and Nilsson, 1995) or its social and political base. It became increasingly elitist and initial popular forms of participation quickly became institutionalized and dominated by the state. This culminated in the attempt in 1984 to forcibly remove the unemployed and under-employed from urban areas to sparsely populated rural areas, with disastrous consequences in terms of loss of life and political support. The lack of consolidation of an effective economic role for the mass of the peasantry had already brought about their economic marginalization from the state-led modernization process. The result was an increasing opting out of the formal system (economy, society and political life) by the majority and the reversion to traditional forms of interaction, usually termed informal.

In parallel, political, military and economic backing from South Africa and other conservative governments worldwide for destabilization of the FRELIMO regime led to a virtual civil war, with armed banditry being used against the state and its representation in social life (eg education and health workers as well as buildings). The war had a devastating effect only possibly matched by slavery, with millions dying from direct or indirect causes and many more being seriously affected in physical dislocation and loss of possessions.[3] Peace only came about after the end of the Cold War with changes in the macro-economic and political circumstances in the region (especially the ending of apartheid in South Africa), and strong pressure (and substantial financial assistance) from the international community. Peace, however, came in the throes of enforced structural adjustment, with the abandonment of socialism and the adoption of free-market liberalism and the strong contraction of the role of the state. The resulting impact in formal employment and economic circumstances is only now being measured.

The role of civil society

In the past century of colonial and post-colonial rule civil society has been largely repressed – albeit for different reasons – except in the brief period before and after independence. Traditional forms of civil society were initially subjugated and then later reactivated in the colonial period as a means to implement wider rule. This was true politically, with traditional chiefs being appointed to rule subordinately to the colonial administration; and also economically, with migrant labour being underpinned by social principles of economic distribution through networks within civil society. Despite its repressive force the state continued to be relatively weak in Mozambique throughout the colonial period – as indeed did market penetration until the last few years. In the post-independence period there was a more concerted effort at state-led forced modernization, but this also sidelined the majority of the population economically and politically, and then eventually socially and culturally. Hence the majority of the population has remained fundamentally linked to traditional forms of civil society in much of the country, albeit in modified form.

In the urban areas this is also the case, and although the forms of modification are different and the state had more impact, the vast majority of the population are not integrated in anything other than a superficial way to formal state and market activities. Recent research has, for instance, shown that only 32 per cent of the workforce in the capital Maputo work in the formal sector, and that only 25 per cent have gained access to land in formal ways for housing (Jenkins, 1999b). In addition, only 15 per cent of the voting population voted in the first ever local government elections in 1998 – less in Maputo, where it was 10 per cent (Braathen and Jørgensen, 1998). This lack of consolidation of formal ways of interaction also affects civil society. As Peter Ekeh has argued for sub-Saharan Africa in general, the undermining of indigenous civil society's political and economic roles in colonial forms of rule has led to the differentiation of 'civic' and 'primordial' public realms (Ekeh, 1975). The former has been dominated by the colonial and subsequently post-colonial state, and has generally not had widespread legitimacy; whereas the latter comprises ethnic, religious and other cultural forms of association, which have been largely alienated from the state, but widely underpin social values.

For many this has led to a separation of both socio-cultural and socio-economic meaning from the formal political and economic context, with different opportunities of expression of these in organizational form. As social and cultural expression was also repressed, civil society has thus not been primarily expressed in organizational form. As Victor Azarya has stated, if the '...focus on civil society remains only in associational life, we may leave out large numbers of people who do not see association formation as the preferred means to solve problems' (Azarya, 1994). This is especially the case in Mozambique, where organizational forms of civil society have long been marginalized and/or subordinated in both the colonial and post-colonial periods. In this situation it is the traditional or 'horizontal' (intra-society) forms of organization within civil society (and modified versions of these) that predominate, and not the relatively recent modern and 'vertical' (state–society) forms – such as those promoted by international agencies in the context of multi-party democracy (eg political parties, the independent media, trade unions and NGOs).

The next section looks at how this has been expressed in the urban shelter sector through the engagement of communities in various housing and urban development projects promoted by the state (central and local) and international agencies in the post-independence period in Maputo.

POST-INDEPENDENCE EXPERIENCES OF COMMUNITY ENGAGEMENT IN THE SHELTER SECTOR

The early post-independence period (1975–80)

After independence the new government organized the establishment of a series of *Grupos Dinamizadores* (GDs) – 'Dynamizing' Groups – in neighbourhoods, workplaces and institutions, initially as a form of socio-political mobilization and organization. These GDs were modelled on local committees formed in the areas liberated and administered by FRELIMO in the northern parts of Mozambique during the liberation struggle, members being elected in public meetings. No general plan of activities for these GDs was established, however, and the development and scope of their activities depended to a great extent on the personal qualities of the elected members. The GDs continued to develop their role in community organization during the latter part of the 1970s, but by the early 1980s increasingly became responsible for a myriad of basic local administrative controls, ranging from registry of residency and permission to travel, to ration card distribution. Although they played a key role in the organization of community participation in some pilot urban development projects, such as the Maxaquene project (see Box 3.1), their role during this period gradually became less that of popular mobilization and more of administrative control.

Several aspects of this project's execution led to the full benefit of what was implemented not being felt by the community, mainly due to the lack of attention given to institutional and political aspects of urban management. The lack of involvement of the local authority meant that when the project was handed over there was neither the capacity nor the inclination to continue the activities. In general, the National Housing Directorate concentrated on the

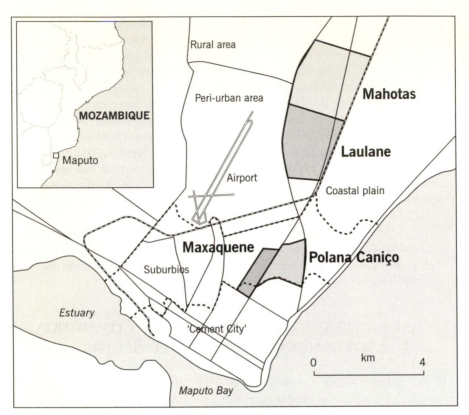

Source: Harry Smith

Figure 3.1 *Case study areas of Maxaquene, Laulane and Mahotas in Maputo*

immediate implementation of the project, and either did not fully appreciate the relevant policy issues, or did not have sufficient resources to raise these issues and try to resolve them.[4] At local level it would appear that city politicians encouraged displeasure with the smaller plot size and voiced this opinion in political arenas such as the council meetings, not for the benefit of the residents, but as an argument against consolidation of what was considered as informal housing in well located urban areas.[5]

Another key issue was the community's involvement in the project implementation. This was encouraged by the project team, and the vehicle used for community mobilization and organization was the GD. At the time of the project these entities were slowly changing their role from being mainly political to being mainly administrative. The extent to which the residents actually endorsed the project is, however, impossible to assess in retrospect as the attempt by the project team to develop independent block committees was quashed at its outset by the political authorities, with the GDs being the only permitted organizational vehicle. By and large it would appear, however, that these were considered by the population as valid vehicles for their opinions.

BOX 3.1 MAXAQUENE CASE STUDY

Maxaquene is an inner peri-urban neighbourhood, or *bairro*, which was partly upgraded by central government not long after independence (see Figure 3.1). Before independence it was part of a vast land concession to the Railway Authority and was fairly sparsely occupied, when it was administered by the traditional chiefs (*regulos*) Malhangalene and Mpfumo. A development plan was drawn up for part of the area in 1971 by the colonial authorities, including a new complex of industrial sites along a new road parallel to the railway and a major new railway shunting yard. During the years 1970–73 the existing population in the area was removed and the development was begun. However, in 1973 all activity stopped due to the growing unrest associated with the struggle for independence.

After independence informal occupation began to grow again, especially south of the main industrial road, and soon reached some 160 inhabitants per hectare. In early 1976 a small part of the Maxaquene *bairro* was chosen by the central government,[6] with UN assistance, for a pilot project in urban upgrading. In line with current UN policy, the need to develop ways of working with the community was emphasized. The population was mobilized by the GD and a structure for community participation in the project was developed through a 'Planning Commission' with members appointed from each relevant neighbourhood 'cell' (part of a *bairro*) to work with the project team. Members of the Planning Commission assisted with a socio-economic survey and subsequently drew up a priority list of problems. Relocation because of the road layout and creation of social amenity areas was also the responsibility of Planning Commission members, with the assistance of the GD.

The upgrading process began in June 1977, and by September 1979 the project area had expanded to include a final total of 300 ha with 36,000 inhabitants in both Maxaquene and neighbouring Polana Canico *bairros*, the latter generally serving as an overflow area (see Figure 3.2). By late 1979 basic infrastructure for the first 10,000 inhabitants in the initial project area had been constructed and paving of one new road was underway to permit public transport access. However, there was a slow rate of construction of community services (such as primary schools and community centres) as this depended on various other institutions. Subsequently, the Planning Commission assisted the project team in subdividing the main surveyed residential blocks to indicate individual plots using simplified topographical techniques.

Early in 1979 the *bairro* was visited by a ministerial commission which was involved in the preparation for the 'First National Meeting on Cities and Communal *Bairros*'. This visit was influential in leading to the passing of a series of resolutions on urban development based on planning concepts inherent in the pilot project. However, the project was criticized from various points of view, including the 'small' plot size. This view was expressed by some residents and was taken up by the press, citing cultural traditions, microclimatic needs and sanitary conditions as necessitating larger plots. This criticism was adopted by the City Council as a reason not to recognize the self-help land demarcation. In addition, in the absence of trained planning personnel, City Council staff also maintained the validity of the (outdated) 1972 City Master Plan, despite its utopian vision of extensive highways and bridges and little economic foundation.

This attitude was somewhat similar to that from the Ministry of Public Works and Housing, of which the National Housing Directorate was a part, which tended to adopt a policy of waiting until adequate resources would be available for full urban redevelopment. Politically the National Housing Directorate was reluctant to follow up the project in the absence of a national housing policy and given that the overall priorities of the government were predominantly rural oriented. Thus at the end of 1979 central government officially ceased its support for the project, indicating that project implementation activities should be the responsibility of the newly formed city council, although the project team recognized that this in fact had a 'complete lack of staff and psychological readiness'.[7]

As a result all project activities ground to a halt, and plans for the provision of community facilities were in most cases not realized, although infrastructure construction in progress continued for a while. The planned social infrastructure and services were finally completed many years later, but without maintenance the latter soon fell into disrepair.[8] Despite an attempt several years later by the city council planning department (which had by then developed a minimal in-house team of technical staff) to regularize the self-help land demarcation, no formal process for regularization could be agreed with the land registry section – due partly to the lack of appropriate land law regulations. The net result in the long term was a partially upgraded urban area in terms of better infrastructure, but continuing informal land allocation, and without any real long-term direct influence on urban development at a national or local level.

Experience in the early 1980s

During the 1980s the development of the involvement of the GDs in shelter-related activities was constrained in that central government controlled most resources (eg land and construction material), with precedence given to the centrally planned projects. As a result there were limited resources with which to develop local shelter-improvement activities. The few local activities that were possible were generally initiated by the city councils and international NGOs, and these usually attempted to work in close coordination with the GDs. This was especially so with respect to the development of local control of land use and construction in residential areas, as in such programmes as the 'Basic Urbanization Programme' of Maputo City Council – illustrated in the Laulane Case Study in Box 3.2.

After local government reorganization in 1979, a new City Council 'Construction and Urbanization Directorate' (DCU) – the equivalent of the Planning Department – was created with a minimum technical staff. By 1983 the DCU had initiated a series of urban interventions, primarily the experimental creation of basic peri-urban sites and services areas and support to self-help house construction.[9] The extreme institutional, financial and technical constraints on the DCU in the face of continued rapid growth in the city's population, with increasing informal occupation of peri-urban land, led the Directorate to develop a deliberate policy of catering for new urban growth rather than attempting to redevelop existing residential areas (such as in the above Maxaquene Project). The DCU thus began a Basic Urbanisation Programme in Laulane concentrating the few resources at its disposal in demarcating relatively sparsely occupied peri-urban areas suitable for housing, to pre-empt informal occupation.[10]

Several key aspects differ in this 'programme approach' from the 'project approach' used in the Maxaquene Project, the main aspect being the imple-

Figure 3.2 *Aerial view of Maputo (1991), showing the 'Cement City' in the background and Maxaquene and Polana Caniço in the foreground*

mentation of the intervention through existing departments of the city council and associated local institutions. Although this was much more difficult to achieve and took considerably more time to develop, there was no crisis when the project was handed over. In fact the continued management of the area was implicitly part of the existing management structures – particularly the lowest level of urban administration, the GDs.

Despite the relative success of this intervention given the resources available, and its potential role as a pilot for peri-urban residential development, the collapse of the national level institution responsible for policy formulation, and the lack of local level political support, led to the impact on policy initially being limited. The experience of this intervention was however fundamental in the formulation of urban development guidelines undertaken by the National Institute for Physical Planning, and the innovative use of appropriate technologies and organizational forms was of considerable importance to land and housing provision in general. In the medium term, however, this intervention was the basis for a further intervention, financed by the World Bank, which reactivated many of the issues raised in the Basic Urbanization Programme, including land use planning, land allocation, registry and transfer rights and regulations, as well as the possible financial and institutional basis for coordinated infrastructure provision. This latter intervention was however implemented in a very different way, as is described in the following section.

BOX 3.2 LAULANE CASE STUDY

Bairro Laulane is a large outer peri-urban neighbourhood partly located on higher land and partly in the low lying coastal plain, used traditionally for agriculture (see Figure 3.1). There is a short and fairly steep escarpment between these, along the top of which the principal northern-bound railway line runs. In the 1950s a relatively small residential neighbourhood was created in the then sparsely occupied southern part of the *bairro* to serve the National Railway Company. At the beginning of the 1970s a large-scale privately financed plan for high income residential development was developed for the central part of the *bairro*. Earthworks were initiated for road construction in the early 1970s, but stopped in 1973 with the rapidly evolving political crisis in Portugal.

Within the DCU Basic Urbanization Programme a subdivision plan was prepared in 1983 for the existing unoccupied land in the higher part of the area in the central and northern parts of the *bairro*. This project covered 194 ha and included approximately 5650 residential plots with provision for basic infrastructure and land reserves for social amenities. Plots were demarcated during 1984 and plot allocation began effectively in 1985. Plot allocation policy was extremely open, applications being accepted from all adults who were economically independent. The plot demarcation and allocation process was carried out involving the local GDs, with weekly meetings and extensive collaboration in the field. The GD was the vehicle for community participation with the relatively small population actually resident in the area demarcated.

Despite lack of funding for infrastructure and shortages of construction material, by 1987 the majority of the plots had been occupied, albeit predominantly using traditional materials and plot layouts (see Figures 3.3 and 3.4). In response to continued pressure from the residents, mainly channelled through the GD, the City Water Company eventually included Laulane within its Peri-urban Water Supply Programme and an electricity network was eventually created in 1992 with World Bank finance. In time also social amenity needs, as expressed by the residents, were attended to, with the construction of a new primary school and, eventually in 1993, the opening of a health centre. Commercial enterprises also began to flourish, especially informal markets and services, but also some formal shops, restaurants and bakeries were constructed. To a great extent these activities were contained within areas set aside in the original subdivision plan for commercial activity (see Jenkins, 1991).

Despite the relative success of the Basic Urbanization Programme in terms of satisfying demand for urban residential land and the need to control rapid urban spread, but effectively using scarce resources and relatively weak institutions, the programme was not substantially continued after 1985. This was affected by the low priority given to residential development for low-income groups by the central government[11] and changing local political interests which emphasized the provision of land to a relatively privileged elite.[12] A proposal for the continued expansion of such residential areas to the north was thus not carried out until the early 1990s (see Box 3.3 – Mahotas Case Study).

Changing context in the late 1980s

In the later part of the 1980s the administrative role of the GDs was firstly built up and then dismantled. Initially the secretary of the GDs and a permanent administrative assistant were financed from central government funds for each

Figure 3.3 *View in 1991 of a plot in Laulane allocated and occupied in 1985*

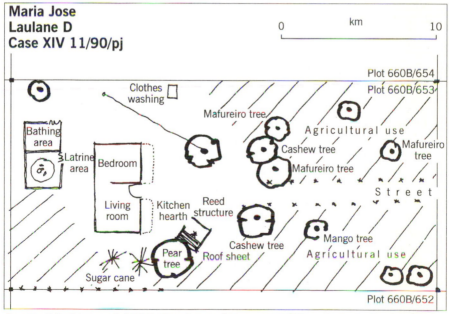

Source: P Jenkins et al (1991) *Housing and Living Conditions in Peri-urban areas of Maputo City*, UNDP/UNCHS, Ministry of Construction and Water Affairs, Mozambique

Figure 3.4 *Layout plan of the same plot in Laulane (see Figure 3.3) showing three constructions – residential, kitchen and latrine – and planted fruit trees*

bairro, mainly to deal with the growing administrative workload, although the secretary had still to be approved in a public meeting. In parallel, attempts were made to set up FRELIMO Party cells at neighbourhood level to continue the parallel party/state apparatus existing at national and local government level, but very few of these cells were in place towards the end of the 1980s. The GDs then were made subordinate to an intermediate level of district administration in the major urban areas, and thus had no direct link to local government structures. As a result, the popular influence of the GDs waned and, as clear directives as to the limits of their administrative role were not issued, the level and type of activity continued to differ considerably from *bairro* to *bairro*, depending on the initiative of the members.

With the deteriorating security situation around the principal and secondary urban centres in the latter part of the 1980s due to the civil war, and the subsequent rapid increase in urban influx, the problems facing all forms of local administrative control became severe. The GDs' capacity to respond to this situation was limited, and increasingly their role was reduced to a few key administrative controls. Local initiatives of communal self-help became increasingly rare and it became difficult for the GDs to solicit sufficient voluntary support for all but essential activities. In many cases the continuing high rate of urban influx and slow rate of supply of house sites put intolerable pressures on the GDs, and these soon became involved in unofficially allocating land and authorizing construction on an individual basis, despite their lack of capacity to control these activities and the formally defined responsibility for this area of the city councils.

Thus, while community participation had been seen as essential to plan and implement housing and urban development programmes in peri-urban areas since the Maxaquene project in 1977, it became virtually non-existent in the early 1990s. Almost the only (visible) community-based organizations other than the GDs of the *bairros*, were the churches, which had an impressive grass roots organizing capacity, as noted in the review of the World Bank pilot project (Jenkins, 1991). The Mahotas Case Study (Box 3.3) represents the involvement of communities in shelter activities in this period.

There is no doubt that the intervention in Mahotas delivered more concrete results faster than the previous two case studies but was probably less spatially useful for the inhabitants (see Figure 3.5); however, this has been done at a very much higher cost in terms of financial and human resources. Despite the definition of the principle of cost recovery, this was never attempted.[13] Legal and administrative problems were alleged to be the main source of delay concerning this, but the difficulty of applying a land improvement tax in a few isolated areas was considered unfeasible in the absence of any overall urban development policy. In this the nature of the project as designed and implemented seems essentially to have been at odds with current World Bank policy.[14]

Despite its serious shortcomings the project did serve to focus attention yet again on a series of key urban development issues which had been highlighted previously in both the Maxaquene and Laulane interventions. These included the need for an urban development policy including clear legal and administrative mechanisms for land use planning, development,

BOX 3.3 MAHOTAS CASE STUDY

Bairro Mahotas abuts on to Bairro Laulane, with which it shares physical similarities (see Figure 3.1). The most northerly area was incorporated within the city limits when these were extended in the 1960s, although at this time most of the area was occupied in traditional form, except for low-lying agricultural land which was developed to supply fresh produce for the urban area. As indicated in the previous case study, Bairro Mahotas was identified in the 1985 City Structure Plan as a priority urban expansion area, but a subdivision plan which was prepared in 1985 was not implemented due to reasons explained above.

As part of the new World Bank Structural Adjustment Programme in 1987 the Mozambican Government requested investment rehabilitation of urban infrastructure and housing.[15] Mahotas was agreed as the site for the 'self-help housing' sub-component, costed at some four million US dollars. This included improving infrastructure for some 1000 plots already provided by the City Council (see above) as well as a new residential expansion area (1500 plots). The target group was finally defined as lower-middle income, although the criteria for this were not quantified formally at any stage. It was decided at central government level that implementation of the whole project would be through specially created project implementation units within the Ministry of Construction and Water Affairs.

In 1988 initial physical, legal and socio-economic surveys of the area were undertaken and investigation of the existing land occupation indicated that the local GD and district administration had been involved in extensive informal plot allocation, as well as there being serious discrepancies within the land registry department of the city council (such as double allocations). As a result it was argued that the project was actually an upgrading and densification project and an in-depth socio-economic and living-conditions survey was carried out to ascertain the relevance of the original proposal for residents, and the possibility of alternative forms of housing consolidation.

The results indicated that the physical, social and economic situation of the majority of the residents was in considerable flux – markedly more so than might have been expected in a 'normal' process of urbanization. The war and structural adjustment were two major factors affecting this, both in terms of family size (rising fast), and food security and incomes (decreasing fast). The study acknowledged the role of kinship in reallocating housing benefits in this situation and identified the existence of informal credit mechanisms underpinning incremental house consolidation processes. Above all it noted the high level of residents who were living in what the World Bank defined as 'absolute poverty'.[16]

Concerning the proposed self-help housing sub-component, the study stressed the need for flexible support packages to be developed through community based and NGOs, as well as allowing this type of institution to provide (and maintain) some of the new infrastructure. The survey also queried the World Bank's approach to land tenure, which was to be linked to cost recovery, and hence might displace a large proportion of the actual residents who would find payments impossible. Finally, the almost complete lack of community or local administration involvement in project design or implementation was noted, with the likely result being a low response in cost recovery and maintenance. The survey was, in fact, effectively the first opportunity for the resident population to express their aspirations for the project. Despite the above recommendations concerning more appropriate mechanisms the project continued to be developed by the implementation agencies as originally designed.[17]

The city council commenced plot demarcation in late 1990, and infrastructure construction began soon after, being completed by 1993. In general, despite the location of an office in the project area little was done to involve and inform the residents about the project. Plot allocation initially concentrated on registration of existing residents, but there was considerable discussion on the allocation process for new vacant plots. The central government favoured a block allocation policy for workers' housing, arguing that this would ensure adequate consolidation as employers could guarantee the housing loans, whereas local government wanted to allocate the land itself. Allocations were eventually made to emergency relocation families (due to drainage problems in the inner city), as well as to employees of the parastatal airline company, but otherwise the plots were allocated by the city council entities. No assessment of economic capacity was entailed and hence there is no way of knowing if the project reached the target beneficiaries or not.

In addition, no final housing credit delivery mechanisms were ever successfully decided on – mainly, it seems, due to the inflexibility and disinterest of the People's Development Bank (BPD) – which was the only formal housing credit institution), despite the implicit subsidy in the project design. The general lack of institutional experience and capacity in this area in Mozambique was also an important factor, together with the very formal and structured way the credit was proposed to be allocated. It is doubtful in fact if many actual plot holders would have been able to gain access to credit through these mechanisms due to low income levels.

allocation, registry and transfer; definition of investment mechanisms for urban development including subsidies and cost recovery; the need for clear relationships between management of the physical and administrative aspects of urban development; and the need for appropriate institutional capacities at local level to be used and developed, both within the state and civil society. To date, however, these issues are still not resolved in Mozambique (Jenkins, 2000).

1990 to the present

Under the new 1990 Constitution, the GDs were abolished and the *bairro* secretaries were to be incorporated into the structure of the city councils. In practice, however, it appears that some of the GDs continue to function in their administrative capacity at local level, or in some cases, have given rise to embryonic neighbourhood committees. Other community-based organizations include family-sector agricultural associations, agricultural cooperatives (both active in the peri-urban areas), and local branches of the women's organization and the youth organization. In general, however, the level of community participation in the mid-1990s was very low, reflecting various factors, such as allegations of corruption and abuse of power among GD members; lack of encouragement by central and local government; lack of responsiveness or capacity to respond to local problems on the part of the city councils; lack of consultation with local residents in the planning and implementation of development projects; and the fact that most of the peri-urban population have more basic preoccupations, such as how to obtain enough food.

Credit: Paul Jenkins

Figure 3.5 *Housing provided by the World Bank in Mahotas*

Conclusions concerning state–civil society relations

The above case studies and related analysis illustrate that constraints to greater community involvement in shelter delivery have been due both to the limited interest and capacity of the state (and latterly the market) to interact with communities and also to organizational weakness at community level. As introduced in the first section of the chapter, this results from the legacy of a long period of repression of independent organizations within civil society. In counterpoint, however, individual households have strong networks within their communities – both geographical and kinship based – as they have to rely on their own initiative in the face of a relatively weak state and market, which do little to facilitate or provide shelter for low-income groups.

The chapter analyses the basis for this in terms of different modes of socio-economic interaction, and suggests that more relevant actions by the state or others would also be based on the dominant forms of socio-economic interaction within civil society. As these forms of interaction are present in many other societies, in parallel with those of the state and market, this socio-cultural basis is appropriate for shelter delivery to the urban poor in a wider way, as opposed to expecting the state, the market or partnerships between these, to successfully provide land and housing for the rapidly growing low-income majority in many urban areas worldwide.

Concerning state–civil society relations in socialist countries in the developing world, White (1985) reviewed the experience of six of these, noting that they all had developed highly statist approaches to socialism, and that all of them had gone through three broadly similar phases:

1   Revolutionary voluntarism
    The application, in a chaotic and rapidly changing post-revolutionary situa-
    tion, of methods of mass mobilization originally developed during the
    politico-military struggle.
2   Bureaucratic voluntarism
    State consolidation and direction of the social economy through a wide
    range of administrative controls, with the aim of rapid development.
3   Reformism and market socialism
    In the light of the development of more complex economic structures and
    diversification of social demands, policies focus on economic efficiency
    (with acceptance of market forces), with a tendency to greater political
    pluralism and cultural diversity.

There are close parallels between this analysis and the above short history of
the relationship between state and community in shelter, with the addition of
a fourth phase of complete rejection of socialist goals – economically in the
late 1980s under structural adjustment and politically in the 1990 Constitution.

THE CURRENT ROLE FOR CIVIL SOCIETY IN SHELTER IN MOZAMBIQUE

As indicated above, civil society has been largely repressed in Mozambique,
despite the brief pre- and post-independence periods of 'revolutionary voluntarism'. The swing to a free-market economy and political pluralism has,
however, not fostered widespread constitution of associational forms of civil
society, although an independent press is now active and trade unions no
longer follow party lines. The churches have also regained much of the acceptance they held with the population previous to the socialist period when they
were heavily restricted (but not banned), and play an important socio-cultural
role in survival. There has also been a growth of other associations such as
ethnic and producer groups. Apart from non-state forms of redistribution such
as those channelled through religious and ethnic associations, kinship forms
remain a major mechanism of socio-economic interchange.

In the rural areas there has also been a resurgence of traditional power,
and much of the public discourse on civil society in Mozambique has been
generated around the role this should play vis-à-vis how the state as local
government is restructured. The international community has tended to see
recently created NGOs as the main protagonists of civil society and these
have received substantial support, especially in development and welfare
work. Few of these have, however, developed as a result of local association
or community interests. As political scientist Jeremy Grest has noted, the
'...study of their implantation and reception reveals something about the
nature of local society, its power relations and its articulation with national
and international flows of goods, resources and ideas' (Grest, 1997). Local
government elections have also now taken place – although as noted above,
with no clear underpinning of legitimacy. It remains to be seen how the local

state will act and whether it will attempt to relate to the needs of the national elite or wider population.[18]

The weak role of the state and role of informal mechanisms is very clearly evidenced in the recent research concerning land access in urban areas such as Maputo (Jenkins, 1999b).[19] The most important mechanism for access seems to have been via local administrative institutions (ie GDs and traditional authorities), which are considered as informal mechanisms of access as no register is kept of such allocations and this is not a formal role (the city council is the only formally authorized entity for land allocation within the urban area). These represented 20–39 per cent of responses on land access mechanisms. Other informal forms of access, such as inheritance or ceding within the family, direct occupation and swopping, were used by between 18 and 25 per cent of respondents. Monetary payment to a private individual for land represented only between 5 and 12 per cent of all surveyed cases.

However, despite this latter finding, between one third and one half of those interviewed indicated that they paid for access to land, suggesting that a significant number have paid for access to land within both the formal and informal mechanisms. Indeed around one third of those who gained access to land through the formal mechanisms (ie the city council) indicated they also paid for access – as did slightly less than half of those who gained access from local level authorities. Overall therefore, while payment for access to land has increased, direct purchase has mainly been at the expense of formal allocation, with mechanisms based on allocation by local authorities and social mechanisms remaining predominant, although these more often now also involve monetary transfer. In most of these cases, however, it would appear that the payment has been for the right to be allocated the land, rather than for the land itself. This form of land access has roots within traditional means to gain access to land in rural areas.

As argued elsewhere (Jenkins, 1998), there is little likelihood that the weak state will respond to the majority lower income population's needs due to its low institutional capacity and lack of political interest. The market in Mozambique is also weak and uninterested in catering for a lower income population with low spending power. The growing commodification of land described above thus represents a rising threat to land occupied through informal mechanisms by the poor. There is thus an urgent need to develop mechanisms to protect occupancy land rights as recognized by the new Land Law, as well as devise more institutionally appropriate and less complex mechanisms for new residential land allocation and development. It is suggested that the key here is to base new land access mechanisms on socially based forms of organization, formalizing these through institutions such as community land trusts which are controlled by the community, although registered by the state, and regulated to protect them from the 'free' market.

This, however, will require strong mobilization at community and higher levels to establish these rights and mechanisms. It is suggested that a key role could be played here by the religious and other community-based organizations (CBOs) which are emerging, with assistance from the fledgling national NGOs.[20] Other important institutions of vertical civil society that could support the political lobbying process would be the independent media and the churches. It is obvious, however, that to be able to confront the state, the wider mobilization of communities around urban issues such as land, and the broadening of the front to deal with these issues will most likely be needed – ie the creation of 'voice'. If this does not happen, the wider part of the population will be obliged to fall back on the 'exit' option (Hirschmann, 1970), which will mean continued living on the fringes of formal life, with the severe exploitation this will increasingly entail.

4 THE STATE, BUSINESS AND THE COMMUNITY: ABATING INDUSTRIAL NUISANCE IN LAHORE, PAKISTAN

Rizwan Hameed and Jeremy Raemaekers

INTRODUCTION

This chapter explores through a case study in Pakistan why, in the cities of developing countries, resident communities are so commonly subject to environmental nuisance from nearby industry.

Approaching from the framework of state, market and community, we can model the problem as a cascade of means by which nuisance might be abated:

- If the state regulators were functioning effectively, the problem would not arise because the town planning regime would segregate sources of nuisance from sensitive land uses, and because the environmental protection regime would largely prevent the sources of nuisance arising even where the land uses were not segregated.
- Where the regulators fail to act effectively of their own accord, business might nevertheless regulate itself up to a point, either because it acknowledges a moral responsibility to society and the environment or, failing that, because it might be sensitive to any market impact of its social and environmental image.
- If the regulators do not act effectively of their own accord, and if business does not regulate itself, the surrounding community might yet force business to abate nuisance by putting pressure upon it, either more or less directly through complaints, demonstrations or even more extreme action, or less directly by pressurizing the regulators to fulfil their remits.

With respect to the first level in this cascade, we have shown how the structural weaknesses of the planning and environmental protection regimes in Lahore constrain effective prevention and remedy of local industrial nuisance (Hameed and Raemaekers, in press). We shall summarize that argument, and supplement it with evidence from factories and surrounding residents about their decision on where to locate.

At the second level, we have described the perceptions of industry about factories' impacts on surrounding residents, and the potential for industry-led initiatives to change industry behaviour (Hameed and Raemaekers, 1999). We shall also summarize these findings, and supplement them with evidence of industry's views on the intermingling of industry and housing.

At the third level, we shall ask whether communities mobilize to try and get nuisance abated, whether they succeed, whether their activity and effectiveness are related to their socio-economic level, and what are their expectations of the state and of business.

Finally, we shall look at a new tool, the environmental tribunal, which has recently been introduced in Pakistan, and ask whether it can deliver environmental justice to less-advantaged citizens where the existing regimes have not.

BACKGROUND

Pakistan is an industrializing nation, in the next wave after the newly industrialized countries of East Asia, although farming is still the largest employment sector. Population is estimated at 130 million, with a growth rate of 2.6 per cent per annum, which is one of the highest in the world. Gross national product (GNP) per capita is about US$500, with manufacturing constituting 18 per cent of gross domestic product (GDP) (Government of Pakistan, 1996). Literacy is low, especially among women and in rural areas. The nation was created as an Islamic state by the partition of India in 1947, and it would be fair to characterize the country as religious, certainly by Western standards. Islam plays a significant role in morality, community welfare and politics, although there is a very wealthy stratum of society with a cosmopolitan lifestyle.

Pakistan is a federation of several provinces, composed of divisions, which are split into districts. Our case study area, Lahore, is an ancient city of five million people and the capital of Punjab Province, commanding the northern part of the vast irrigated plains of the Punjab. The city is bounded on the north and west by the River Ravi, and India lies close to the east (see Figure 4.1). Manufacturing accounts for at least one quarter of its economic output, with textiles accounting for 21 per cent of the 850 or so large scale industries (defined as those employing 20 or more workers as per the census of manufacturing industries in Pakistan). Other important sectors are metal parts fabrication, basic metal industries and food processing (Government of Punjab, 1998).

Municipal committees or corporations govern the urbanized parts of districts, while those parts which are still rural remain under district councils. Thus the 343 km² built-up part of Lahore District is governed by Metropolitan Corporation Lahore, which holds the usual range of local government powers, including planning and building control and nuisance abatement, and the remaining rural parts by District Council Lahore. The district councils acquired planning and building control powers only in 1997.

Overlying this structure is the 2269 km² Lahore Metropolitan Region. It was delineated under the Lahore Development Authority Act 1975, which created the Authority. The region includes the built-up part of Lahore District

Source: Rizwan Hameed

Figure 4.1 *Lahore and neighbouring territories*

(the Corporation area) and the remaining rural parts of the district (under District Council Lahore), as well as part of the neighbouring rural Sheikhupura District to the north across the River Ravi, and part of Kasur District to the south (see Figure 4.2).

Lahore Development Authority is charged with a range of functions including the preparation, updating and implementation of the Metropolitan Development Plan; exercising land use and building control; preparation, implementation and enforcement of schemes for environmental improvement, housing, transport, health and education facilities; preservation of objects or places of historical importance; and the creation of agencies such as the Water and Sanitation Agency. The Authority thus holds planning powers in parallel with the Corporation itself throughout the Corporation's area, and with Lahore, Sheikhupura and Kasur District Councils outside the Corporation's area. Moreover, it reports to a different provincial government minister.

There is yet another complication! In the east of the Corporation's territory lies the Cantonment, an administrative island of 93 km^2, controlled by its own Board. This area was set up under British rule, under the control of the military. Its Board deals with all matters relating to planning and development, and with the delivery and maintenance of infrastructural services and public amenities. The Cantonment has always been excluded from spatial planning exercises carried out for the city as a whole.

Environmental protection within the Metropolitan Region is the remit of a provincial agency, the Environment Protection Department Punjab (EPDP).

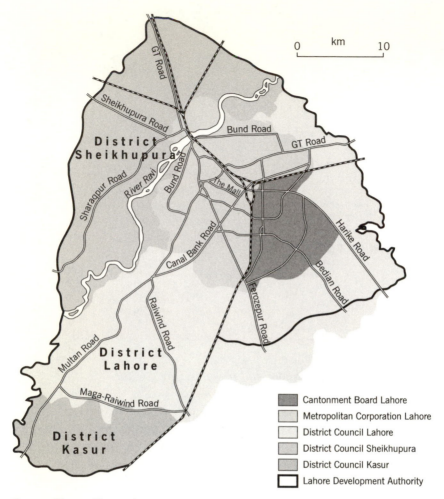

Cantonment Board Lahore
Metropolitan Corporation Lahore
District Council Lahore
District Council Sheikhupura
District Council Kasur
Lahore Development Authority

Source: Rizwan Hameed

Figure 4.2 *The areas of jurisdiction of planning agencies in the Lahore Metropolitan Region*

METHODS

Information was mostly collected during 1997 and 1998. Surveys of the distribution of industry in the Metropolitan Region identified 15 clusters (see Figure 4.3). These were defined as geographical concentrations of primarily large scale industrial units, whether existing side by side with other land uses in a haphazard manner (13 fell in this category), or neatly segregated from other land uses in planned industrial estates (two clusters). The degree of intermingling of industry with housing varies within the 13 non-estate clusters, although it tends to be greater in those lying within the densely developed parts of the city than in those on its periphery. Some factories also exist throughout the city outside the clusters identified.

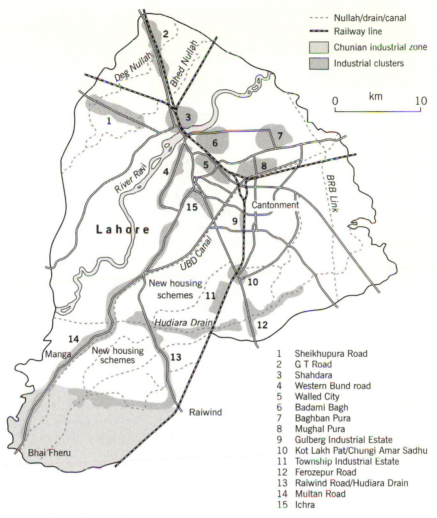

Legend:
- - - - Nullah/drain/canal
▬▬▬ Railway line
Chunian industrial zone
Industrial clusters

1   Sheikhupura Road
2   G T Road
3   Shahdara
4   Western Bund road
5   Walled City
6   Badami Bagh
7   Baghban Pura
8   Mughal Pura
9   Gulberg Industrial Estate
10 Kot Lakh Pat/Chungi Amar Sadhu
11 Township Industrial Estate
12 Ferozepur Road
13 Raiwind Road/Hudiara Drain
14 Multan Road
15 Ichra

Source: Rizwan Hameed

Figure 4.3 *Industrial clusters in the Lahore Metropolitan Region*

The clusters were used to select firms and communities for guided inter-views. Representatives (usually owners or managers) of 23 large scale firms from across the 15 clusters were interviewed. The firms were chosen to cover different ages, types of ownership and waste streams, but all situated close to housing. One residential community from each industrial cluster in the Metropolitan Region was also interviewed, in groups of five to seven persons. The communities interviewed were those surrounding the factories of the interviewed firms. We were thus able to cross check information from firms and communities against each other.

Officials of regulatory regimes at federal, provincial and local levels were interviewed to gain access to data, to identify cases, to clarify institutional and legislative issues, and to seek explanations of operational weaknesses.

THE PROBLEM OF INDUSTRIAL NUISANCE

We illustrate here the problems of industrial nuisance and intermingling of housing with industry. More information may be found in Hameed and Raemaekers (in press).

Industrial air emissions make up an increasing proportion of total air pollution in Lahore Metropolitan Region, rising even faster than vehicle emissions (Government of Pakistan/Joint Research Committee–International Union for the Conservation of Nature and Natural Resources, 1992; Environmental Protection Agency Punjab, 1993). Near a chemical complex at Kala Shah Kaku, half to two thirds of residents suffered from vomiting, sore eyes, sore throat, chronic cough and chest pains.

At least 1100 industries in the Metropolitan Region discharge waste water containing acids, alkali, ammonia, chlorine and heavy metals without treatment into drains and sewers which fall into the River Ravi. Samples of waste water collected from various industries show contamination levels in all cases exceeding the national environmental quality standards (Environmental Protection Agency Punjab, 1993; Ministry of Environment, Local Government and Rural Development, 1997).

This poses a health threat, because the river is used for irrigation, recreation, livestock watering and domestic purposes. One quarter of the land around the city is irrigated by municipal sewage water and sludge, laced with metals like cadmium, chromium and lead (Younas et al, 1997). Most of the city's water is drawn from the underlying aquifer, to some extent recharged from the River Ravi. Contamination of the city's water supply has been recorded, including concentrations of heavy metals (Ministry of Environment, Local Government and Rural Development, 1997). Industrial effluent is also often discharged directly on to land, exposing surrounding residents to risk of heavy metal and chemical poisoning.

Solid industrial wastes also contribute towards land pollution. Such wastes are either dumped with municipal solid wastes (often in low-lying areas without using modern sanitary landfill techniques) or fly-tipped (sometimes immediately outside the premises and sometimes on to open land) or burned at any convenient location.

The impact of several types of industrial nuisance is aggravated by the juxtaposition of polluting industries and housing (Qadeer, 1983). We did not have the resources to survey the extent of juxtaposition systematically, but Figure 4.3 indicates at city scale the mingling of the two land uses, and Figures 4.4 and 4.5 illustrate it photographically.

PERFORMANCE OF THE REGULATORY AGENCIES

Environmental protection

Why does the environmental protection regime not effectively control industrial nuisance?

Credit: Rizwan Hameed

Figure 4.4 *Juxtaposition of industry and housing: an iron and steel mill in the middle of a residential area (Baghban Pura cluster)*

Credit: Rizwan Hameed

Figure 4.5 *Juxtaposition of industry and housing: textile mills surrounded by housing (Western Bund Road cluster)*

One obstacle is that EPDP lacks trained staff and basic physical resources, and staff morale is low (Hameed and Raemaekers in press). Another is that EPDP staff tend to focus on problems of water pollution, whereas our interviews showed that residential communities are more worried about air pollution, noise, vibration and waste disposal.

A third obstacle is beyond the control of EPDP. There have existed national environmental quality standards which the provincial EPDP could enforce, using powers under the national Environmental Protection Act 1997. The standards had, however, never been activated by the federal government, and the powers awarded to the federal protection agency by the 1997 Act had never been devolved to the provincial ones. This is because the federal government had never convened the Pakistan Environment Protection Council, which could do so. In August 1999, the council was eventually convened. It approved a revised set of standards, delegated powers to the provincial agencies, and instructed implementation to begin on 1 January 2000. However, the council then again delayed implementation in response to representations from industry. Thus the present position is that the necessary approvals have been made, but implementation is withheld.

Lacking the necessary powers itself, EPDP has sought the cooperation of other agencies at district level which have powers that could be harnessed to control industrial nuisance. Thus it has asked district administrators and Metropolitan Corporation Lahore to prosecute offenders under their public nuisance powers. This has produced little effect, partly because of corruption within those organizations, and partly because of the endemic protraction of litigation. Unfortunately, both are characteristic of the country. There is a culture of contesting regulatory controls through the courts, tying up processes almost indefinitely.

EPDP has also sought the help of the Punjab Industries and Minerals Development Department (henceforth called the Industries Department), a provincial body charged with strategic oversight of industrial location, and which has, over the years, had a fluctuating power to license factories. As a preventive measure, EPDP asked the Industries Department to request firms seeking a no-objection certificate from it also to seek an environmental impact statement clearance from EPDP. But again, some Industries Department area offices have not complied. This reflects another characteristic of the institutional culture: territoriality of agencies, which are not necessarily ready to cooperate towards a common goal greater than the legal remit of each, especially when the one seeking help is of low status, as EPDP certainly is.

Land use planning

Why does the planning regime not effectively segregate industry from housing? We present here a perspective derived from case studies of the factories and communities in the industrial clusters.

Most houses in the majority of our 15 clusters were built without approval (building permission and planning permission are fused into one process). Development control was strongest in those communities falling under Lahore

Development Authority, the planning agency with the best staffing and resources. It was weakest on the outskirts of the Metropolitan Region, under the district councils, which until recently had neither the capacity nor indeed the powers to exercise building control or to make their own development plans.

One source of weak control is the conflicting planning policies applying to some of the clusters, because within the municipal limits there are two concurrent development plans: the 1966 Master Plan, which is followed by the Corporation (Government of the Punjab, 1973), and the 1980 Structure Plan followed by the Authority (Lahore Development Authority et al, 1980). Thus there are concurrent plans followed by two agencies with overlapping territories, both holding planning powers! In fact, even in this mess the mingling of factories with housing could have been prevented, reduced or removed, if only the later 1980 Structure Plan had been implemented in a spirit of cooperation between the two agencies. The reasons this has not happened include points of legal detail, but the underlying one is the organizational territoriality referred to above, not helped by the agencies reporting to different ministers.

This confusion over planning powers is aggravated further, in the case of industrial development, by lack of clarity on whether the local planning authorities or other licensing agencies have the final say on granting location clearance. One of these other agencies is the Industries Department. For example, it licensed factories to set up in Zarfishan Street and Shalimar Town, in contravention of the 1966 Master Plan followed by the Corporation.

The lack of clarity about which permissions in reality carry weight not only allows problems to arise, but also interferes with the planning authority's ability to put them right if complaints are lodged. For example, if the Corporation sought to close down or require relocation of an offending factory which had been licensed by the Industries Department, the factory owner could take the matter to court and obtain a stay order on the grounds that permission had been granted by another government agency.

Finally, some of the juxtapositions simply arose before regulatory powers were created. For example, the factory at Kala Shah Kaku was set up in 1962 in Sheikhupura District, whereas the district council did not obtain planning powers until more than three decades later.

The problem with control of house building is somewhat different: the question is not which agency's approval carries most weight, but whether permission to build is required at all. Questioning of residents indicated that some built without permission because they perceived that, outside the municipal limits or in a *katchi abadi* (unauthorized housing development), no such permission was required. In this they were in fact correct, since the district councils only acquired control powers in 1997, while inside the municipal limits the government regularized *katchi abadis* in later years after they had been built, leading people to believe that permission was not required in the first place.

The representatives of some communities, where some or most residents had gone through the process of obtaining a building permit, expressed their dissatisfaction with the regulations and the approval process. They pointed out that people do not seek house-plan approval because of difficulty in understanding the regulations and the procedures, and due to corruption and delays in the process. Some commented that those on low incomes do not seek permission because the standards do not allow low-cost houses – a familiar complaint in developing countries. Others argued that finding an architect who could design the house for a low fee is also difficult, and that those with low incomes have neither the income nor the desire to spend money on preparing a house plan which will obtain building clearance.

When asked how people deal with building inspectors, respondents invariably replied that inspectors rarely visit. If they do, people pacify them with bribes. If the inspector refuses a bribe and reports an unapproved house, a fine is usually levied, on payment of which the house plan subsequently submitted is approved. This obviously reinforces the perception of residents that approval is a purely bureaucratic tool for levying a tax, as opposed to a means of promoting a better and safer environment.

CAN INDUSTRY REGULATE ITSELF?

Even without effective regulation by the authorities, industry might regulate itself to a level more satisfactory to local residents. Afsah et al (1996), reporting on their experience as 'participant analysts' in six large developing countries (China, Indonesia, Philippines, Brazil, Mexico and India) have found that regulatory agencies are '...not the sole source of pressure on plants to improve their environmental performance. Local communities and market agents also play important roles.'

It is easy to take a cynical view that industry takes advantage of apparent immunity from prosecution. But this is not the whole story. Factory owners and managers we interviewed were often ignorant of the origins of pollution, the options for abating it and the cost of these options (Hameed and Raemaekers, 1999).

There is therefore a case that a 'regulate and enforce' approach needs to be supplemented by a 'facilitative' approach, which accepts that non-compliance arises partly from ignorance, and that the remedy therefore lies partly in understanding, educating and working with industry to create the conditions in which initial compliance is more likely, obviating the need for enforcement (see Prior, in press). Interestingly, some of the residents interviewed also saw cooperation within industry and between regulators and industry as a way forward:

> 'Their factories always make a profit and, if they want, they can solve this problem, maybe by taking joint action such as pooling money and resources to construct where possible a common treatment plant for many factories.'
>
> 'Government should try to negotiate the matter with the industrialists and assist them in finding appropriate solutions to the problems.'

The Environmental Technology Programme for Industry (ETPI)[1] is an example of such a facilitative approach and includes demonstration projects with volunteer firms (Hameed and Raemaekers, 1999). It is obviously encouraging that industry has itself taken the initiative.

We should also beware of taking a one-sided view of industry's attitude with regard to land use planning. Housing moves in on factories as much as the other way around: housing had located close to existing factories in 9 of our 15 clusters. This must raise doubts in factory owners' minds about the seriousness with which residents view industrial nuisance. Asked why they located close to factories, or tolerated factories opening close to their homes, residents did indeed confirm that proximity to employment, as well as to other conveniences, were important determinants of choice. They also cited initial lack of awareness of the nuisance problem.

When asked about juxtaposition, factory owners and managers defended themselves by arguing variously that, at the time they set up, the area was empty (seven cases), there were only a few scattered houses nearby (one), there were already factories in the area (two), the nearest housing was at a reasonable distance (one) and still is (one), the factory was in a planned industrial estate (two), or the area was declared in 1947 as an industrial zone (one). All also stated that the population around their factory expanded in later years and that no government agency took any action to prevent or remedy this.

It is no surprise that, under the circumstances just described, firms feel little moral responsibility to clean up their acts. They can readily argue that they are meeting the most important public interest at this point in the nation's development by providing economic benefits.

Nevertheless, firms that do not feel moral pressure might respond to market pressure for a more environmentally responsible image, especially through the globalization of trade. The WTO is requiring that nothing will be imported from member states who do not follow the ISO-9000 quality management and ISO-14000 environmental management standards. Many firms in Pakistan have ISO-9000 certificates, but to date only two have ISO-14000 certificates; so far as we know, no company operating in Pakistan is accredited to award them. Joint enterprises with foreign firms are another route by which environmental management standards might be introduced into Pakistani industry. The Lahore Chamber of Commerce and Industry asserted that there is an urgent need to make industrialists aware of this matter. Our sample of 23 firms interviewed contained three indigenous exporting firms and three foreign joint enterprises. Thus one quarter of the sample, which was random with respect to these variables, is in categories potentially subject to external pressure to raise standards, suggesting a positive prospect nationwide in this regard. One foreign joint enterprise in our sample had significantly improved its standards.

ACTION BY SURROUNDING COMMUNITIES

If firms feel no moral responsibility to improve their performance, and experience no market pressure to do so, they might yet respond to pressure from the surrounding communities. A number of authors cite examples of success-ful action by local residents in developing countries (Cribb, 1990; Hartman et al, 1997; Huq and Wheeler, 1993; and Khator, 1991). Afsah et al (1996) argue that:

> 'neighbouring communities can have a powerful influence on factories' environmental performance... Where formal regula-tors are present, communities use the political process to influence the tightness of enforcement. Where formal regulators are absent or ineffective, "informal regulation" is implemented through community groups or NGOs.'

We found a degree of resignation among residents due to a mixture of low environmental awareness, other priorities, fear and inability to mobilize. Notwithstanding this, interviewees expressed some moral indignation at indus-try:

> 'Industrialists should be forced to feel their moral responsibility to protect the environment, as fresh air and water are impor-tant for health of the people.'
> 'They should not be allowed to play with the lives of the people through uncontrolled emissions.'
> 'Either they should adequately control nuisance or they should be forced to shift their factories to some other place.'

The low expectations of the responsiveness of industry applied also to the regulators, as the following quotes illustrate:

> 'Officials in those agencies are in alliance with the industrial-ists. If somebody complains to them, they will take bribes from the industrialists and do nothing against them, since they are more powerful.'
> 'No one in these agencies listens to you.'
> 'On visiting the offices, you often will not be able to find the concerned officers at their desks.'

Nevertheless, a majority of respondents were clear that the regulators should act:

> 'After all, it is these agencies alone who are supposed to make sure that the industrialists install and use pollution-control facilities.'
> 'These agencies can influence industrialists to abate nuisance because of the statutory powers given to them for this purpose.'
> 'Basically, it all depends upon the government. If it wants to see something done and asks these same agencies to do it,

they will get it done, just as they successfully implemented anti-encroachment campaigns in Lahore in the recent past' (ie they cleared streets of traders illegally encroaching on pavement and road space).

Ten of the fifteen communities in our interview sample had complained either to a factory or to regulators. Even the communities near the two planned industrial estates had complained. Industrial discharges from both estates had caused public sewers to overflow, and air emissions from one estate had also caused a problem. Ignorance of the role of agencies was clearly a limitation: more than one third of the respondents were unaware of EPDP and its role. Some of those who had heard of the name were unsure of its functions.

In three of the communities only individuals had complained, but collective complaints had been lodged by seven. In two cases formal CBOs had been formed, although one had later disbanded. In five communities no complaints had been lodged. In two communities spontaneous demonstrations followed a gas leak and explosions respectively.

Several commentators report that communities that are richer and better educated are more likely to protest and are more effective when they do so (Afsah et al, 1996; Hartman et al, 1997; and Hettige et al, 1996). We too found in Lahore that poorer communities are less likely to complain. The five communities that had lodged no complaints were among the six poorest in the sample, whereas five of the seven that took collective action were the wealthiest in the sample. This raises the issue of environmental justice. If regulators respond to pressure from communities, then they will tend to take action to improve the environments of the wealthier ones because they mobilize better. This emphasizes the need both for the regulators to have equally sound information on all types of area, and for the poorer communities to be the focus of efforts to empower them to assert their rights.

Success of complaints, even by the wealthier communities, was in any case low. Only four of the ten communities that had lodged complaints had achieved some success. Our small sample showed no relationship between the success and income: some success was achieved by two low-income communities and two wealthier ones. Yet, despite their lack of success, some communities intended to continue protesting.

NEW DEVELOPMENTS

A new arrival on the scene is the environmental tribunal, set up under the Environment Protection Act 1997. The federal government, which has refused to convene the Pakistan Environment Protection Council, the key to empowering EPDP, was forced to set up the tribunals by the Supreme Court of Pakistan, which set a deadline of October 1999. At present there are only two tribunals, one in Lahore and one in Karachi, to cover the nation, although two others may be set up. The chair of a tribunal is a judge of the High Court, appointed by the federal government, which must consult with the Chief

Justice about the appointment. Of the other two members, one must be technically qualified for the role.

In principle, these tribunals could cut through the Gordian knot of forces that constrain effective abatement of industrial nuisance. They have spectacular powers of fining, imprisonment and requiring restoration of the environment. They have already addressed some cases, including two in our sample, but both are ongoing, and it is too early to assess performance. Normally, the tribunal will respond only to a referral from a provincial environmental protection agency (EPDP in the case of Lahore) in the event of a firm failing to comply with an environmental protection order issued by that agency. However, a complainant can also go directly to the tribunal if the agency does not act within 30 days on a complaint made to it.

There are limitations. First, the recipient of an environmental protection order can appeal against both the order to the tribunal and the decision of the tribunal to the High Court. Thus the trap of protracted litigation is not escaped. Second, with just two or potentially four tribunals in the country, their capacity for business is clearly limited, and their physical remoteness will be a practical obstacle to complainants who do not chance to be from the cities where they sit. Third, the process is still likely to be daunting to the ordinary citizen in the street.

Still more recent than the tribunals are monitoring cells set up by the military government that took power on 12 October 1999, at the federal and provincial levels, with army teams visiting the civil departments with the sole objective of tracing corruption and improving performance. The public can complain directly to the army monitoring teams. The military government has also created 13 new accountability courts for the trial of the corrupt, and has undertaken to create 23 more courts (Dawn, 2000).

CONCLUSIONS

A report by the World Bank (2000) presents an upbeat view of the potential of non-traditional approaches to pollution abatement in developing nations (more information can also be found on the Bank's New Ideas in Pollution Regulation website at http://www.worldbank.org/nipr). How does our study of Lahore live up to this optimistic view?

We attempt in Table 4.1 to list the main obstacles to the effective abatement of industrial nuisance in Lahore, and possible remedies. In keeping with the theme of the book, we have tried to characterize obstacles in terms of mental or organizational institutions, but the distinction is not always clear.

Two of the biggest obstacles are institutionalized corruption and litigiousness. These are widespread in Pakistani society, and barely susceptible to localized measures targeted at particular sectors. Yet even here, action is being taken against corruption at the level of the organization, through the monitoring cells and accountability courts. We highlight below some other approaches that hold promise.

Table 4.1 *Obstacles to the abatement of industrial nuisances in Lahore, Pakistan, and possible remedies*

Factor	Mental obstacle	Organizational obstacle	Possible remedies
THE STATE *Environmental protection agency*		Low competence due to few trained staff, little equipment, poor leadership	Training, funding, stable leadership, all led by provincial government
		Powers not activated	Activation by Pakistan Environment Protection Council
	Organizational territoriality leading to...→	Low status, leading to inter alia...→	Due recognition by provincial government
		...lack of cooperation from other agencies	Lead from provincial government
	Low morale		All of the above, leading to successful action
Local planning authorities		Overlapping jurisdictions	Sorting out by provincial government, with legislation if necessary
		Confusion about priority of permits from local planning authorities, EPDP, Industries Department	Federal/provincial governments issue guidance
	Perceived by clientele as a bureaucracy rather than a public service		Elimination of corruption and clarification of regulations; the former is being addressed now through monitoring cells and accountability courts. In the longer term, palpable contribution to environmental quality
	Perceived acceptability of buying and selling permits, leading to...→	...corruption	Tricky! Example of senior officials, politicians; adequate pay; punishment; perhaps even threat of removal of functions
INDUSTRY	Lack of respect for regulators		Strengthening of regulators' status and competence
	Sense of immunity from regulation and enforcement, due to actual...→	...ability to evade regulation and enforcement	Powers to regulators; elimination of corruption among regulators; change of culture in the judiciary to despatch of cases; refusal to hear cases unless there are prima facie strong grounds, etc

continued overleaf

Table 4.1 *continued*

Actor	Mental obstacle	Organizational obstacle	Possible remedies
INDUSTRY (continued)	Lack of perception of stewardship responsibility		Facilitative programme of education, eg that being run by Pakistan Chamber of Commerce and Industries – opportunity for aid agencies, international NGOs, religious organizations. 'Name and shame' programme by EPDP in collaboration with the media, targeted at firms sensitive to it
	Interpretation of residents' behaviour as according environmental quality a low priority		Change in signals sent by residents. Acceptance of stewardship responsibility
	Ignorance of technical solutions and fear of their cost		Facilitative programme of education, eg ETPI. Opportunity for aid agencies, international NGOs
		Large number of independent actors	Movement by, eg chambers of commerce to create associations of industry
THE COMMUNITY	Ignorance of environmental matters		Education – low literacy and low schooling suggest staff intensive awareness raising by NGOs, EPDP, perhaps via pyramidal training, and aural media campaigns in addition to paper media. EPDP make data available to communities
	Low priority accorded to environmental quality		Increased wealth. Understanding of environmental matters
	Fear of industrialists		Dissemination of protest success stories
	Lack of faith in regulators		Effective regulation and enforcement
		Limited ability to mobilize	NGOs seed and support CBOs in the affected communities. Possible role for religious organization, eg via sermons

One is pollution charging, promoted in the World Bank report as a supplement to the traditional 'command and control' approach to pollution control. The 1997 Federal Act enables pollution charging, and the government intends to introduce it. It has marked advantages in principle, but it should be borne in mind that to work well it needs a lot of information, for example, local abatement cost data which allow the charge to be set at the right level locally to achieve the desired goals. At present such data are generally lacking, but projects such as the ETPI will help to produce it.

Second, the new environmental tribunals do offer a specific means of strengthening the credibility of EPDP, and offer citizens a comeback if EPDP fails to act on their complaint. In the short term, this could be the strongest spur to community mobilization. The tool would be even stronger if some form of legal aid service were available.

Third, there is a strong role for a facilitative approach to be taken in a number of ways. For a start, EPDP, though still awaiting permission to implement powers and standards, can focus in the interim on non-legal tools such as seeking partners in the NGO sector to strengthen its campaigns of public education, and cooperating with the media to 'name and shame' offenders. The latter measure will work with relatively large firms having a market or shareholders sensitive to image, whereas much of the local industrial nuisance is caused by quite small firms slotted into residential areas and which are insensitive to image.

Then there are clear opportunities for aid agencies and NGOs to intervene to help industry to develop awareness of, and technical competence in, pollution abatement. The ETPI is an example. Aid agencies and NGOs can also help communities to develop environmental understanding, and the confidence and ability to campaign for better environmental quality.

The problem is multi-faceted, and the solution must therefore be so too. We remain cautious about how applicable some of the approaches to abatement promoted by the World Bank (2000) are to a country at Pakistan's state of development. Yet we believe that our analysis indicates that it is possible to move on a number of fronts in mutually reinforcing ways towards more environmentally and socially sustainable industrialization. To do so requires the three facets of community empowerment, effective state machinery and willing industry.

5 URBAN PUBLIC TRANSPORT: THE DEVELOPMENT OF A REGULATORY ROLE FOR NGOs IN PAKISTAN

John Russell and Ghulam Abbas Anjum

INTRODUCTION

Urban public transport in Pakistan

'No one would use it unless they had to.' This comment by a bus passenger in Lahore sums up the deplorable state of public transport services generally in Pakistan's cities today. A typical journey for a passenger will involve scrabbling for the privilege of being crammed like a sardine against other passengers inside – or hanging on for dear life to the outside – of a battered old (mini) bus, being driven at breakneck speed by an underqualified driver, and constantly jolted around as he brakes, accelerates and weaves around the multiple obstacles in the carriageway. If you did happen to get a seat you are likely to face a wait before departure until the bus is full to capacity or more. Reaching your destination you may be set down in the midst of the melee at a junction rather than at an authorized bus stop. To reach your bus route in the first place may well have involved a long walk, since many areas of the city are ill served or have no services at all. It may take even longer to get back home in the evening if the driver decides to cut the route short and turn around because there are no longer enough passengers for it to be profitable. If you are a woman, as a Muslim it will be unacceptable for you to use public transport at all in such circumstances.

Such is the plight of the urban bus passenger. Yet some of Pakistan's cities are already vast and urbanization is proceeding rapidly. The need to travel over longer distances within urban areas is growing as a consequence, and so too is the market for urban public transport services; or it would be if acceptable services were on offer. Relatively few people can afford motorcycles let alone cars, and other alternatives such as taxis and rickshaws are expensive; so public transport should be ideally placed to meet much of the increasing demand, and it should be profitable to provide services which do so.

What then is going wrong? Many of the problems are rooted in the inadequacies of the systems in place for regulating the provision of urban bus services, in Pakistan as in other less developed countries (LDCs). Over recent years a start has been made in seeking to address these inadequacies and, following a brief discussion of the problems, a case study is presented below of a recent reform of the regulatory framework in Faisalabad, Pakistan, which involves the devolving and administration of regulatory powers through an NGO. This reform has produced major improvements in the quality of public transport in Faisalabad. It also has interesting implications for relations between the state and civil society as regulator and regulated, and for the limits of their roles in these capacities.

The regulatory role of government

Regulation is conventionally seen as one of the key roles of governments. Markets must be regulated in the interests of consumers and the more general public. Urban development must be regulated, to avoid or alleviate the negative effects of market breakdown and a monopolistic land market, if not to positively capitalize on the environmental and efficiency gains which can derive from coordination and good planning. Only governments are in a position to institute such regulation and theoretical debate focuses not on the principle of regulation, but on the extent of regulation that is desirable and on the means of regulation required as a corrective to market failure.

The actual means of regulation employed varies with the economic sector and nature of the activity involved. In the UK it ranges from self-regulatory bodies, for example, for the press and for some professional and financial institutions, with the threat of government regulation held in reserve, to full-blown legislation and enforcement through the police force itself or through other government agencies. Regulatory bodies are often established as separate quangos at 'arm's length' from government rather than constituting part of the government bureaucracy itself. Recent examples are the regulatory offices for the privatized utility and railway companies. This arrangement has advantages for government ministers and senior officials in that they are no longer directly responsible or accountable for the individual decisions made by the regulators, and pressures or temptations to intervene directly are correspondingly reduced. Power to act, in circumstances where the government is unhappy with regulatory performance, is retained through the ability to replace a regulator.

Poor regulation or over-regulation can, of course, be worse than the disease that regulation is intended to cure, and total deregulation can be the preferable alternative in circumstances where regulation is likely to be corrupt or maladministered. This risk is, in general, more likely to arise in developing than in highly developed countries, in that the institutional capacity necessary to support effective regulatory systems, in terms of staff expertise and political infrastructure, is more likely to be lacking. Markets grow more complex and in need of more sophisticated regulation, however, as the economy of a country or region grows. Urban public transport services are a case in point, where the need for regulation increases as the size of urban areas, the urban economy, and the market for such services grow.

Urban public transport regulation

The regulation of urban public transport services as a sector presents many of the difficulties and dilemmas associated with decisions over how and to what extent to regulate economic activity. Effective quality controls are essential for road safety if for no other purposes, but even in developed countries the imposition of either fares controls or quantity controls over service levels has been controversial. Indeed in the UK, such controls have been deemed to be counterproductive, and were deregulated under the Transport Act of 1985 for urban areas except in London.

In LDCs urban bus services have generally been subject to extensive regulation, but that regulation has tended to be weak where it needs to be strong (over vehicle quality controls, for example) and strong where it should be weaker – for instance in applying fares controls or quantity controls restricting the number of buses operating on particular routes (Armstrong-Wright and Thiriez, 1987; Kwakye, 1994; Roth and Diandas, 1995; Gwilliam, 1997). The result has been services that are less effective, less reliable, of poorer quality, and fewer in number than would have been provided under a supportive regulatory regime.

Over more recent years there have been moves to reform and to reduce the burden of overregulation in many countries, to varying degrees and with limited success. Some countries, most notably Chile, fully deregulated quantity and fares controls but with mixed results: the emergence of cartels fixing fares and exacerbated traffic congestion leading to a partial re-regulation (Darbera, 1993).

The regulatory regime in Pakistan

Pakistan exemplifies problems that are typical of those which exist in many other LDCs. Overzealous and discriminatory regulation failed to prevent the near total collapse of the inefficient, publicly owned services in the 1980s, and it has been concluded that 'inappropriate controls over fares and other ill administered and ill conceived regulations', together with inadequate traffic management and a lack of clear policies, have undermined the role of public transport in Pakistan's cities (Russell and Anjum, 1997).

Periodic attempts at improvement have been made but new public transport initiatives have generally been short-lived and have ultimately been ineffective; again a common experience in other LDCs. A prime factor in their failure has been the retention of regulatory controls in the hands of the established bureaucracies, which are ineffectual and often corrupt.

In most LDCs, governments control fares, but it is exceptional for such fares regulation to be informed on the basis of reliable financial analysis. Typically operators are crudely placed under pressure to keep fares low, without compensation and despite rising costs (Briggs, 1989; Armstrong-Wright, 1993). Pakistan is no exception. Fares are held low as a policy, seeking to extend affordability on welfare grounds, but the government does not compensate the operators for the loss of revenue involved. Consequently the operators are forced to cut services, and marginal routes or route sections which become unprofitable are not operated. Service levels are therefore inadequate, and instead of the policy helping the poor, there are few if any

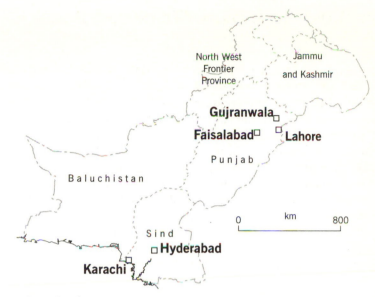

Source: Harry Smith

Figure 5.1 *Map of Pakistan showing Faisalabad and other Punjabi cities with new public transport initiatives (Lahore and Gujranwala)*

services in poorer areas. Furthermore, fares are not reviewed regularly or increased in line with inflation, and fare increases have often only been authorized following operators' strikes (Russell and Anjum, 1997).

It is in this context then that a new, but very different attempt was launched, in order to improve the lamentable public transport services in the city of Faisalabad (Punjab Province – see Figure 5.1). This initiative involved some radical changes to the existing regulatory system, which is the prevailing one throughout Pakistan.

The Faisalabad initiative: regulation through an NGO

In 1994, government officials founded an NGO to operate and regulate stage carriage bus services in Faisalabad. The NGO, the Faisalabad Urban Transport Society (FUTS), in effect assumed delegated responsibility for most aspects of public transport regulation. It can be seen as an innovative regulatory model, providing an alternative to that of direct bureaucratic control by government agencies, but it also represents an interesting development affecting the role of civil society in Pakistan, with potentially wider implications.

The findings presented below summarize the results of an analysis of the performance of the FUTS scheme, based largely on survey work conducted or supervised by Dr Abbas Anjum in 1995 and 1996, and reported in Anjum and Russell (1997) and in Russell and Anjum (1999). They demonstrate the relative success of the FUTS regulatory framework to date and are followed by a discussion of the implications of this success in the context of current policy developments in Pakistan and the Punjab Province.

The Faisalabad Urban Transport Society

Formation

Faisalabad is a large industrial centre and one of the fastest growing cities of Pakistan, with an estimated population of around two million. Desperately poor public transport existed there until recently, as a result of the collapse of publicly-owned services and the restrictive nature of the regulatory controls imposed on private operators. Almost the only public transport available was in the form of small, unpopular, Suzuki ten-seat vehicles. Would-be passengers resorted to alternatives such as the more expensive autorickshaws (low-powered, low quality, three-wheeler forms of taxis), or horse-drawn tongas (see Figure 5.2), or they cycled or walked (Faisalabad Divisional Commissioner, 1994). Following representations made to the then prime minister of Pakistan, Benazir Bhutto, during her visit to Faisalabad in 1993, the Divisional Commissioner Faisalabad[1] initiated a public–private partnership by creating an NGO to run public transport in collaboration with the local operators. Thus FUTS came into being early in 1994.

Although it was organized by senior provincial government officials in Faisalabad, the society has the legal status of an NGO. It is therefore regulated by the laws of a social company, with a constitution approved by the Social Welfare Department of the Punjab Government. In principle any adult can become a member of the society, but in practice membership is dominated by private minibus operators. Reflecting its 'social' status the society's stated objectives – which include improvements to urban transport, traffic management, road safety, the environment and adult education – are wider than would be the case for a normal public transport agency or operator (FUTS, 1993). The provision of public transport services is nevertheless its real purpose.

Administration

The society is administered through a governing body mainly composed of chief government officials, most of whom have functions concerned with the planning, regulation and operational control of public transport in Faisalabad. The four office bearers of the management committee of the society are all provincial government officials, including the Divisional Commissioner who is the president of the society, and the secretary of the Regional Transport Authority (RTA), which is the provincial government agency ordinarily responsible for the regulation of public transport services in the Faisalabad region. An administrator is responsible to the management committee and the governing body for the actual running of the society.

There is provision for a matching number of appointments to the governing body from the general membership of the society. Half of these should be by election at the annual general meeting, but to date no nominees have been appointed or members elected by the private operators. They prefer to register their views, make complaints and raise any other issues of concern with the administrator, which are then considered in meetings of the governing body. This has acted as an effective liaison mechanism, and survey results in 1996

Credit: John Russell

Figure 5.2 *View of traffic on the streets of Faisalabad*

indicated that the operators were satisfied with the way the current system was working. They were fearful that 'representatives', once elected to the governing body, might not genuinely represent their collective interests, and therefore did not wish to take up their places on the board.

Operation

FUTS operates stage carriage services, with a fleet composed entirely of minibuses. Initially, private-sector operators were doubtful about the society, but once confidence was established membership grew rapidly, and by 1999 some 850 vehicles were operating on FUTS routes.

The operators make vehicles available to the society through an annually renewable agreement. The agreement relates to specific vehicles, and is subject to the condition of the vehicle being approved by a committee appointed by the society. Vehicles are otherwise the responsibility of the drivers/owners.

Crew staff (driver and conductor) are employed by the operator who is responsible for their performance meeting requirements under the agreement with FUTS. Crews must treat passengers with courtesy; they must not charge more than the fixed fares; and they should not allow smoking or the playing of music in the vehicle. Overloading is not permitted, buses must only stop at authorized stopping points, and the vehicles must be kept clean and in good condition. Violations of these terms and conditions are punishable by fines, with the threat of termination of the operator's agreement for more serious or persistent violations.

Staff employed by FUTS are responsible for route allocation. They are headed by the administrator, who manages the society's affairs, assigning duties to other staff, entering into agreements with operators, and levying fines for violations. Security guards posted at terminals and other route-end check-posts keep a record of arrivals and departures and issue duty slips. These records have made it possible to eliminate the practice of route shortening. Mobile supervisors, provided with motorcycles, oversee service operations along the various routes. They check that there is no overloading, that drivers stop at the specified points, and that there is no route deviation. The society's security guards and mobile supervisors generally perform these duties efficiently, in marked contrast with the practice of the traffic police.

The society generates funds through monthly service charge and welfare fund payments by the operators, supplemented by the fines collected for violations. It also profits from running its own shops and a filling station, and its financial position is very sound. Substantial annual surpluses are being generated, which have been invested in the construction of an office building and the main terminal, as well as the shops and filling station. In addition, it has made donations to charities and to the traffic police for the purchase of equipment.

REGULATORY REGIMES

Route network

FUTS defines the entire route network, terminals, and bus stops for its own services, with the RTA obliged to rubber stamp its decisions. Stop signs have been installed by the society on all its routes, where previously no indication was given of stop locations. In February 2000 a network of 13 routes was operating, converging on the main terminal and running through the city centre. Shelters were provided only at the new central terminal, but a new shelter design had been commissioned.

Route permits

Public transport route permits in the city are formally the responsibility of the RTA Faisalabad, which is authorized to specify the routes and determine the type, the size, and the number of vehicles operating the specified routes.

In practice, FUTS has assumed the responsibility for the planning, operation and control of its own services. The society allocates permits and specifies the routes in discussion with operators. Operators consult with FUTS about potential routes, assess passenger demand, and then apply to it for a permit. The society specifies the size and type of vehicles. Routes are allocated to operators on a 'first come first served' basis, with no formal maximum set for the number of vehicles on a route, but FUTS has tried to steer new entrants to routes where less vehicles are operating.

Suzuki routes still operate alongside and in competition with FUTS services on some routes. These Suzuki services are still under RTA regulation, but some are operated illegally without permits.

Fares

Public transport fares are legally determined by the provincial government. Despite this, FUTS has been allowed to set fares for its own services; prior approval for fares revisions is still required from the Punjab Government but in practice this is seen to have been a formality. In effect the FUTS is being treated as a private institution that can run bus services and set fares for its own purposes, thereby creating a mechanism for circumventing the government fares controls. Maximum and minimum fares for FUTS services have been set at approximately double the government controlled levels (see Table 5.1), and no concessionary fare has been granted to students, in contrast with other stage carriage services.[2] These higher fares are the chief attraction to operators to join the society.

Safety

A motor fitness certificate must be obtained at six-monthly intervals for all public transport vehicles, from the Motor Vehicle Examiner (MVE), under the official system. Generally this appears in reality to be a paper based formality rather than meaning actual inspection of the vehicle. By contrast, the vehicles operating under the control of FUTS are examined daily by FUTS supervisors, who identify defects, record the need to do repairs, and check that the repairs are done.

Enforcement

Responsibility for most important aspects of on-street traffic regulation and enforcement is with the traffic police. Operational controls of hours of operation and route coverage are conditions of the route permit issued by the RTA.

Enforcement systems in Pakistan are generally weak and they are seen to be a source of graft for the traffic police and other officials. The lack of effective controls over urban bus operations has led to numerous abuses by drivers. Abuses include route deviation, route shortening, irregular hours of operation, waiting for full loads, dangerous driving practices (Government of Pakistan, 1995) and overloading. In theory no standing passengers are allowed on stage carriage services, but in practice gross overloading is the norm.

In Faisalabad, FUTS has established its own much more effective system, outlined above, under which drivers are fined for committing violations, and backed up by the sanction of exclusion from the society. The traffic police intervene only when drivers are involved in more serious traffic offences.

THE EFFECTIVENESS OF NGO-BASED PUBLIC TRANSPORT REGULATION

It is evident that the new NGO form of regulation in Faisalabad has proved to be a success and that it has promoted major improvements in services. Table 5.1 summarizes an analysis of the performance of the two regulatory regimes,

Table 5.1 *Comparison of regulatory approaches*

Elements	Government bureaucratic regulation	NGO-based regulation (FUTS)
Quantity control	RTA specifies the size, type and number of vehicles	In theory RTA, but in practice FUTS, specifies the size and type of vehicles for its own services
	Routes allocated to operators on a discretionary basis	Routes allocated on 'first come, first served' basis in discussion with operators
	Frequent delays in issuing route permits	No specified maximum number of vehicles per route
Fares control	Government fixed fares charged	Fares determined by the society
	Maximum full route fare: Rupees 6.25	Full route fare: Rupees 12.0
	Students given concessionary fare	No student concessionary fares
	Fares increased as a result of operators' strikes	Fares increased in consultation with the operators
Route network	RTA defines the route network	FUTS defines the route network
	No consultation with operators	RTA has to rubber stamp FUTS decisions
	No specific criteria	FUTS specifies the location of all bus stops and installs clear signs
	Lack of bus stop signs	Routes amended in response to passenger and operator opinion
Safety regulation	Vehicle fitness certificate obtained from the MVEs every six months	Fitness certificate from the MVE plus vehicles examined daily by FUTS supervisors
		Defects must be repaired within a specified time
Enforcement	Weak and muddled system	Strict enforcement by FUTS staff
	Provides opportunities for corruption	Adequate staffing level
Monitoring	No monitoring of services	Regular monitoring and consultation with operators
	Lack of qualified staff and more responsive procedures	Responsive procedures
Corruption	At all stages of regulation	Very little evidence of corruption
	Linked to red tape and bureaucratic procedures	The one incidence so far detected was firmly dealt with

Source: Based on findings from field survey visits (1995–1996): as in Russell and Anjum, 1999

based on survey findings, which shows that the achievements of the NGO approach have been marked when compared with the government system.

Service improvements under FUTS have been rapid and substantial. A summary analysis of the factors behind this success is given below.

Improvements in service

The FUTS fleet has largely replaced the Suzukis in Faisalabad. The remaining Suzuki services mainly cover areas not adequately served by the FUTS network. A rapid transformation occurred because the FUTS provides a quality of service which Suzuki operators are unable to match (Anjum and Russell, 1997). User surveys were conducted in 1995 (pilot) and 1996. The 1996 results confirmed

Table 5.2 *Service comparison under two regulatory regimes*

Indicators	Government bureaucratic regulation	NGO-based regulation (FUTS)
Bus occupancy	Legally no overloading allowed but In practice gross overloading	Passengers guaranteed seat Overloading largely eliminated by imposing fines
Reliability	Drivers always wait for additional passengers at terminals and en route bus stops	Drivers don't wait for additional passengers at en route bus stops
	Frequent route shortening	Route shortening eliminated by establishing check posts on each route
	No checks on service performance	73% of the passengers satisfied with service reliability
	None of the users satisfied with service reliability	
Hours of operation	At the mercy of drivers Drivers withdraw service during off-peak periods Many complaints and passengers not sure about off peak departures	Fixed by the FUTS (6.0 am to 10.0 pm) Same level of service operated throughout this period No complaints from passengers
Waiting time	No predetermined timetable Lower waiting time on routes with a large number of vehicles	No predetermined timetable Average waiting time reduced
Comfort	41% of the passengers complained about comfort aspects	An overwhelming majority of the passengers satisfied with comfort aspects
Safety	In Lahore, minibuses involved in 40% of the total (191) deaths from road accidents in the year 1994[1]	One fatal accident over three years 62% of the passengers satisfied with safety aspects 31% of the passengers complained drivers irresponsible and risk accidents
Fares	Unrealistically low Overcharging in bad weather and for evening services	Higher but realistic Overcharging eliminated during FUTS hours of operation[2]

Notes:
1 Minibus data only for Lahore for ease of comparison
2 The only complaints related to increased charges for services outwith FUTS hours or to legitimate fare changes on two modified routes
Source: Data collected in field survey visits (1995–96): as in Russell and Anjum, 1999

that the FUTS service had attracted most of its passengers from Suzukis (37 per cent), tongas (24 per cent) and autorickshaws (12 per cent).

FUTS offers greater capacity and a better quality service to passengers, at realistic fares. It is providing services that are more efficient and far more reliable. It is notable that FUTS services ran as usual, and despite some harassment by other operators, during a three-day strike in July 1996. Passengers are assured a seat; the buses stop at designated stops; and there is strict adherence to specified routes.

Off-peak demand is generally well satisfied, but service levels do not adequately meet demand in peak periods on some routes. Since overloading is not allowed, and no additional buses operate in peak hours, passengers must either wait longer or switch to alternative modes. The user survey results showed concern over the inadequate number of FUTS vehicles. With the operation of two additional routes subsequent to this survey the number of minibuses operating has been increased. Nevertheless, peak-period capacity remains a problem. In principle this can be addressed either by operating larger-capacity vehicles on some routes or by introducing more minibuses, but more minibuses would exacerbate traffic congestion problems on road sections where public transport is already delayed. There are obstacles to the supply of good quality vehicles of either type. The federal government has recently moved to address this problem, but the measures taken to date assist only the largest cities such as Lahore.

The FUTS network is still being extended and developed, with routings being adjusted in response to pressures. The central area is well served but elsewhere the coverage is more uneven, with some areas inadequately served. In some of these areas, however, road conditions are unsuitable for the operation of minibuses and Suzuki services would need to be retained.

User survey responses clearly demonstrate the relative popularity of FUTS services. The majority of the Suzuki passengers surveyed indicated that they use Suzukis mainly because an adequate FUTS service is lacking, and they complained about the comfort and reliability of the Suzukis. A majority also stated a willingness to use FUTS services, where provided. By contrast, the most common reasons for their use of FUTS services, given by the majority of passengers, were the guaranteed seat and service reliability. A summary comparison of service provision under the alternative regulatory regimes is presented in Table 5.2.

Fares, incomes and social exclusion

Passengers' views about FUTS fares were obtained in the December 1996 survey. To obtain a representative picture, passengers were randomly selected and interviewed at stops along different sections of the route network. The results indicated surprisingly little dissatisfaction. Only 11 per cent of passengers interviewed were concerned that fares were too high and indicated they would prefer a cheaper alternative mode if one was available on their routes. Thirty-one per cent considered the fares slightly high, while the majority of passengers (54 per cent) were satisfied with the fares. The remaining 4 per cent gave no opinion because this was their first trip on a FUTS service.

These findings, of course, reflect only the views of users, who by definition, can afford to pay, and are not representative of the views of the population as a whole. The survey results also indicate a middle-income bias among passengers. Passengers on FUTS services are drawn from somewhat higher income groups compared with those of Suzukis, while passengers on both types of service are predominantly from middle income groups. Lower-income groups cannot afford to use FUTS services regularly, and the lowest-income groups cannot afford to use public transport at all. The poor walk, and overall a large majority of trips in Faisalabad are made on foot.

The passenger interview surveys in Faisalabad were not designed to explore the views of users on the basis of income and it is unfortunate that very little information is available about the access needs of low-income and lower-middle-income groups, and research is needed to assess these needs. Not only is it unclear what their access needs are, but also whether and to what extent public transport services (whether cheaper or not) could help to meet those needs. It is clear, however, that at present there is no means to provide public transport services at affordable fares for low-income groups which effectively meet their needs, whatever the regulatory regime.

It seems unlikely from the evidence available that the higher fares of FUTS services are giving rise to additional social exclusion to any substantial extent. The cheaper Suzuki services are still available, although on a reduced scale, and overall the increased level of service provision means that access by public transport has been increased. In addition, the higher quality of FUTS services in general and the absence of overloading in particular, have reduced social barriers to the use of public transport by women.

Improving the regulatory regime

There have been a number of previous attempts over the years to improve urban public transport in Pakistan. None of these have succeeded, and it is significant that all have operated essentially within the existing regulatory framework, with only minor or temporary modifications.

A distinctive and vitally important characteristic of the FUTS is that it is operating outside the official regulatory system. In the FUTS context the key officials wear two hats. As members of the government bureaucracy, they are constrained to apply the established bureaucratic procedures and find it difficult to initiate reforms. Within FUTS, wearing their second hats as members of the governing body of an NGO, they have more freedom to directly influence the planning and management of public transport services, within a decision-making process that also directly involves the operators. Improvements in service have been made possible through the bypassing of procedures associated with inefficiency and corruption. In effect, the officials have been freed from entrapment in their own government systems (Anjum and Russell, 1997).

The effective self-enforcement of operational regulations by FUTS has been a prominent feature in its success. Several factors are vital to the effectiveness of FUTS's enforcement regime. The level of enforcement activity and the staffing committed to it are far higher, and this, together with the reasonable fares, mean that drivers have less incentive to resort to abuses. FUTS is free of the nefarious activities of operators' 'unions' or 'associations' which have been linked with corruption and political interference in public transport organizations elsewhere in Pakistan. Most important of all, there is little evidence of corruption within FUTS itself, and the only recorded instance by 1997 had been dealt with firmly by dismissing the member of staff concerned.

Fares control

Fares control has been the most crucial factor influencing the level and quality of service provision. The FUTS has provided a mechanism to set fares at realistic levels which have allowed operators to make profits and to increase service provision and service standards, bypassing the usual government controls. Fares were fixed initially in 1994 by the FUTS without any formal approval from the provincial government, and the society has retained the freedom to increase its fares, although the 1997 increase did require the formal prior approval of the provincial government because of a legal challenge of FUTS powers. The government appears to be content to leave the fare setting to the NGO but to retain the right to intervene.

Decisions to change FUTS fares at present involve an informal process of consultation between officials and operators. The operators applied to the FUTS management for a general increase in fares in December 1996, to allow for inflation and a relative increase in the price of fuel. Wider opinions among operators were sought by the administrator concerning the extent of the increase, before fares for FUTS services were increased by 20 per cent in February 1997. A substantial increase was thereby agreed amicably, in contrast with the situation in other cities, where only after the disruption of three-day operators' strikes were fares increased in August 1996.

This increase kept fares at approximately double the government controlled level, but was still inadequate to cover inflation over the previous three years, and represented a substantial decrease in real terms from the 1994 levels. It is essential that the fares are reviewed regularly, and in times of high inflation an annual cycle of review and increase is needed, but as yet FUTS has no regular fares-review procedure in place. This needs to be addressed promptly, or the benefits of escaping from government fares controls risk being rapidly eroded.

Traffic management

Public transport in Pakistani cities operates in a difficult environment. The mix of slow and fast moving traffic, physically poor road conditions, lack of awareness and flagrant violations of traffic rules, a lack of basic traffic management and illegal roadside parking create chaotic conditions and congestion. As a result, public transport travel times increase during peak periods in the central area and elsewhere. The implementation of effective traffic management measures could make services safer and more efficient (Anjum and Russell, 1997).

FUTS is not able to directly influence traffic management in the city. The society has, however, provided funds to assist the traffic police with the purchase of motorcycles and radio communication, as a result of which the police are somewhat better equipped to regulate overall traffic in Faisalabad. In addition, the relatively well organized and supervised on-street operation of FUTS services has resulted in a better flow of traffic, in that unauthorized stopping and unruly behaviour by bus drivers is often a root cause of traffic jams at and around road intersections and bus stops.

The attractiveness of FUTS services has in itself resulted in other indirect improvements. The numbers of smaller autorickshaw and Suzuki vehicles in use on the roads has declined, as they have been replaced by fewer, larger capacity FUTS minibuses.

With well supervised FUTS service operation and a better equipped traffic police, alongside this decline in the number of autorickshaws and Suzukis, overall traffic conditions in the city did somewhat improve. Discussions with shopkeepers, pedestrians, drivers and traffic police in 1996 all confirmed improvements.

Evolving regulatory change

Initially a maximum age limit of three years was specified for vehicles under FUTS operation. This limit proved too ambitious a condition for operators and they could not afford to replace vehicles at the prevailing market price for new minibuses, which was very high. Consequently, a relaxation to allow four-year-old vehicles was agreed in January 1996. In addition, operators of new vehicles were granted exemption from the donation to charity then required from operators, as a financial incentive to encourage investment.

Still facing severe difficulties, the operators requested that more appropriate quality control conditions be applied, rather than strict adherence to an age limit. In February 1997 the society accepted this argument and amended its regulation. Vehicles up to a maximum age of ten years are now allowed to operate, subject to the approval of a three-person committee appointed by the society. This committee is authorized to examine thoroughly the condition of all vehicles at the time of entering into and renewing agreements with operators, while the operator is still obliged to obtain vehicle-fitness certificates from the MVE.

Again at the request of operators, a requirement placed on the operator of each vehicle to contribute a substantial annual sum to specified charities has been withdrawn. This requirement had originally been introduced to reflect the society's wider social objectives, but in actuality had no bearing on its functions.

These examples indicate that the forum provided by FUTS is promoting greater flexibility in decision making, and a learning process for both operators and officials, strengthening mutual understanding and capabilities. The regulatory framework is still evolving.

REPLICABILITY AND SUSTAINABILITY OF THE NGO MODEL

Replicability

Although not widely publicized, the success of the FUTS scheme has attracted interest at the highest levels within the Punjab and from other provinces. The federal government also commissioned an evaluation of the performance of FUTS services from the National Transport Research Centre, which reported favourably (Idris, 1996).

Growing interest has not been widely translated into action, however. Changes of provincial governments as well as the national government intervened following elections early in 1997, and reshuffles of official positions did not help to promote follow up. Nevertheless in Lahore, the capital city of Punjab Province (see Figure 5.1), an NGO was formed in June 1997, for the introduction of better quality bus services on a few priority routes in the first instance.

Lahore is a much larger city (population of about six million) with established minibus operators and active operators' associations, so that the introduction of an NGO-based regulatory system is a more complex process, and a cautious approach was adopted. The Lahore Transport System (LTS) is similar to FUTS but there are some important differences. Full size (60-seater) buses were introduced on several routes along major roads in what was seen as a first phase. A lower full route fare was fixed, at only three-quarters of that in Faisalabad. Similarly, although the student concessionary fare was raised, it was retained, and still without operator compensation. Also, the president of the Local Bus Owners Association and two members of the provincial assembly (supposedly representing passengers) were nominated by the provincial government to the governing body.

The LTS started on one route with 12 buses and by March 1998 over 60 buses were operating on three routes. The services compete with minibuses which still operate under government controls. This small-scale start in part reflected an insistence on better quality full-size buses, which have been in short supply.

More recently the Government of the Punjab has commenced the introduction of a new route franchising system on major bus routes in Lahore, in association with a federal government initiative which permits the duty free import of full-size buses, subject to some conditions, for urban stage carriage operation. Under this scheme, the regulatory implications of which are discussed later, the LTS NGO, still in its infancy, has not been in a strong enough position to bid for any of the initial round of franchises. Consequently the prospects for further expansion of the LTS seem limited, and any expansion which did occur would take place within the franchise scheme rather than on the Faisalabad model.

More promising perhaps is the very recent announcement of the formation of a new NGO to operate in Gujranwala, another major city of the Punjab, which is closer in size and public transport characteristics to Faisalabad.

Given the will, the FUTS model can readily be replicated in other cities faced with comparable situations to that in Faisalabad. In order to promote the FUTS model and more effectively transfer its success to other areas in Pakistan, better training arrangements are seen as essential, and explicit support for both training and the supply of new vehicles is needed from the federal government. In other LDCs, with similar regulatory problems and similarly deficient bureaucracies, it should also be possible to emulate the FUTS success. That success, however, is likely to depend on key officials, as in Faisalabad, and the impetus for reform must be maintained and politically supported throughout the process of implementation.

Sustainability

The success of the FUTS is now so well established that it seems unlikely that the gains made will be reversed through a clawing back of the control in to the government bureaucracy. Nevertheless the following issues are of concern and could influence the sustainability and future development of the NGO regulatory regime.

Legality

There are three areas that appear to contravene the prevailing law dealing with public transport services. First, the RTA is legally responsible for the planning, regulation and control of all stage carriage services within its jurisdiction. In practice the NGOs regulate their own services, and the RTA secretary rubber-stamps NGO decisions, but pressures remain from the ambivalent position in which this places the RTA and its secretary. Second, the government has treated the FUTS and the LTS on an exceptional basis by authorizing them to increase fares, whereas other operators and even other social companies operating public transport services have not been treated in the same way. Third, a concessionary fare to students is a legal requirement, yet none is given for using the FUTS services, apparently in contradiction to the law. Clarification of the legal framework to resolve these issues would help to ensure sustainability.

Fares review

The sustainability of the FUTS' success depends not just on retaining its independent ability to set fare levels, but on its use of this ability to ensure that fares are maintained at realistic levels through a regular review process. Only then will further investment and associated quality improvements be possible.

Corruption

The FUTS' success derives also from its clean administration, but this is still too dependent on a few officials in key positions, such as that of the administrator. The openness of the governing body as a decision-making forum does provide a degree of protection against the emergence of corrupt practices within FUTS. Operators can, for instance, directly report their complaints to the governing body, which acts as a restraint on the actions of individuals in senior positions and makes it more difficult for corruption to become re-established.

Representation

It would promote greater transparency and accountability within the FUTS decision-making process if the operators were to take up the representation to which they are entitled on the governing body. Legitimate concerns underlie their reluctance to do so, however, and these need to be addressed. With operators present as representatives at governing body meetings there may need to be areas of reserved business, for discussion and decision by officials only, if for example, matters of particular financial interest to individual operators were involved. Passengers' representation would also be desirable, since effective, independent representation of passenger interests is important in the assessment and monitoring of service performance in the longer run. Considerable difficulties are faced in seeking genuine consumer participation in the shorter term, in the absence of any organized public transport user groups. In the meantime no representation is likely to be preferable to representation by politicians, as on the LTS governing body, whose presence will inevitably be seen to compromise its independence.

Training

The FUTS model is seen to be an example for public transport regulation in other cities, but it has neither qualified staff nor training facilities. For FUTS to effectively build on its success, needs for staff training will have to be addressed. Training is also required in order to effectively promote the transfer of FUTS success and experience elsewhere.

A FUTURE FOR NGO REGULATION?

The Faisalabad NGO can hardly be seen to represent any conscious or serious attempt on the part of government to strengthen civil society and extend the role of NGOs. It is even questionable, given the composition of its governing body and with a management committee composed exclusively of government officials, whether it is a genuine NGO at all. It can be characterized as a government organized NGO (a GONGO?) and its NGO status can be seen as just a convenient legal device, used by a resourceful government official, in order to bypass blockages in the arteries of the government bureaucracy responsible for public transport regulation. Viewed in this way the FUTS merely represents an alternative type of agency arrangement, designed to provide regulation at arms length from the government, and perhaps only an interim arrangement pending necessary reforms to the regulatory bureaucracy itself.

Public transport regulation is inherently a government function, whatever the agency arrangements, and it cannot simply be transferred to a genuine NGO. In any arrangements that are made for regulation through other agencies, it is clear that accountability will be retained by an effective government. The role of any 'non-governmental' agencies involved in regulation will therefore be to provide a regulatory regime on behalf of government. The rationale for the use of any particular mechanism is simply that it is able to deliver that regulatory regime more effectively than alternative mechanisms.

However, FUTS is more than just a more effective regulatory bureaucracy, it actually takes responsibility for running bus services, and is analogous more to London Transport than to a traffic commissioner's office in the UK context. It engages constructively, directly and continuously with the operators in order to provide those services, and it has established an open and effective forum for discussions between operators and regulators. It is also notably free of corruption and can be seen as having developed a 'service culture' to a degree that is remarkable in the context of Pakistan today.

In contemporary Pakistan the government bureaucracy itself has proved incapable of delivering effective regulation, and radical changes are required for the existing government systems to work well. The prevailing bureaucratic culture would need to shift from one where typical attitudes are characterized as 'doing favours' to one in which bureaucrats see themselves as 'providing services'. The same holds true for many other LDCs. In the near future there seems to be little prospect of such radical reforms being widely and consistently implemented.

It is in this international context that, more generally and throughout LDCs, NGOs have been acquiring an increased role in urban development and the delivery of services, and with growing support from international aid agencies (see, for example, United Nations, 1996, and Hague, 1997). In this context also the Faisalabad NGO regulatory experiment can be seen to have wider significance and perhaps to act as a useful model. Its significance has been assessed as follows:

> *'The importance of the NGO (FUTS) regulatory experience in Pakistan as a model is that it has resulted in greater freedom of decision making and a more open system of regulation; a system which operates on the ground, and is interactive with the operators who deliver the services. As a legally private body it has provided an effective arms length mechanism, with accountability both upwards to government, and significantly also downwards to the service providers, if not yet to the service users. This is in marked contrast with the modus operandi of the official government system. There is clear potential for the wider application of this model for public transport regulation both in Pakistan and elsewhere.'* (Russell and Anjum, 1999)

Developments over recent years in the Punjab, under the Muslim League federal and provincial governments since 1997, did not suggest that this potential was about to be exploited, although the success of FUTS was acknowledged. In the introduction of the NGO model in Lahore, a very cautious approach was adopted, and it was not encouraging that politicians were placed on the governing body as representatives of users' interests. This risks undermining the independence of any regulatory role and weakens the function of the NGO as an 'arms length' mechanism. There was strong government interest in urban public transport but this concentrated on the new franchise initiative in Lahore. Under the new military regime urban transport problems may not be given the same priority, but there are signs of renewed interest in the NGO model, with the initiation of the new NGO in Gujranwala. This is planned to follow the FUTS pattern more closely and to involve both minibus and full-size bus routes.

Whatever the immediate extent of the prospects for replication elsewhere, there is no doubt that public transport regulation in Pakistan in this new form, using NGO status, has proved far more effective than government bureaucratic regulation to date. The achievements of NGO-based regulation are impressive.

Key factors involved in this success have been realistic fares, the involvement of private operators in decision making, freedom from the constraints of government bureaucracy, and the strict enforcement of service standards. It has also demonstrated there is a market for better quality services at higher fares in Pakistan.

Moreover, the Faisalabad experience has acted as a learning process, raising awareness and understanding about public transport issues, a process of vital importance given the absence of expertise, and one which acts as a means for strengthening civil society. The NGO has provided an effective 'arms length' mechanism for decision making, which has circumvented many of the problems associated with government bureaucracies. In the absence of more radical reforms, this mechanism offers the best prospects for further improvements to public transport services in Pakistan in the medium term.

The new franchise scheme in Lahore offers an alternative means to the achievement of improvements in the quality of urban public transport services. However, even if the franchise scheme proves highly successful there, it will not be easy to build on or generalize that success swiftly. Success depends on the existence of financially strong, locally based operators; it is labour intensive for the provincial government as the franchising authority; it is very dependent on scarce and specialized expertise; and it leaves the effectiveness of key aspects of regulation dependent on successful reform of the government's RTAs. It does not therefore offer a model that could readily or rapidly be transferred to cities elsewhere in Pakistan, other than perhaps a few of the major metropoli.

Elsewhere the replication of FUTS style NGO schemes could be expected to yield more rapid improvements. Moreover, such schemes provide a means for the mutual education of operators, officials and potentially user representatives, thereby continuously raising awareness and performance standards. They can offer more in terms of watering the roots of a strengthened civil society than a more exclusive and 'higher tech' franchising approach.

In other LDCs, with similar regulatory problems and similarly deficient bureaucracies, it may also be possible to emulate this success. An NGO regulatory model may even be worth considering for adaptation and application to the regulation and delivery of services other than public transport.

6 INFORMAL DEVELOPMENT IN THE MARKET SOCIALIST CITY: THE CASE OF THE FLOATING POPULATION OF BEIJING

Ralph Throp

INTRODUCTION

China's Floating Population

Since the late 1970s, Chinese state socialism has been restructuring through the introduction of market-orientated economic reforms. This restructuring has led to far reaching changes in the relationships between the state, market and society. Structural changes in the Chinese economy and society have caused corresponding changes to the character and structure of Chinese cities. One of the most visible of these changes is the growth of enclaves of rural–urban migrants. These migrants have brought new models of informal development to cities that have a long history of development carried out and rigidly controlled by the state.[1]

It is estimated that there are now as many as 100 million such migrants in Chinese cities. These migrants exist on the periphery of both the state apparatus of the socialist system and the opportunities offered by emerging markets. In the language of Chinese officials the people who make up this wave of migrants are known as 'the floating population', as they are living away from their officially registered place of residence. They are a heterogeneous group, more male than female, comparatively young and well educated. They are most often single and of working age, and may be engaged in one of a variety of occupations, in construction work, as short-term contract workers in state-owned enterprises, in textile manufacture, waste disposal and recycling, and working as domestics or nannies and in a range of small-scale service occupations.

As a phenomenon, the growth of the floating population has had both positive and negative impacts on life in Chinese cities. On the positive side, its members make an important contribution to China's urban economies. They provide a pool of low-cost labour that is in high demand by China's newly market-oriented industries; they work in a variety of low-paid service sector jobs and run a myriad of small businesses. They have also had the effect of injecting vitality and vibrancy into the grey and monotonous cities of the state socialist period and have changed their character just as profoundly as has the explosion of shopping malls and postmodern office towers which has occurred in the 1990s. On the other hand they are also linked with many of the urban ills which are facing Chinese cities. In social terms, the floating population has been associated with rising crime levels and deteriorating social order. The growth of migrant enclaves has also caused a physical decline in the environment of Chinese cities, which during the state socialist period were renowned for having avoided the problems which were seen as attendant on areas of informal development or 'shanty towns' in other countries.

Work and Civil Society in Zhejiang Village

The community of Zhejiangcun, or Zhejiang 'Village' in Beijing, which is the main subject of this chapter, is one of the best known and most distinctive migrant communities that has emerged in recent years. Most of its residents are migrants from the Wenzhou area in Zhejiang Province in southern China. Zhejiangcun has developed with startling rapidity, despite periodic government repression. The population of the 'village' now numbers over 100,000, the vast majority of whom are rural–urban migrants.

Zhejiangcun has a unique and complex set of social relations both within the community and linking it to the rest of the city (Ma and Xiang, 1998; Xiang, 1998). Economically, the whole community is geared up to function as a large, flexible factory, producing textiles for the Beijing market and beyond. The migrants operate a model of household-based production known as the Wenzhou Model (Parriss, 1993) which involves the use of simple equipment and traditional technology to make copies of existing garments. Relationships between producers and suppliers of raw materials are complex and varied and large networks are called into play to meet orders and source supplies. On a social level, the role of powerful individuals in the community is very important as mediators within the community and between migrants and the representatives of the state (Xiang, 1998).

Despite the large size of its population, Zhejiangcun has been virtually ignored by the Chinese urban planners, although not by the officials of Beijing's district governments, who have demonstrated a new entrepreneurial spirit in their dealings with the migrants. Zhejiangcun has no local government of its own; informal networks among residents provide all social organization and local services. Housing, industry, markets and services have all been developed by the migrants themselves.

Chapter Structure

The objective of this chapter is to show how, in the case of the floating population of Beijing, informal social and market mechanisms are substituting the state in urban development. It is therefore in three parts:

- The trajectory of Chinese urban development from traditional Chinese development, to the period of state socialism, and moving into the period of market reform is reviewed.
- The ways in which aspects of the state, market and society are reflected in the development of the spaces created by the migrant community of Zhejiangcun in Beijing are discussed.
- Finally, it is argued that in the case of this community, informal development, based on markets and traditional relationships is replacing the formal mechanisms of the socialist state.

STATE, MARKET AND CIVIL SOCIETY IN CHINESE URBAN DEVELOPMENT

China has always been viewed as a unique example of urbanization both because of the scale of the country and also because of its exceptional responses to the issues raised by urbanization and development. For this reason Chinese cities have long been of interest to Western scholars of urban planning and development. Until the 1980s, the focus of most of this interest was the creation of an ideal type of the 'Chinese', or the 'socialist' city (French and Hamilton, 1979). During the 1960s and 1970s, in particular, there was a great deal of academic interest in the Maoist model of development, which was perceived by Western observers of Chinese cities as a viable, radical alternative to the development models used in other developing countries (eg, Russell, 1971).

Since the reforms and revolutions of the 1980s, however, the familiar categories and distinctions that formed a background to this work – socialist, capitalist, Chinese or Western – have become obsolete. As with other countries that have adopted state socialist systems in the 20th century, and have recently been reforming these systems, the attention of researchers has turned to the study of the particular institutional arrangements which are driving and influencing development in specific places, at particular times, and often to the potential for the autonomy of the individual from the state which results.

In China, market reforms are rapidly changing the relationships between the state, and the other 'partners' in development. To understand this process in terms of a transition between state and market is insufficient as it ignores the role of the social structures embodied in the various concepts which are often pulled together under the label of 'civil society', and in which both the state and the market are embedded. The relationship between these three interrelated but opposing components of society, and particularly the nature and role of civil society, has become the focus of an increasing proportion of research into Chinese development and planning.

As has been pointed out in the introductory chapters of this book, the definitions of civil society are many and varied. In the Western context, the development of the concept of civil society is linked to the institutions of Western liberalism and modernity that developed from the Enlightenment of the 18th and early 19th centuries. This school of thought defines civil society in a modern vertical form that could perhaps be encapsulated as being made up of institutions which are formed and operated on the basis of voluntary, reciprocal associations such as neighbourhood, family and church, and which mediate between the individual at the bottom of a hierarchical polity and the state at the top (Berger and Neuhaus, 1977).

In the context of former state socialist countries, civil society has come to be associated with this Western idea of civil society, with an added dimension that focuses on the autonomy of the individual from the state. However, as Jenkins has pointed out in Chapter 3, such a modern definition of civil society may not be appropriate where either society retains a strong traditional element, or where state repression has weakened political, social or cultural associational structures, as in the case of many state socialist countries including China. In such cases, civil society may take the form of traditional institutions that are often temporarily submerged by the institutions of state socialism, and which have been presented with an opportunity to re-emerge during periods of market reform.

In China at the beginning of the 21st century there is a proto-market system, in which some goods and services are allocated under the system of state planning and some by markets, and which leaves little room for the institutions of modern civil society. Distinctions between the state and market sectors are blurred to say the least, and civil society in terms of voluntary organizations which would be recognized in the West is in its infancy, or submerged by the institutions of the socialist state. Relationships between the state, market and civil society are constantly being renegotiated.

Many functions, which were previously in the domain of the state, are now increasingly carried out by market mechanisms. China remains, however, basically a corporate society (Nee, 1989, 1992; Nee and Su, 1996) in which interest groups that might be regarded in the West as civil society such as women's or youth groups and trades unions are directly controlled by the state. Unofficial organizations are the subject of suspicion. Established state institutions such as urban planning, while they may have evolved to develop links with and mechanisms to deal with markets, are still strongly embedded in the state sector and do not relate to civil society. The state also retains at least partial control, through ownership and regulation, of much of the market sector. In this situation of partial market reform, the most successful institutions are those that have access to the resources of both state and market (Nee, 1989, 1992).

TRADITIONAL CHINESE URBAN DEVELOPMENT

The roots of many of these institutions can be found in past development practice. The history of Chinese urban development is extremely long, and shows a remarkable degree of continuity over three millennia, from the earliest slave societies through China's long period of semi-feudalism and into the state socialist period. Throughout this long history, the state has retained a strong role in the process of urban development, while the market and civil society have emerged to different degrees at different times. Feudal China was governed by a highly centralized system of which the Emperor or 'Son of Heaven' was the apex.

The agents of this authority were the meritocratic elites of the bureaucracy and the military. In imperial China, cities were administrative centres that served as nodes of imperial authority. Capital cities, such as Beijing, were at the top of the urban hierarchy and as such became the focus for huge concentrations of resources. Cities had a strongly orthogenetic role, reinforcing traditional values and organizing agricultural production, markets and taxation.

China has a long history of involvement of state officials in commercial activity through state monopolies and contracts, a situation that is reflected in post-reform China. The state also had a strong role in regulating urban development. The order of the built environment reflected the order of society in which the size of the building, its internal arrangement and its architectural decoration were already determined by the owner's social position. All urban land was owned by the state in the person of the emperor, as the Chinese saying goes: 'All land under the sun belongs to the Emperor'.

From the mid-19th century onwards, the weak Qing state in China was no longer able to retain the degree of state control which previous governments had achieved and lost control of large sections of the country, including major cities, to domestic rebels. Due to their military superiority, the Western trading and colonial powers were able to force the Chinese government to sign a series of unequal treaties that granted them extraterritorial enclaves or 'concessions' in coastal cities such as Shanghai and Tianjin, which became known as Treaty Ports. In these cities the pattern of state-controlled urban development was not followed and European-style civil society played a stronger role. Some of the first modern developments in Shanghai, for instance, were instigated and carried out by voluntary associations. In Beijing, the late 19th and early 20th centuries saw the beginning of modernization and the emergence of urban development that reflected the institutions of Western style civil society in the form of hospitals, schools and churches.[2]

China's earliest migrant communities developed in the Treaty Ports during this period. These communities were well organized, with social institutions which, in addition to aiding migrants and their families, carried out local government functions on behalf of the state including tax collection and military levies (Rowe, 1986). In the early mid-20th century, the weakness of the state meant that it was possible for individual households to move to urban areas and establish themselves in vacant buildings. In the inner city of Beijing, for example, it is still possible to see former ancestral temples which were taken over in early squatter invasions by rural–urban migrants in the 1940s and are today still occupied by the original squatters and their families, with the sanction of the municipal government. The areas where these buildings stand are, however, now the subjects of intense pressure for market-driven development.[3]

THE STATE SOCIALIST PERIOD

When the Chinese Communist Party (CCP) came to power in 1949, the socialist system of government that was implemented retained many features of the traditional Chinese system as well as the many new 'Maoist' ideas developed by the leadership of the CCP, and borrowed ideas from the established social-ist state of the Soviet Union.[4] The system was highly centralized and bureaucratic. As in imperial China, ultimate authority rested with the strong central leadership, which existed in symbiosis with the bureaucrats who ran the Leninist Party State and the Peoples Liberation Army.[5] State officials not only controlled but also planned and directed urban development through the state planning of the economy and direct control of production.

During the early part of this period, many Western observers were struck by the apparent success of the Chinese model of urban development. In the cities of the capitalist developing world, informally developed shanty towns and favelas were seen as the physical manifestation of the marginality of the urban poor. Extreme poverty, unemployment, crime, poor or insufficient housing and infrastructure, environmental degradation, epidemic disease and above all, a 'culture of poverty' (Lewis, 1976a, 1976b) were noted features of such communities. Although this perception of informal settlements later changed, the general lack of capacity in developing countries to deal with the problems of such areas did not. Chinese cities, by contrast, were perceived as uniquely successful in the developing world in avoiding many of these problems. In reality, this apparent success was the result of two important factors: state control of the movement of population, and state control of the process of urban development.[6]

The physical movement of people during the state socialist period was controlled by the *hukou* (household registration) system[7] (Chan, 1994, 1996) as part of China's planned economy. The *hukou* system effectively bound Chinese, and particularly rural Chinese, to a single place of residence. The most important function of the *hukou* system was to classify people according to their place of residence as either 'agricultural' or 'non-agricultural'.[8] For people who were born after the system was introduced, *hukou* status was inherited from the mother and could not otherwise be transferred, even by marriage, to an urban dweller. Although travel within China was never officially banned,[9] by restricting the locations in which people could live, the *hukou* system acted as an effective internal passport system (Chan, 1994, 1996). Legal migration from rural to urban areas was permitted only as a tiny trickle. Illegal migration was extremely difficult because households could only draw the rations of food to which they were entitled under the state socialist system from their registered place of residence, and also because it was illegal to privately rent urban housing.

The urban development process was also controlled as part of China's system of economic planning. A process of project-specific development was used in order to achieve rapid industrialization. The main actors in this process during the state socialist period were the *danwei* (work units). Industrial development was encouraged at the fringe of existing urban centres so new development tended to form a ring around the existing historic core of the traditional city. *Danwei* applied for permits to acquire land at the edge of the city from the municipal government. Compensation was paid to the land's original occupants at a level that approximated to the use value of the land over a number of years.[10] Investment came from the state budget, as part of the planned investment in production. Construction was carried out by state-owned construction enterprises.

The *danwei* were the urban communities of the state socialist period. As well as being centres of production facilities, the *danwei* also carried out important social functions. They were responsible for providing welfare services, often referred to as the 'iron ricebowl', to their employees. This meant that as well as factories, *danwei* compounds typically contained housing and services including schools and medical facilities for their workers. Housing was rented at nominal cost from their *danwei*. Work units, and therefore their managers and officials, thus had a tremendous control over the lives of their employees as instruments of state control as well as service delivery. This was particularly true of housing. Enterprise managers allocated households their housing. In theory, this could mean that housing was allocated according to need rather than demand. In practice it left ample scope for corruption. The managers also had an important role in weakening the horizontal development of civil society because they restricted the social networks of most urban residents within their individual work units (Davis et al, 1995).

In spite of the changed institutions and rhetoric, however, there were many parallels between the traditional Chinese city of the imperial era and the new socialist cities which began to develop after 1949.[11] Chinese cities during this period were essentially closed and inward looking. Work units were usually set in walled compounds, which contained in a single module most of the services and facilities which would be required by their residents. In this they were a similar phenomenon to the walled wards of the traditional city, whose gates could be locked at night. These wards, often, like the *danwei*, specialized in a particular industry or trade. The mix of functions within the work-unit compound meant that the need to travel long distances was minimized and the walking scale of the city was retained (Davis et al, 1995).[12]

THE REFORM PERIOD

Since China began the introduction of markets into its society in the late 1970s and early 1980s, the illusion of poverty-free cities has dissolved. What Castells and Sheridan (1977) referred to as the 'classic link between urbanization and industrialization' has been re-established. The perception that China was a poverty-free society formed by Western observers of Chinese cities in the state socialist period was a false one. It has become apparent that China's 'poverty free' cities were achieved through the use of what Chan (1994) refers to as 'invisible walls' of state institutions which sealed them off from their rural hinterlands and thus held cities and countryside in an artificial equilibrium. This was implemented by strict control of the movement of population through the *hukou* system and the rationing of day-to-day household necessities such as grain and cooking oil.

Urban growth which was so strictly controlled by the institution of state planning, has exploded under the new market-based system.[13] Market-driven development in the formal sector has increasingly led to the growth of functionally specific areas, based on Western models, such as central business districts, and 'new industrial districts' such as special economic zones and economic and technological development zones. Many researchers have described Chinese cities of this period in the tradition of Burgess' 1925 study of the development of Chicago, in terms of concentric rings of different types of development. The inner area is made up of the historic core of the city; the middle ring is composed of state socialist era development, constructed using the project-specific development model by work units; and there is an outer ring of market-driven development.[14] In reality, the restructuring taking place is more complex. In Beijing, as well as pressure for development on greenfield sites at the edge of the city, there is intense market-driven development activity in the city centre, and along the ring roads and axials which make up the city's primary road network.

This market-driven development may be divided into two sectors, the formal and the informal. Formal development is carried out by state owned or formal private sector development companies.[15] Informal development is carried out by Beijing residents, or migrants to the city, in order to provide extra space to accommodate their households, or from which to operate a small business, or to generate income rent by letting to another household. In reality this kind of informal construction has been an important factor in the lives of Beijing's ordinary citizens for a long time. They have used the central open space of their traditional *si he yuan* courtyard houses as a source of infill space for small-scale development. In Beijing's inner city today there are very few *si he yuan* houses which still retain an open central courtyard. In most cases it has been reduced to a narrow corridor by crammed-in informal construction.

One of the major changes that has accompanied the growth of markets and market-driven development in many Chinese cities is the massive increase in rural–urban migration. Since the late 1970s this trend has been driven by both push and pull factors. In rural areas, agriculture has been progressively decollectivized causing productivity in this sector to rise. At the same time millions of agricultural workers were left underemployed or unemployed and therefore unable to make a living from the land. By 1995 it is estimated that the rural agricultural labour surplus numbered some 150–200 million workers. Commentators suggest that by the turn of the century this total may well reach 400 million (Xiaoli and Wei, 1997). At the same time, the growth and restructuring of China's urban economies has created rapid growth and demand in urban employment.

While the *hukou* regulations have never officially been abolished, from the 1980s onwards there has been more freedom of movement to urban areas. In 1983 the Chinese State Council issued new regulations under which peasants involved in non-agricultural work in towns were allowed to gain residential status, provided they did not claim any state benefits, including food or housing. They were called 'households with self supplied food grains'. Mark One of the main regulatory changes which made this possible was the Number One Agricultural Document: this was issued by the Chinese government in 1984. This document allowed people who had rural *hukou* registration to travel to small towns in order to work or do business. As there was no way that such migrants could gain access to their rations of grain, they were forced to either carry provisions with them or buy food on the market. Migration was thus only possible when and where markets for essentials such as food existed. Later government documents have allowed migration from rural areas to larger cities for similar purposes (Chan, 1994, 1996). This relaxation was followed by a rapid expansion in the growth of urban floating populations.

CASE STUDY: THE DEVELOPMENT OF ZHEJIANGCUN, BEIJING

Urban–rural migration to Beijing and characteristics of the floating population

The latest figures show that the number of rural migrants in the whole of Beijing Municipality, including its rural counties, is around 3.6 million – 24 per cent of the total population of the city (Beijing Municipal Statistical Bureau, 1998). In total, about 1.8 million migrants now live in Beijing's urban districts. Most of them live in the area on the fringe of the city proper, between the predominantly formal development of the city's urban districts and the mainly informal development of the rural districts.[16] Approximately 25 per cent live in the four districts of the inner city, and 75 per cent live in the four inner suburban districts, Chaoyang, Fengtai, Shijingshan and Haidian. This means that rural–urban migrants now number one in four of Beijing's population (see Table 6.1).

This migration has been caused by a number of factors, both positive and negative. Recent research shows that migrants have thus been driven by both push and pull factors to make the move to Beijing. The main reasons given by migrants asked about their motivation to move to Beijing were both to take advantage of money-making opportunities (55.4 per cent) and shortage of land in their original home area (19.6 per cent) (Liu and Liang, 1997).

Compared to the native population of Beijing, the migrants are comparatively young, and a high proportion are male.[17] They are also relatively well educated; only 3.2 per cent are illiterate or semi-literate while 79.1 per cent are educated to at least junior middle school level and 7.1 per cent have been to college (Beijing Municipal Statistical Bureau, 1998). Their length of stay in Beijing varies. A high proportion (58 per cent) are transient visitors, leaving

Table 6.1 *Beijing's floating population as a percentage of total population*

Area	Total population	Floating population	Floating population as a percentage of total
Urban districts	7,512,000	1,813,518	24.1
Inner city	2,691,000	368,434	13.7
Inner suburbs	4,821,000	1,445,084	30.0

Source: Adapted from Beijing Municipal Statistical Bureau, 1998

Table 6.2 *Members of Beijing's floating population by housing type*

Housing option	Total	%	Inner districts	%	Inner suburbs	%
All households	1,813,518	100	368,434	100	1,445,084	100
Rent	750,674	41.4	105,494	28.6	645,180	44.6
Self-build	45,316	2.5	2437	0.7	42,879	3.0
Purchase	4975	0.3	1186	0.3	3789	0.3
Relatives	82,071	4.5	32,080	8.7	49,991	3.5
Hotel	91,949	5.1	46,882	12.7	45,067	3.1
Workplace	783,851	43.2	162,663	44.1	621,188	43.0
Other	12,398	0.7	5129	1.4	7269	0.5

Source: Adapted from Beijing Municipal Statistical Bureau, 1998

within the year. There is, however, some continuity of residence with 19.6 per cent remaining in Beijing for between one and three years, and 19.4 per cent staying for over three years.

The main factor in the location of migrants on arrival in Beijing is their place of origin. The migrant enclaves in Beijing are known as villages and are usually named after the native province of their residents, or their main occupation. The five largest migrant enclaves in the city are populated by people from the provinces of Zhejiang, Xinjiang, Henan and Anhui. In reality, the migrants in each village tend to come from one or two neighbouring counties. Zhejiangcun, for instance, was named after Zhejiang Province because the residents of Beijing had not heard of Wenzhou Prefecture, from where most of its residents originate. In addition, there are a number of smaller enclaves such as 'Eyeglass Village' and 'Lumber Village' which are named after their economic speciality.

The enclaves have grown through a process of chain migration. Successful migrant business people have recruited additional labourers from their place of origin, providing houses and employment. Once established in the city these new migrants have left their original employers and set up their own businesses, recruiting in turn from their contacts in their home area. Approximately 75 per cent of migrants found their first jobs in Beijing in this way, through relatives or contacts from their place of origin (Ma and Xiang, 1998).

The development of Zhejiangcun

The development of Zhejiangcun demonstrates how informal networks outside the control of the state have replaced formal mechanisms of either state or market in the development of housing and other facilities for the floating population.[18]

The Community of Zhejiangcun is the largest and one of the most distinctive of the migrant village communities in Beijing. It is mainly populated by migrants from Wenzhou Prefecture in Zhejiang Province. This prefecture has a long history of business activity and its residents have a reputation as entrepreneurs. It also has a serious historic problem with shortage of land supply. These two factors have led to a tradition of migrating away from the area in order to 'make a fortune' (Liu and Liang, 1997).

Zhejiang Village specializes mainly in garment processing and marketing. At the beginning of the 1980s, when the Cultural Revolution was over, there was increasing demand for service industries from Beijing residents who began to complain of the inconvenience of obtaining meals, buying clothes and getting their possessions repaired. In this situation, the skilled clothes manufacturers of Wenzhou were welcomed in Beijing and this gave them their opportunity to gain a foothold in the city.

Over 50,000 of the Zhejiangcun residents are engaged in this business. This concentration of textile businesses supplies over 90 per cent of the winter clothing and leather jackets on the market in Beijing and is therefore significant to the economy of the city as a whole (Liu and Liang, 1997). Its exports extend beyond China's borders, particularly to the former Soviet Union (Xiang, 1998). In their business activities, the residents of Zhejiangcun employ the traditional system known as the 'Wenzhou Model' (Ma and Hanten, 1981; Liu and Liang, 1997). This is a system of manufacture that is based around the household. Traditional social networks are used to source raw materials, facilitate cooperative working and carry out marketing. The whole village acts as a flexible factory with the migrant's homes as workshops within it. They make use of simple equipment and traditional technology to make copies of existing products for sale on the market (Liu and Liang, 1997).

Xiang (1998) described the business networks in Zhejiangcun as a series of overlapping networks:

> *"Zhejiang Village" is a big company as well as a big factory. Each of the producers and merchants has built a network of personal relationships. Based on these networks, each merchant has close contacts with 20 or more households engaged in producing, and vice versa. Producers delivering products to their co-operators or merchants collecting garments from producers is the basic, but most important practice in the community. Producers and merchants frequently call at each other's homes to discuss the styles and prices of garments. In doing so, information about the outside market disseminates quickly and smoothly within the community. The frequent communication also enables producers and merchants to get to a tacit agreement in their co-operation, so that no time is wasted on bargaining.'*

Zhejiangcun is located in Nanyuan (South Garden). This area is a former imperial hunting ground to the south of the centre of Beijing, only about four kilometres from the central commercial district of Qianmen and five kilometres from Tiananmen Square (see Figure 6.1). Versions of the story of the origin of the community vary. It is generally agreed that it was founded in the early 1980s by Wenzhouese businessmen returning homeward from Batou in Inner Mongolia and, finding a ready market for their stock in Beijing, deciding to stay where they were and rent accommodation in the city (Xiang, 1998). The population quickly grew to 10,000. Between 1986 and 1989 the population of

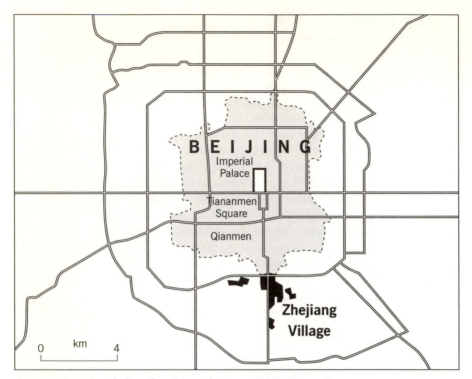

Source: Harry Smith, based on Ma and Xiang (1998), Figure 2

Figure 6.1 *Map of Beijing, showing the location of Zhejiang Village*

Zhejiangcun rose rapidly, and environmental degradation associated with overcrowding developed. By the end of 1994 the area had approximately 110,000 residents. Of these, only about 14,000 had Beijing *hukou* status while 96,000 were migrants. By 1995, all the formerly agricultural land between the work unit compounds in the area had been infilled by informal development.

Zhejiangcun now covers the area of 24 administrative villages. The native Beijing residents, although they lived in areas that were designated by the government as villages, have long since ceased to be involved in agriculture. A migrant community has grown up here for a number of reasons. The first is its excellent geographical location for commercial activities, only a few kilometres away from Beijing's busiest commercial districts. It is also close to a long-distance bus station. More significantly, Nanyuan, on the edge of the city, is a place where the urban and rural administrative systems overlap (Liu and Liang, 1997). This situation leads to a degree of ambiguity in terms of regulation and gives the migrants a degree of freedom from state control.

The most characteristic form of development in Zhejiangcun is the big yard or *da yuan*. In contrast to the informally constructed neighbourhoods of many cities in other less developed countries, these informally constructed walled compounds offer migrants basic versions of many of the services that are provided to urban *hukou* holders in the work-unit compounds of the state socialist era. There are now some 46–48 *da yuan* in Zhejiangcun which house 30,000–40,000 of the Wenzhouese migrants. The first *da yuan* were constructed by native Beijing villagers in order to take advantage of the booming market for accommodation for Wenzhouese migrants; the model was then taken up and applied on a larger scale by Wenzhouese entrepreneurs.

According to Xiang (1998) the first *da yuan* was built when the village committee of Dongluoyuang Village decided to clean up an area of derelict land, and constructed 240 basic rooms for rent to Wenzhouese migrants on the site. The rent from these rooms subsequently became the village's main source of income. The next *da yuan* to be constructed was a similar project constructed by a local village, but all subsequent ones have been constructed by the migrants themselves.

Land for *da yuan* is rented by Wenzhouese entrepreneurs directly from the heads of the village in which they wish to build. This is only possible because the land in question is classified by the government as rural rather than urban and is therefore owned by the village rather than the central government. In Beijing, planning consent for development is granted at different levels of government depending on the size of the development and value of the investment it involves. The largest developments are considered by the Capital Planning Commission which has representatives of the central and municipal governments. Medium-sized developments may be granted consent by the municipal government. District governments regulate only the smallest of developments and the construction of temporary structures. This framework is important in understanding the development of the *da yuan*. The need to obtain planning consent for development is often avoided altogether by agreement between village heads and the Wenzhouese developers not to report the new *da yuan*'s existence to the relevant authorities. An alternative is to apply for planning consent for the construction of 'temporary' rather than permanent buildings. Planning consent for temporary construction can be granted by the district government, which is usually much more amenable to the migrants than is the municipal government.

Finance for the construction of *da yuan* comes from two sources. The first is money pooled by a group of three or four successful businessmen who have usually made their money in the garment industry. The second method of raising the necessary finance for the construction of a *da yuan* is through prepaid rents. It is quite common in Zhejiangcun for a compound's developers to collect rent before building is complete. Tenants may be required to pay two or three months' rent in advance when they apply to a developer for housing. Tenants are also encouraged to pay rent as a lump sum for as long as six months to a year. The price charged will be lower if the rent is paid in this way. By pre-charging rents the developers of *da yuan* can recover their investment in just a few months (Xiang, 1998).

Construction workers for the buildings are mainly 'construction teams' from nearby provinces such as Hebei, themselves migrant workers. Some local Beijing residents, previously agricultural workers, can also be seen to be taking part in the construction process. Few Wenzhouese are directly involved in construction. This does not mean, however, that the developers of compounds need to travel to Hebei in order to recruit construction workers, as there are many such construction teams working in Beijing.

Due to the rapid development in Zhejiangcun, and its informal nature, the area's original infrastructure is under serious pressure, although it is still superior to many rural areas which lack sewerage altogether. Services in the area which were largely constructed during the state socialist period were built to serve a much smaller population than now uses them, designed as they were without taking the migrant influx into account. The sewerage system is particularly obsolete and overloaded. Major problems exist in garbage collection services (Liu and Liang, 1997). Public toilet facilities are privately run, and are shared between many households. The *da yuan* usually provide their residents with public toilets and running water systems. *Da yuan* also often employ staff to look after the security of the compound. Some yards also employ cleaners to deal with garbage collection and disposal. These public services that are provided by the migrants themselves are limited to the *da yuan*.

Social facilities in Zhejiangcun have been developed by individual migrant entrepreneurs. In the largest *da yuan* in Zhejiangcun, fee-based services such as day-care centres, beauty salons, grocery stores, telephone services, clinics and entertainment facilities are privately run, mostly by the families of the *da yuan* developers. The first kindergarten was opened in 1988; the first food market opened in 1989. Since 1990 clinics, barbershops and repair shops have been set up. A government-run post office and bank have also moved into the area. Interestingly they are both located in the same building and distance themselves from other privately-run services in the area.

Despite the size of the population of Zhejiangcun, which would normally be expected to qualify for the administrative status of a town, it has no formal institutions of local government or social control. Social organization is informal – the main instruments of control are the clan based 'gangs' whose role 'falls somewhere between facilitation of local autonomy for the provision of services and outright extortion of residents' (Xiang, 1998). Traditional networks based on 'blood ties' and place ties (Ma and Xiang, 1998) are still the most important for the daily life of the community. The role of powerful individuals in the community is very important – their most significant role is to mediate in conflicts between different families, which are usually business related, and between the migrants and the agents of the government.

Different government institutions display markedly different attitudes to the migrants. Lower levels of government and individual enterprises are involved in symbiotic relationships and partnerships with the migrant community. The central and municipal governments have, until very recently, been interested only in regulating them, accepting their presence reluctantly.

Between 1986 and 1995 there were five attempts to clear the Nanyuan area of migrants. Between 1986 and 1989, as the environment of the area deteriorated, the municipal government adopted a series of eviction policies, none of which was successfully implemented. In 1990, immediately prior to the Asian Games being held in Beijing, 2000 members of the police force cleared Zhejiangcun of its migrant population. The migrants left – but returned when the Games were over. The most recent attempt to eradicate Zhejiangcun came in November 1995, when Fengtai District organized a force of 2000 people to clear the illegal construction: out of 47 *da yuan* 22 were demolished. The markets in the area, however, many of which were owned, or partly owned by district governments were not demolished, and the migrants motivation to return therefore remained. The migrants had become adept at playing hide and seek with the authorities, retiring to villages further away from the city at times when the authorities seek to expel them and returning when pressures relax (Xiang, 1998).

CONCLUSION

Urban development in China has a long history of state control from which the development of migrant enclaves such as Zhejiangcun represents, in many respects, a significant departure. During China's long imperial era markets were an important part of urban development, but the strength of the imperial bureaucracy was such that the state was able to exercise strict control until the final decline and fall of the imperial system in the 19th and early 20th centuries. During this period contact with the European powers and the US led to the first introduction of Western-style civil society to the process.

The establishment of the communist People's Republic of China in 1949 led to a renewal of state dominance of development in China's cities. A strict top-down model of development based on economic planning and social control was applied. The state-owned work unit compound was the expression of this system.

The reintroduction of markets to the Chinese economy has provided opportunities for new forms of development to emerge. The development of Zhejiangcun and other migrant villages in Beijing and elsewhere is an example of how it is possible for alternatives to emerge on the fringe of both the state and the market.

Is this a sign of the emergence of civil society in China? This depends on perspective. Clearly there are significant institutions at work in Zhejiangcun which are to a large degree independent of the state. There is, however, little sense of a Western-style civil society composed of institutions such as democracy, free press and civic institutions emerging. The civil society of Zhejiangcun is an altogether more coercive phenomenon. It is characterized by traditional relationships between bosses and workers and between clan and family members which have their roots in the rural origins of the migrants, and in traditional Chinese society from before the socialist revolution. Development remains in essence top-down. Housing and facilities are constructed by entrepreneurs who control access to housing and profits from services, and also act as mediators between the migrants and the state. Their position is bolstered by the coercive power of the 'security forces' that they control.

As with many phenomena of transitional China, it remains to be seen whether the migrant villages are themselves transitional or longer-term features of China's cities. Recently it has been possible to detect changing attitudes to the migrants among officials of the Beijing Municipal Government.

In 1999 the government announced a new initiative to provide housing for migrants in Beijing known as the 'Five Experimental Areas Programme', consisting of government sponsorship of areas with housing specifically for migrants. The government will offer subsidies for such housing in five locations in Beijing, including Zhejiangcun. The Beijing Government is also planning to establish *wailai renkou xiao qu* ('small districts for population coming in from outside') in Chaoyang, Haidian, Fengtai and Shijingshan Districts.[19] It remains to be seen what these signs of an increasing willingness on behalf of the Chinese state to engage with the migrants portend for migrant communities such as Zhejiangcun.

7 URBAN MANAGEMENT AND COMMUNITY DEVELOPMENT IN METRO MANILA

Michael Carley and Josefa Rizalina Bautista

INTRODUCTION

Metro Manila is the focus of the economic and political life of the Philippines. It is home to around 12 million people, putting it on the list of the world's 20 largest urban regions, with a population growing by around a million new residents every five years. Within the city-region, there are 17 local government units, in eight cities and nine municipalities. The overall metropolis occupies over 640 square kilometres on Luzon Island, along the eastern shore of Manila Bay at the mouth of the Pasig River. The river bisects the city, flowing from its new settlement areas to join the sea at old Manila.

These geographic features provide some focus to the vast, sprawling metropolis, although many residents relate more strongly to the city's old market places, such as the Paco Market, as well as to vast new indoor shopping malls, some a kilometre long or more, as can be found in the high-rise centre of Ortigas City. Traffic congestion in and around the metropolis is fierce, with buses, the colourful Jeepneys, modelled on ex-army style jeeps from the Second World War, and a growing number of private cars and trucks jostling with motorcycles, horse carts, motorized and bicycle rickshaws and floods of pedestrians. Despite various measures, including banning odd and even registration numbers on alternative days, severe air pollution and many hours devoted to daily commuting are facts of urban life. Air pollution is said to exceed WHO recommendations by 300 per cent; 70 per cent of the city-region's air pollution comes from motor vehicles with 50 per cent of the total vehicles in the Philippines registered in Metro Manila (Development Academy of the Philippines, 1996).

The oldest part of the region is the City of Manila, occupying only around 6 per cent of the built up area. Its focus is the original Spanish fortified town (Intramuros, or 'within walls') and harbour. There are also a series of important urban subcentres, a number of which have eclipsed the old centre in terms of economic vitality and as a focus for daily life, as shown on the map. These

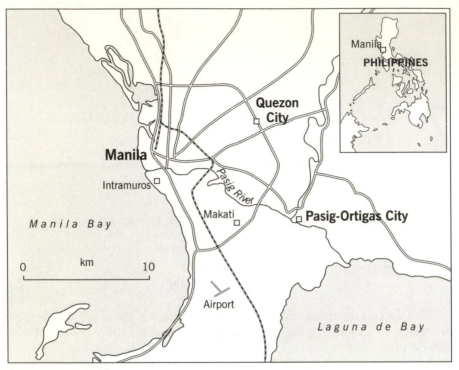

Source: Harry Smith

Figure 7.1 *Map of Metro Manila*

include Makati, the business centre, Quezon City, the university zone to the
north-east, and Pasig-Ortigas City to the south (see Figure 7.1). There are
currently three distinct CBDs and more are coming on stream. The urbanization of Metro Manila is linking up to spreading urbanization in nearby regions,
such as the resort area of Taygaytay and new developments around the Subic
Bay-Clark economic zone (Cabanilla, 1996).

The metropolitan area exhibits the usual range of economic vibrancy,
conjunction of extreme wealth and poverty, and environmental degradation that
characterize many of the world's megacities. First-time visitors may be surprised
to find more than 60 skyscrapers, housing Asian and multinational businesses,
but the perceptive visitor may also notice that one-quarter of the region's people
live in squatter settlements – which are of various degrees of permanency, with
around half of these lacking adequate water and sanitary services.

There is population pressure and an intense housing shortage, in part
because of substantial rural to urban migration and, in the early 1990s, the
arrival of many people displaced by the huge volcanic eruption of Mount
Pinatubo. The squatter population has doubled from 1.65 million in 1982 to
3.5 million in 1996 (Development Academy of the Philippines, 1996). Health
indicators show major differences between squatter and non-squatter areas,
such as a variation of infant mortality rates from 76 to 210 per 1000 live births
(Hardoy et al, 1992). Social and environmental problems in Metro Manila

include lack of clean water and adequate sanitary facilities in squatter settlements, poor housing, water and air pollution, flooding and poor solid waste management (Abracosa, 1996a). Diarrhoea and lung disease are two of the five most common causes of morbidity (Gozun, 1996).

In squatters' neighbourhoods, many self-build projects are in evidence. Commonly the first stage on the housing ladder is construction of the *barong-barong*, a makeshift house built of salvaged materials, such as flattened tin cans, scrap lumber, cartons or billboards. However, typical of squatter settlements, the neighbourhoods, or *barangays*, of poor residents demonstrate enormous ingenuity in their diversity of housing types. These show a progression from the temporary *barong-barong* to multi-storey concrete construction, one floor at a time as finance permits. These may also include rooms for rent for recent arrivals, sometimes on an eight hour per day 'bed share' basis.

ORGANIZATION OF THIS CHAPTER

What is less obvious to the casual observer is the institutional and social framework of governance that underpins daily life in Metro Manila, or the role of vertical organizational integration, as described in the first chapter, as a prerequisite for sustainable development. The term describes a positive linkage between the neighbourhood–city-region–national urban policy framework for the management of the city-region and the empowerment of its citizens. Where such integration is lacking, bottom-up community initiatives are frequently undermined by top-down interests, and sustainable development is unlikely to be achieved (Carley and Christie, 2000).

With this in mind, this chapter looks at organizational developments in Metro Manila and their contribution to urban development. In particular it looks beyond urban management at its usual level of the city or the municipality to examine institutional initiatives at the lower, neighbourhood level and the higher, city-regional level. At the latter level, governance is undertaken by the Metro Manila Development Authority (MMDA). At the neighbourhood level the operation of the lowest spatial unit of Filipino local government – the *barangays* – is examined. For many people, particularly in squatter settlements, the *barangay* provides the main, or the only, point of linkage between government and civil society. This issue of the management of cities is of critical importance in the Philippines – with around 60 per cent of the country's population now resident in urban areas, compared with only 33 per cent in 1970 (Abracosa, 1996a).

Between city-regional governance by the MMDA and the *barangays*, are the municipal assemblies (*sangguniang bayan*), created for each city or municipality, which coordinate with the metropolitan government in administration and legislation. Each *sangguniang bayan* is composed of a mayor, vice-mayor, councillors, the captains of the *barangays*, and representatives from other sectors, the latter appointed by the President of the Philippines upon recommendation of local units of central administration. The mayors are the presiding officers in their respective areas of jurisdiction.

The chapter begins at the neighbourhood level, with a description of local government and self-management initiatives in the *barangays*. These 'bottom-up' political units of from 2000 to around 6000 people are a unique, formal unit of neighbourhood governance. They were recently reconstituted in a modern sense, but their historical precedent goes back to the pre-Spanish period from around the 13th century. Continuing with the theme of vertical integration, the chapter also discusses, more briefly, urban management at the 'top-down' level of the city-region. Tackling issues such as traffic congestion and the provision of public transport at this regional level, conditions quality of life for all residents of the city-region.

A final section examines these organizational initiatives, and discusses their linkage and the extent to which an appropriate organizational framework contributes to community and urban development. In particular, it is suggested that the experience of the *barangays* could be of interest to a wider constituency in other large cities around the world.

A Visit to the Barangay

Within the larger spatial context outlined above, the city is differentiated into a series of urban villages or neighbourhoods. These are the *barangays*. On a visit, an observer might take an interest in groups of men patrolling the community's clean streets at night or, in daytime, in an environmental improvement project along a riverside, a neighbourhood waste management project or just in mixed groups of women and men huddled in animated conversation near a roadside structure, possibly elevated on stilts or else standing on a concrete pad. This structure may be of concrete, if the neighbourhood is moderately prosperous, or even of plywood. This is the *barangay* hall, the centre of neighbourhood governance. Outside could well be found a list of names of men and women – the officers of the *barangay*, frequently with their pictures and an enumeration of their responsibilities (see Figure 7.2).

The night-time patrol would be of guards or *barangay tanods*, ensuring the neighbourhood sleeps peacefully through the night, and remains relatively free of burglary. The discussion group would be *barangay* officials and residents, and they could be discussing any of a number of aspects of local governance including public safety, drinking water quality, primary education, the working of the local informal economy or even traffic calming on neighbourhood roads. If traffic calming is under discussion, for example, *barangay* officials and residents probably will not wait for local government at the city level to act – they might well organize their own traffic calming methods. These might consist of concrete humps or just a large truck tyre cut open and nailed down on the road as an instant, inexpensive hump. This is typical of *barangays* – within the context of the existing political power structure, they are a focus for local action in community development.

Both poor and rich neighbourhoods have *barangays* but, in the squatter settlements, the city's chronic housing shortage is evident. To ease pressure, some tenement housing projects have been constructed by the government,

Credit: Michael Carley

Figure 7.2 *A typical* barangay *hall*

one of which is the Bagong Lipunan Improvement of Sites and Services
(BLISS) programme, initiated by Metro Manila's governor. The government
has also developed resettlement projects around Metro Manila accessible
mainly by bus transport. But the *barong-barong* is most common in squatter
barangays.

Local political subdivisions that have elected officials include cities and
municipalities; during the Marcos regime the ancient *barangay* was reinstated
within this framework of elected officials as the most local political unit in the
Philippines. The *barangay* serves as the primary planning and implementing
unit of government policies and programmes in the community; as a forum
wherein the collective views of the people are expressed and channelled to
senior levels of government, and as a legal mechanism by which neighbourhood disputes are mediated by elected officials without drawn-out recourse to
higher courts.

For example, in order to reduce the load of the courts, local committees of
citizens called pacification committees (*lupon tagapayapa*) have been
organized to effect extrajudicial settlement of minor cases between *barangay*
residents. In each *lupon* there is a conciliation body (*pangkat tagapagka-
sundo*), the main function of which is to bring opposing parties together and
effect amicable settlement of differences. The committee cannot impose
punishment, but otherwise its decision is binding.

HISTORY OF THE BARANGAY SYSTEM

Current *barangay* organizational arrangements can be traced back through six centuries of Philippine history. In pre-Spanish times, it was known as a *balangay*, probably named after the sailboats the ancient Malays used in fleeing to Filipino shores from Borneo, also called *balanghai* and *biniday* in other parts of the archipelago. Each boat carried a large family group, and the master of the boat retained power as leader, or *datu*, of the village established by his family. This form of village social organization can be found as early as the 13th century in Panay, Bohol, Cebu, Samar and Leyte in the Visayas, and in Batangas, Pampanga and Tondo in Luzon. Evidence suggests a considerable degree of independence as small city-states with their heads known as *datu*, rajah or sultan.

Barangay villages sometimes grew to include 100 extended families, but they remained isolated from one another. Except on Mindanao, the part of the Philippines where Islam never lost its foothold, no larger political grouping emerged. For some centuries therefore the *barangay* was usually the largest stable economic and political unit, rather than the smallest, as it is now. This fact facilitated Spanish conquest in the 16th century, since resistance remained uncoordinated and sporadic.

The Spaniards retained the *barangay* as their basic unit of local administration in the islands; however, the *datus*' once hereditary position became subject to Spanish appointment. *Barangays* lost their political independence and thus importance, even as the leaders became figureheads, and later mere tax collectors, for a colonial regime. The term *barangay* evolved to that of the Spanish term *barrio*, although the original *barrios* in the early days of Spanish rule were the housing areas that sprung up along new roads between *barangay* areas.

The *barangays* experienced indirect changes during the American rule beginning in 1899, when the US government reorganized Filipino local government. However, local institutions and native customs and habits were generally respected and the natives of the islands, both in the cities and rural communities, were given the opportunity to manage local affairs. Under US administration, there was a *barrio* lieutenant with four councilmen constituting the *barrio* council.

During the period of independence a Barrio Charter programme was implemented in 1959 to give the new powers to local communities. A Presidential Assistant on Community Development (PACD) and similar development agencies were created. More programmes and projects were initiated to provide material or economic assistance. The number of *barrios* proliferated to 32,000 in 1969 and over 40,000 a decade later.

Given this history of reconstitution of local government powers and the creation of new units, the transfer of local governance arrangements to newly reconstituted *barangays* in 1975 was not difficult. Now it is estimated that there are around 42,000 *barangays* in the Philippines, working within the country's 62 cities and 1,570 municipalities. New *barangays* can be created, divided, merged, abolished or their boundaries substantially altered, by law or ordinance of the provincial legislature or city council, subject to the approval by a majority of the votes cast in a plebiscite to be conducted in the local government unit directly affected. The modern *barangay* can be created out of a contiguous territory which has a population of at least 2000 inhabitants, certified by the National Statistics Office (NSO), except in cities and munici-palities within Metro Manila and other highly urbanized areas, where such territories shall have an NSO-certified population of at least 5000 inhabitants.

FUNCTIONS OF THE BARANGAY

A range of social service functions can be carried out within the remit estab-lished for *barangays* by national legislation. These include running local schools including *barangay* primary and high schools but also providing for the establishment of non-formal education in the community, including adult education; providing childcare and day-care centres for pre-school-age children; promoting housing refurbishment schemes; and carrying out environmental and public service duties, including street and river cleansing, and rubbish collection. The *barangay* councils can pass environmental measures related to solid waste management and sanitation, protection of ecosystems (coastal and river water, forest areas in rural communities) and measures to abate public order concerns including matters related to illegal activities such as drug use, noise pollution and excess traffic within their juris-diction. The council also serves as the executing body that implements national and MMDA programmes in the Metro area.

The *barangay* can also organize public meetings or lectures to discuss community problems such as poor sanitation, inadequate nutrition, low liter-acy rates and drug abuse, and convene assemblies to encourage citizen participation in government; or adopt measures towards the prevention of neighbourhood ills such as vandalism, juvenile delinquency and child abuse. There are also economic development functions. According to the local government code of the Philippines, the *barangay* council can assist in the establishment, organization and promotion of cooperative enterprises that will improve the economic well-being of residents, and provide for the organi-zation of community brigades or community service units.

Given this latitude of action, it is a common if a little facetious claim on the streets of Manila that the *barangay* captain – the *punong barangay* – has more powers than the municipal mayor or provincial governor.

Eleven elected officials administer *barangay* affairs in the council or *sangguniang barangay*: the *punong barangay*, also a member of the munici-pal assembly; seven council members; a chairperson of the youth council; and a secretary and a treasurer. *Barangay* officials' terms of office are for three years and they may not serve for more than three consecutive terms in the same position. The seven council members are elected by the *barangay* population at large (rather than in wards) with the one getting the highest number of votes automatically becoming the *punong barangay*. The secretary and the treasurer are both appointed by the *punong barangay* with the concurrence of a majority of council members.

Interestingly, these are paid positions, albeit with modest remuneration. Each *punong barangay* receives around 1000 pesos per month (about US$25) and each member, *barangay* treasurer and *barangay* secretary around 600 pesos per month (about US$15). In addition, cities and municipalities may provide honoraria, allowances and other emoluments to their *barangay* officials, which may include medical care, free tuition for family members at state colleges or universities located within the province or city to which the *barangay* belongs; civil service pension eligibility on the basis of the number of years of service to the *barangay*; and preference in appointment to government positions after their tenure of office, subject to the requisite qualifications and the provisions of the rules of the Civil Service Commission.

Finance of the Barangay

What distinguishes the *barangay* system from many other community development efforts around the world is that *sangguniang barangay* are entitled to modest grants from state coffers, and have modest revenue-raising authority. External grants, the main source of income, include an 'internal revenue allotment', one of the non-tax sources of funding to local government from which *barangays* derive a share to boost their financial capability, based on the computation of gross national internal revenue tax collection. This yearly share is used for the mandatory payment of compensation of *barangay* officials.

There is also direct funding from higher government units. Provinces, cities and municipalities are mandated to provide a minimum amount for each *barangay* in their annual budgets. Other funding sources are from local revenue sharing schemes provided by the Local Government Commission, including shares from the proceeds of basic property tax, shares from the proceeds of tax collected by the province on sand, gravel and other quarry resources, and shares of the proceeds of a community tax collected locally through the *barangay* treasurers.

The *barangay* may levy other taxes, fees and charges to finance its operations, including the delivery of basic and other social services. For example, there are an increasing number of public sanitation facilities (including public standpipes, toilets and baths, and laundry areas, many connected with public market places) for which control has been transferred from municipalities to *barangays*, which then decide their own user fees and management regimes. These are reported to be more successfully managed at this local level, with income derived used for such diverse local benefits as upgrading footpaths, funding child care, building basketball courts or subsidizing cooperative retail outlets (Gozun, 1994a). Finally, the *barangay* is empowered by the local government code to enter into contracts and to engage in entrepreneurial ventures, with the assumption that what is earned is ploughed back into community projects.

BOX 7.1 SOLID WASTE MANAGEMENT IN THE BARANGAYS

Solid waste pollution is ranked as the most serious environmental and social problem in Metro Manila (Abracosa, 1996a). Many squatter settlements are located along the easements of canals and waterways. Inappropriate dumping in river courses contributes to flooding in squatter areas, which contributes to degradation of water supplies, leading to ill health. In Metro Manila, 700 tons of garbage is said to be dumped in waterways daily. With 6000 tons of solid wastes generated daily, the continued availability of disposal sites is also a growing problem (Development Academy of the Philippines, 1996). To counter this problem, many *barangays* have organized local waste collection, sometimes with policing, not only to avoid inappropriate dumping, but as a means of 'kerbside' collection of pre-separated waste and as a valuable source of employment in the recycling industry. An initial difficulty, now mainly overcome, was to convince senior local government units that *barangay*-level action on solid waste was a worthwhile addition to their formal collection procedures, and also for *barangays* to learn to work with, rather than in competition with, existing commercial firms (Furedy, 1992).

Smokey Mountain

In past years, two of Metro Manila's open dump sites, Smokey Mountain and Payatas, became infamous due to global media focus on the numbers of people who scavenged over the smoking piles. However, this apparent horror at conditions reflected a simplistic view of the social economy of the dumps. When government attempted to close Smokey Mountain, the scavenger households, through their *barangays*, resisted the move to curtail their main source of income and to destabilize their communities and way of life, however unpalatable these might be to observers. Working through the *barangays*, substantial efforts at community development were undertaken with successes including new housing, community facilities, a school and organized employment in recycling businesses (see Figure 7.3).

Barangay Mameltac

Barangay Mameltac borders a sanitary landfill site. Here, through innovation in the *barangay*, full-time management staff and 'garbage pickers' are engaged in solid waste management which brings both economic and environmental benefits – in the words of the *barangay*'s chief Jose Evangelista Jr, 'making open dump scavenging into the dignified and profitable occupation which it ought to be'. The garbage pickers are employees of a firm which sells on recyclable materials to dealers in the city. The number of garbage pickers is regulated to safeguard income levels and children are banned from the site. Workers receive free medical care. Benefits include employment to community members and benefits to the recycling movement. Grace Flores, who has raised four children on a garbage picker's income, gives a quick rundown of treasures from the heap: plastics; solid aluminium as in basins and kettles; soft drink cans; lead wire; and yellow bronze, such as tap heads. Garbage picking at the site starts at four in the morning, after the midnight haul of trash and when there is just enough light to begin work.

Barrio Ugong KILUS

Translated as 'women with the common goal of a progressive nation', and organized by the *barangay* chair, this group took the lead in a neighbourhood recycling project.

Groups of women in every neighbourhood have been deputized to buy recyclable waste from households and then sell it on for a profit to a junk dealer. The *barangay* provided pushcarts, weighing scales and attractive uniforms. An ecology centre has also been set up where employment is available turning materials like old paper from used telephone directories and recycled metal into baskets, table lamps, fruit stands and small rubbish bins.

Barangay Integrated Development Programme

With resources from the Ayala Foundation, this programme provides resources and technical assistance, including training for Metro Manila *barangay* leaders on community waste management strategies and business planning in the recycling field. With this capacity, a number of *barangays* have established successful projects, for example, Recycling Technology Industries, which turn scrap cloth from a jeans factory into high quality paper (Gozun, 1994b).

In addition to the waste management activities set out in Box 7.1, other *barangays* make money through activities as diverse as flower growing and tourism. Advantages of, and constraints on, barangay action are discussed in the concluding section.

BARANGAYS AND PARTY POLITICS

Barangay politics in the Philippines generally follow the pattern of politics at the municipal and provincial level. In general, *barangay* captains tend to be associated with the ruling political party in the municipality. This can be politically expedient because the mayor of the municipality can dispense political favours to the *barangay* captains, for example, by way of influence over special allotments of funding appropriated by the local legislature, or funds generated from political and business supporters, including the congressional representative within whose jurisdiction the municipality lies. Congressional representatives wield strong local power because they also hold special funds for distribution to their constituents.

These funds can legitimately be used for a wide range of purposes, such as *barangay* road construction, purchase of a fire truck or ambulance and employment retraining programmes at various local levels. Where the *barangay* captain is not of the political party of the current mayor, provincial governor or congress person, difficulties arise in generating additional funds for *barangay* projects. However, *barangay* officials need not necessarily be formally attached to national political parties by way of active party affiliation or participation in party processes.

MANAGING THE CITY-REGION – THE MMDA

Turning to the strategic level, development in Metro Manila is coordinated by the MMDA, which has a broad range of functions. In 1975, Manila and its

Credit: Michael Carley

Figure 7.3 *A community-run recycling business in the* barangay *at Great Smokey Mountain in Manila*

contiguous cities and municipalities were integrated by presidential decree to function as a single administrative region, also known as the National Capital Region. It has since been given the powers of a fully fledged development authority, in response to prevailing political currents, as well as to the rapidly changing demands of metropolitan governance. The MMDA is vested with the powers and attributes of a corporation (including the power to make contracts, sue and be sued, and hold, transfer and dispose of property). It is intended that the MMDA shall plan, monitor and coordinate functions and in the process, exercise regulatory and supervisory authority over the delivery of services within Metro Manila, albeit without diminution of the autonomy of local government units concerning 'purely local matters'.

The following general tasks are allocated to the MMDA:

1   The formulation of medium- and long-term socio-economic and physical development plans consistent with national development objectives and in coordination with national government agencies and local government units.
2   The translation of medium- and long-term plans into policies, standards, rules and regulations for metro-wide services.
3   The monitoring of metro-wide programmes and projects to ensure consistency with the medium- and long-term plans.
4   The enforcement of rules and regulations.
5   The installation and administration of a unified metro transport ticketing system with powers to fix, impose and collect fines and engage in all measures of traffic management and enforcement.

Organizationally, the authority is intended by the state to bridge a gap between urban and national governance. The governing board and policy-making body of the MMDA bears out this intention. This is the Metro Manila Council, composed of mayors of the constituent cities and municipalities, the president of the Metro Manila vice-mayors league and the president of the Metro Manila councillors league, and as non-voting members, the heads of the Federal Department of Transportation and Communications, Department of Public Works and Highways, Department of Tourism, Housing and Urban Development Commission, and the Philippine National Police. The council is headed by a chairman, who is currently appointed by the President of the Philippines. The chairman is assisted by a general manager and by three assistant general managers: for finance and administration, for planning and for operations. Liaison between the MMDA and the highest levels of government is through a cabinet officer for regional development, who is charged with briefing the President of the Republic on issues confronting the region (Abracosa, 1996a).

The functions of the MMDA appear straightforward (Republic of the Philippines, 1994). They include:

1   *Development Planning.* To ensure an integrated development approach consistent with the country's National Physical Framework Plan for 1993–2022 and the Medium-term Philippine Development Plan for 1998–2003.
2   *Urban renewal, zoning, land use planning and shelter.* To assist in the formulation of development guidelines and the enforcement of zoning rules and regulations, and land use plans, directed at preserving/rehabili-tating the urban environment which will lead Metro Manila towards a stated goal of 'global urban competitiveness'.
3   *Traffic and transport management.* To attain more efficient arrangements through effective traffic and transport management.
4   *Environmental management.* To enforce environmental rules and regula-tions and environmental improvement projects.
5   *Solid waste management.* To undertake solid waste disposal management activities and practices in an efficient, cost-effective and environmentally safe manner.
6   *Flood control and sewerage management.* To anticipate and manage calamities, such as flooding, and to coordinate emergency functions.
7   *Public safety and disaster management.* To promote disaster prevention, mitigation and control, and actively participate in rescue operations.

PROSPECTS FOR EFFECTIVE METROPOLITAN GOVERNANCE

Having established that an apparently reasonable organizational framework for governance exists, this section examines the extent to which it is achieving a degree of success in urban management and constraints on that achievement.

The challenge of subsidiarity and cooperation

The interwoven economic, political, socio-cultural and environmental aspects of the life of the 17 local governments currently under the wings of the MMDA, underpinned by their contiguous location, makes regional governance a realistic prospect for Metro Manila. However, it is in the actual balancing of many crucial elements where the challenge of the MMDA realizing its vision rests. One issue is that, for all the apparent logic of the organizational framework in theory, in practice unresolved questions of subsidiarity intervene in governance and management processes.

One issue has to do with power relationships between the MMDA's administrative and regulatory intentions and the political control exerted by the chief executives of the 17 local authorities. Despite their membership on the Metro Manila Council, the Philippine's local government code has also greatly empowered these chief executives to act independently of the MMDA, where local interests seem of paramount economic or political importance. This means that virtually all of MMDA's strategic functions and planning actions cannot be dictated to the local authorities, but must always arise from consensual participatory processes, which will invariably involve a lot of 'horse trading'. As is frequently the case in the management of city-regions, charismatic local leaders have a strong political constituency that cannot be bent to regional ends without substantial accommodation. This holds true even when the chair of the MMDA is appointed by the President.

A second issue has to do with the devolution of functions to appropriate levels in what is a complex institutional structure of governance. For example, some commentators on Metro Manila have called for increased devolution of urban and environmental management authority from central to subsidiary local government units, where there is local knowledge, and a closer link between policy planning, monitoring and regulation (Abracosa, 1996a). This question permeates the institutional system, and it is a characteristic of the application of the principle of subsidiarity that there is no one right answer as to the appropriate level for functions to be carried out (Smith, 1985; Frenkel, 1986). For Metro Manila, concerns range from devolution of environmental management and control from central to regional and local government, and equally the transfer of functions, such as aspects of waste management, from cities to *barangays*.

There are always tensions where a higher level is reticent to give up power or financial control, whatever the efficiency gains. However, devolution is about more than simply transferring responsibility from one level to another. For example, other commentators have noted that previous devolution of health functions to local governments was unsuccessful because 'local government units were not ready to take on the responsibility of maintaining the devolved services and workers' (Basaen, 1996). 'Renationalization' was called for in that case. Subsidiarity is a continuous process of consensual reallocation of the functions of governance, rather than a scientific arrangement that can be determined with any precision.

Institutional and regulatory weakness

There is a significant strategic problem that conditions all aspects of governance in the city-region and its long-term prospects in a variety of sectors. This is that, despite the MMDA's commitment to strategic planning, current land-use planning arrangements are extremely weak, allowing virtually uncontrolled land development and urban sprawl. This in turn is identified as having knock-on effects on virtually every serious problem area facing the metropolitan region: transport congestion; air and both fresh and sea water pollution; and flooding of both overcrowded and inappropriately located squatter settlements and also new suburban developments on low-lying floodplains (Abracosa, 1996b). Uncontrolled land use coupled to lack of sewage facilities is said to be degrading both fresh and sea water resources, with rivers already 'biologically dead' (Abracosa, 1996b). Traffic congestion has become one of the major factors which may limit the economic potential of the city-region. The problem is recognized by central government, which speaks of 'fragmented solutions lacking comprehensive direction and coordination', 'a largely uncontrolled process of land development' and 'lack of a comprehensive and enforceable land use plan' (Abracosa, 1996a).

The problem stems from two bases. First, and probably related to US influence on the land-use planning system, is continued reliance on a weak zoning model of land-use planning. The basic assumption of this model tends to be that the state has little business meddling in private property rights and that almost any conforming development ought to be construed as positive. At best, the role of planning is to channel development into appropriate pockets in the city-region. This can be compared with, say, a European style strategic planning model which assumes that the state has a legitimate role in pursuing a common good and that some developments, or locations of developments, may be antithetical to this common good and ought to be refused. The second problem derives from the first, in that the basic assumption is that the less planning the better and that even where zoning is in place, variations ought to be allowed. In Metro Manila, even when the zoning plan is in place, variations are commonplace.

Hard on the heels of weak land-use planning is weak 'demand led' transport planning. Some developed countries have very recently given up this demand-led approach due to a chronic failure to ever match road supply with demand, and in dawning recognition that traffic volumes expand to fill available road space, no matter how amply provided (Owen, 1995). But in developing countries trying to 'modernize', private automobility is considered the *sine qua non* of modernity. Metro Manila still has in place the rudiments of a sustainable transport network with an emphasis on public transport and cycling, but there are very few people who would accept that these are part of a modern transport system, or that one would ever take public transport when a private car was available. Such very common attitudes disfavour the majority of low-income households which remain car-less (or car-free) and increasing congestion causes substantial deterioration in their quality of life and their ability to gain employment without long, debilitating journeys.

The power of pressure groups

Where planning is weak, pressure groups such as those of real estate developers, hold sway over development prospects and market forces dominate over strategic land-use planning processes. In Metro Manila, and in the absence of effective land use regulation, local development preferences – including improving the property tax base and other revenue fiscal considerations of local government as well as real estate market forces – are often the dominant influences. *Barangays* may make significant progress on local issues, but they have only marginal control over processes of land development.

Failure to develop a multi-sectorial institutional and strategic approach

Sustainable development in Metro Manila requires considering:

> '...simultaneously the problems of uncontrolled land use, solid waste management, air and water pollution, flooding, rapid population increase, overloaded infrastructure, traffic congestion, blighted squatter settlements, water shortages and public health risks. Many different kinds of management problems are closely linked to each other.' (Abracosa, 1996a)

Despite its broad range of strategic functions, the urban development perspective within the MMDA is still very divided and limited by perceptions of zoning and other similarly narrow approaches to regional development. The fact that the different zones within Metro manila are linked by common air, water corridors and land use base suggests that a much broader approach to sustainable development planning is necessary. This broader approach would tackle the problems cited above in a creative and integrated manner, including solutions such as replacing end-of-pipe pollution control with more effective control at the source of pollution (Carley and Spapens, 1998). Sustainable development planning would link economic, social and environmental concerns, and it would establish strategies ranging from the short- to the long-term. Such a development plan must be visionary in order to garner wide political consensus. It must also be practical, with monitoring procedures built in and provisions for frequent revision on a cyclical basis (Carley and Kirk, 1999).

Barangays' *power to affect positive social change*

By design, that is in terms of the mandates set out in the Philippine local government code, the *barangay* serves as a reasonably powerful vehicle to affect social, environmental and economic change. This is by virtue of the *barangay* government's immediate access to its citizenry, and its executive and legislative, and to some extent, judicial powers, for example, in the settling of community disputes. Because of its powers, the *barangay* council can enact as well as ensure the proper execution of laws that will spur development results.

In reality, as is true in many community arrangements, the translation of potential into reality is highly dependent on a number of factors. In their favour, and beyond the intrinsic conflicts in any capitalist system with significant levels of income disparity, *barangays* do meet the criteria set out by Sharp (1992) for community empowerment at the micro level. The first of these is stated to be the most important: the right to organize, or to create a community through institutions and collective organization. The *barangay* system also does well against the remaining criteria, which are: representative government at all levels; a community-based approach in government programmes; the introduction of paid community facilitators; and support of local government for community initiatives. The degree of support of course varies considerably from area to area.

A second factor that affects the influence of local organizations is the initiative and quality of local leadership, and the degree to which they are willing to represent the interests of their constituents. Certainly a degree of strategic outlook, innovation and resourcefulness is needed to bring *barangay* governance up to the level aspired to in the local government code. Success in local level development in *barangays* is strongly identified with the strong leadership of key individuals or 'champions of the community' (Gozun, 1994a).

In general, however, those who have been elected to *barangay* leadership have usually come from the ranks of retirees or local personalities politically close to the municipal or city leaders under whose wings the *barangay* councils serve. For obvious reasons, very few people in current employment are willing to run for *barangay* positions, mainly because of the low levels of compensation and the general orientation, particularly in urban areas, for anyone with a modicum of qualifications to go for more prestigious jobs in urban centres, rather than service in local councils or offices. There are exceptions in media-prominent cases where qualified professionals have been elected to leadership of a *barangay*, including one in Makati (one of Metro Manila's plush areas) whose *barangay* captain was a former cabinet secretary. It is also not surprising to find that many aspirants to political leadership, even at the *barangay* level, must reach some accommodation with the values and the practices of the existing power elite. In this the Philippines is no different from any other country.

Barangays' *capacity for self-development*

In general, *barangays*, through their respective councils, have been given latitude by the local government code to make decisions within their areas of responsibility, as indicated above. This decision making breeds confidence, in part by 'learning-by-doing' which doesn't mean always getting things right. Beyond this, central government, through the Department of Interior and Local Government (DILG), also develops programmes and projects for implementation at the *barangay* level, in which case, roles and responsibilities related to the particular project thrusts are spelled out in programme documents. It is also reported that local *barangays* have worked directly with the MMDA to devise community waste management schemes, and with municipalities to organize more efficient local service delivery by partnership between residents and government employees (Gozun, 1994a).

Recent fieldwork suggests that *barangays* have fostered self-reliance among local communities and helped them maximize local problem-solving capacities (Bautista, 1999). This is because they are now given the opportunity to set the direction of their community development without direct supervision from city or municipality governments, but also through the process by which *barangay* captains regularly meet with their corresponding city or municipal mayors to coordinate and collaborate on programmes and to agree resource allocations from the municipality itself. *Barangay* initiative is also reported to have speeded action on matters of direct concern to communities (such as health protection, waste management, public order concerns and settlement of minor disputes) as people actually living in, and familiar with, the communities are able to deal with concerns in a more direct and efficient manner. *Barangays* are also said to have engendered an enhanced sense of, and concern for, community well-being, as *barangays* have developed distinct identities.

However, there are disadvantages to the current system, albeit in terms of policies and resources rather than in terms of the *barangay* concept itself. These include instability of resource provision, with on average around 80 per cent of *barangay* funding sourced from the national government's internal revenue allotment (IRA) to local government. This makes funding vulnerable to collection performance of the national tax agency, and also national political views on local government funding. For example, in 1998 senators decided that the best way to trim a 'bloated' national budget was to cut local government's IRA stipend. One result was to bring local governors and mayors onto the streets to put pressure on the national legislature. Only *barangays* with large commercial establishments in their jurisdiction are able to weather such variations in funding because of local charges they are able to levy.

Barangays – *national movement or individual success stories?*

No formal study has yet assessed the degree of achievement of the *barangay* programme at the level of the nation. The apparent success of *barangay* as a form of neighbourhood governance charted here may rest more on the leadership qualities of individual *barangay* officers in their respective jurisdictions, rather than on *barangays* as a purposive and systematic national programme of neighbourhood governance.[1]

However, under current arrangements, there is an office at the DILG, which is a national government line department, solely dedicated to *barangay* affairs. The Local Government Academy, the DILG training arm, offers *barangay* training programmes on, for example, management, planning and environmental management. There is also a national federation of *barangay* captains that discusses common concerns and also acts as a lobby and advocacy group.

Under the guidance of DILG, the *barangay* have successfully arranged public consultations and convened community groups for consideration of new projects that affect the community. This has been most notable with environmental impact assessments (EIAs) where public hearings are arranged through the office of the *barangay* captain. The EIA system provides that developers secure a *barangay* permit as part of a set of local government permits that are intended to ensure that a new development is being sited correctly within the *barangay*'s zoning ordinances. Although the general weakness of land use planning, and the possibility of corruption, can weigh against good decision making, there is a general move toward more recognition of the need for improved EIA and land use decisions.

CONCLUSION

This chapter has explored some unique organizational arrangements for local governance in the megacity of Metro Manila. Of course such a city-region faces enormous problems, not least from dramatic population growth, due to rural to urban migration, coupled with explosive urbanization: no institutional arrangements, however strategically organized and based on principles of democratic empowerment and management efficiency, can be a panacea for such problems. Appropriate institutional arrangements are necessary, but not sufficient without attention to overall social objectives, strategic planning functions and the empowerment of citizens at all levels. As we have suggested, the MMDA has all the necessary strategic functions – it looks good on paper, but it faces major constraints on its ability to govern such a sprawling city-region effectively.

The 42,000 *barangays* are unique in constituting a formal level of local governance, and there is some preliminary evidence that they are making positive contributions to local development in the Philippines and in Metro Manila. They are also making one other positive contribution to governance in the Philippines: like all local government units, *barangays* are federated into a national association. With its elected leadership, it is able to put neighbourhood-level issues on the political table by raising a common voice on issues in national debate. Recently, this channel has been used by *barangays* in partnership with other local government units, in demanding a higher share of the national IRA, as well as sufficient funds for the exercise of devolved functions.

Carley (1999) argued that neighbourhoods must be the 'building blocks' of national sustainable development efforts. If that is the case, then it can be said that the Philippines, for all its problems, may be at the forefront of organizing its society locally to work towards sustainable development. If it could also bring regional planning and national urban and transport policies into line in this effort, real achievement would be possible.

8 WHEN COMMUNITY DEVELOPMENT BECOMES A POLITICAL BARGAINING TOOL: THE CASE FOR STRUCTURAL CHANGE IN LOW INCOME HOUSING PROVISION IN COSTA RICA

Harry Smith and José Manuel Valverde

*'Every four years the money gets lost here... The money gets lost, and those who are affected are the poor.' (*Community leader in Rincón Grande de Pavas)

INTRODUCTION

Community development has a long tradition of central government support and regulation in Costa Rica, and has often been related to low-income housing projects. Critics, however, have seen a clear case of co-option in this regulation. In addition, the relations between communities and the state have often been based on politicians and government officials offering land, infrastructure or housing in exchange for votes and other support during elections, a practice known as clientelism. This is a precarious way for communities to gain access resources, including housing, as it is highly dependent on the outcome of elections every four years.

The situation this chapter describes is therefore one of highly centralized and politicized governance, where national party politics reach all the way down to neighbourhood level and central government politicians and officials have direct links with community leaders. Within this context, an enabling approach aimed at strengthening community self-management was attempted in several settlements under the National Plan Against Poverty (1994–1998), including Rincón Grande de Pavas, in San José, which this chapter examines as a case study. This case clearly illustrates the lack of continuity in the relations between the state and specific communities and its adverse effects on housing. The other main themes that emerge as significant are the need for real political and administrative decentralization, in particular, in a country as centralized as Costa Rica, and the related need for capacity building at community level, especially the strengthening of community organizations' capacity to lobby and negotiate. These are themes that are directly relevant to other national contexts, in both the developing and developed worlds.

The chapter first describes the general context of relations between the state, the market and society in Costa Rica from 1986 to 1998 and provides a brief insight into how this has affected life in the case study area. It then examines the rhetoric and practice of community development in relation to the implementation of housing programmes and projects. The roles of community and the state in housing delivery are then analysed in the case study area, providing the basis for conclusions on community development and low-income housing in Costa Rica, as well as for recommendations that suggest ways of supporting community initiatives.

RELATIONS BETWEEN STATE, MARKET AND CIVIL SOCIETY (1986–1998)

Crisis and structural adjustment

Costa Rica shares some of the socio-economic characteristics of the rest of Central American countries such as a small economy, high external debt, housing deficit, and a medium level of urban population but a high urbanization rate. However, other aspects differentiate it from its neighbouring countries: it is the most stable democracy in the region; it has a relatively developed welfare system; poverty levels are well below those prevalent in the region; and it ranks highly in the United Nations (UN) human development index.

One of the experiences this country shares with its neighbours and, indeed, with Latin America in general, is to have suffered the severe economic crisis in the early 1980s, which had a profound impact on the relations between state, market and civil society. The crisis in Costa Rica reached its peak between 1979 and 1982, for various reasons. In summary, the weaknesses of the Costa Rican development model were exposed when the external debt crisis broke out – by 1982 the rapidly growing per capita level of external debt had reached an unsustainable level. After decades of growth and gains in social welfare, for the first time socio-economic indicators suffered a severe setback.[1]

In order to respond to this crisis, the Costa Rican government initially resorted to stabilization measures implemented with financial support from the US, which had strong geopolitical interests in the region at the time. Stabilization was followed by a process of structural adjustment, imposed by the International Monetary Fund (IMF) and the World Bank. This process was implemented through four letters of intent and three structural adjustment programmes (SAP), as a condition for loans. Briefly, the objectives of these programmes were to promote exports; to promote non-traditional agricultural production; to reform the financial sector; and to transform the public sector. The transformation of the public sector was to be achieved through an improvement in its efficiency and through cutting back its participation in the economy.

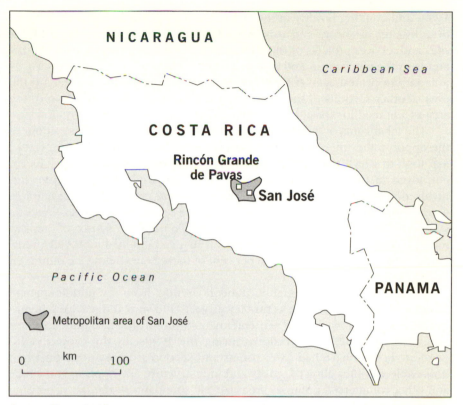

Source: Harry Smith

Figure 8.1 *Location of Rincón Grande de Pavas*

In summary, in Costa Rica a process of economic, social and institutional adjustment began, as a consequence of the international development of a new model of accumulation, although with certain specific traits, especially in relation to decentralization and community participation.

Adjustment on the ground: life in Rincón Grande de Pavas

During this period of structural adjustment new urban settlements have been established: Rincón Grande de Pavas, with an area of 140 hectares and an estimated population of around 40,000 in 1997 is an example. It is located about eight kilometres west from the centre of San José, the capital of Costa Rica (see Figure 8.1). In the early 1980s this land was uninhabited, consisting of paddocks and coffee plantations; today it is one of the large low-income areas in the Metropolitan Area of San José.

A dead end in terms of road network, lodged between two deep ravines, and in the flight path of the Tobías Bolaños airport, Rincón Grande is a home for low income households who could no longer afford rents elsewhere in the San José Metropolitan Area, who have come to San José from rural areas in search of job opportunities, or who have left Nicaragua fleeing violence in the

1980s and grinding poverty in the 1990s.[2] In the eyes of the housing authorities, this area has been seen as both a solution, when chosen as a location for sites and services projects or the relocation of households from squatter settlements in the city centre, and as a problem when it became notorious for its militancy in protest against government housing policies. Its notoriety in the eyes of other sections of the capital's society is due to the perception of the area as a hotbed for social unrest, delinquency and crime.

The inhabitants of Rincón Grande, however, make the best they can out of the opportunities there are both within the neighbourhood and in the rest of San José, to which there is regular access by bus. Most of those with jobs are employed in the service sector (68.9 per cent), while the remainder are involved in industry (29.8 per cent). There is a clear gender divide in employment, with women working more in the service sector, especially in domestic service (48 per cent of employed women), while the main source of employment for men is the building industry (36 per cent of employed men). However, incomes are very low, 70 per cent of these being below the minimum wage (Cordero, 1996).

Income levels vary throughout Rincón Grande, from the middle-income settlements built by the state as turnkey projects and sites and service schemes in the 1980s, to low-income settlements resulting from state relocation on greenfield sites or land invasions during the 1990s. In the former, solid concrete houses have had extra rooms and second storeys added on when household incomes allowed, roads and infrastructure are in place and shops and other commercial premises are relatively abundant. In the latter, housing ranges from shacks built out of scrap to basic concrete houses supplied through government subsidies; infrastructure can be practically non-existent or very basic, and commerce is less prevalent. In addition, squatter settlements tend to cluster on the edges of the 'formal' settlements, often in vulnerable areas such as the steep banks of the ravines.

The different circumstances in each of the settlements that make up Rincón Grande have given rise to different agendas and, often, friction and confrontation between community organizations and between communities. This has coloured the whole process of community development and participation, as is examined later on. What all community organizations have shared, however, has been the need to engage with central government, given the strong centralization of the Costa Rican state, despite the current rhetoric on decentralization, an international trend that is also present in Costa Rica.

Decentralization and community participation as deregulation and privatization mechanisms

The trends towards decentralization and towards the strengthening of civil society participation in development are partly a result of the departure of some sectors of transnational capital from previous centralized state models of social and political organization. The new economic model that is being promoted by international capital, in particular in countries on the capitalist periphery such as Costa Rica, seeks the formation of decentralized states, more supportive of private enterprise, with borders open to trade and an increasingly flexible labour force.

In the case of Costa Rica, SAPs went hand in hand with the emergence of a political discourse among the political parties, and in the government, that was very favourable to the promotion of decentralization[3] processes and to the strengthening of civil society participation. However, in practice effective processes towards these aims have not been fostered or supported. On the contrary, in recent years it would seem that the channels for negotiation and consensus have been closed. One of the sectors most affected by this is the community.

In parallel with the closure of these channels used by community organizations with a certain lobbying capacity, some economic sectors have promoted two new forms of labour organization, as a way to achieve the necessary and unrestricted support for new economic and social policies: these are the *solidarista* movement and labour joint-stock companies. The first was established in the 1950s and its main aim was to create collaboration and understanding among workers and employers. This type of organization thrived during the process of structural adjustment and became a kind of 'alternative' organization to the trade union movement. Its main attraction is its accomplishment of some material benefits for workers, such as loans, advantageous credit systems, leisure facilities and others (Trejos, 1991). It is estimated that there are about 2000 *solidarista* associations.

Labour joint-stock companies (*sociedades anónimas laborales*) are private firms, established by mobilized workers,[4] who are offered the opportunity to provide services to the institutions where they formerly worked. Currently there are around 150 of these firms (Paz, 1998). While *solidarista* associations play a role in managing labour conflict through regulation and co-option, labour joint-stock companies help demobilize labour and partially or totally privatize some public services. In both cases, these movements are seen by the hegemonic sectors as a form of state decentralization and as a strengthening of civil society's role in development.

As for the community, the different social compensation programmes applied since the beginning of the structural adjustment process in 1982 have made repeated calls for community participation as an essential element of programme implementation. However, studies of these show that community participation has been largely absent, although some programmes implemented within the framework of the National Plan Against Poverty during the Figueres Administration (1994–1998) took this into account. Valverde (1998), referring to this programme, points out the following hurdles in the way of some of its decentralizing aims: the lack of decentralization in decision making and in competencies at the different levels; and the absence or limited participation of local actors in project design, implementation and evaluation.

In summary, although the rhetoric of SAPs, against the background of globalization, promotes processes of decentralization and strengthening of civil society participation, in practice the opposite has happened in Costa Rica: day by day the channels for participation become more constricted as the state increases its role in enabling economic transformation. This is looked at in more depth in the next section, using housing as an illustration.

THE COSTA RICAN COMMUNITY MOVEMENT AND HOUSING

Costa Rica is a country with a long experience in the organization at grassroots level of peasant associations, trade unions and community organizations. This experience is considered by some authors as key to the process of formation and consolidation of democracy in Costa Rica (see Rojas, 1989, especially the article by Valverde et al).

The years following the great crisis of capitalism in 1929 are usually noted as the starting point of the social and political processes that underlined the development of the country until the end of the 1970s. Towards the end of the 1930s the first community organization movement, known as the Movement of Progressive Boards (*Juntas Progresistas*), rose in the poorer quarters of the capital city of San José. It was a movement that emerged under the influence of the Communist party, whose purpose was to fight for a solution to the problems of lack of infrastructure and basic services in poor communities, as well as to support the grassroots struggle against the high cost of living and unemployment. In 1939 the pressure of these boards and of other grassroots organizations resulted in the approval by the Legislative Assembly of the Associations Law, an instrument that during the following years allowed the creation of many more progressive boards, in the neighbouring provinces of San José, Heredia and Cartago.

Institutionalization of the Costa Rican community movement

Around 1948, the civil war in the country was the starting point of a new period of national development. From the political point of view, this new period is characterized by a gradual and incremental process of increasing state intervention in the economy and society, and by the deployment of various mechanisms to channel and institutionalize ('co-opt') negotiation around social conflict.

Within the framework of this 'new project of society', in the 1960s the state gave a strong impulse to a new form of community organization: the so-called community development associations. From the beginning this movement had political and financial backing from the state, as a way to check the continuing rise of the progressive boards.

On that occasion the Commission on Social Affairs at the Legislative Assembly noted the following:

> '*The bases on which Costa Rica rests as a sovereign and democratic country, which are individual effort, social equality, respect for liberty and for the dignity of the individual, as well as for the republican institutions, may be weakened if system-*

> *atic efforts are not made so that both the agents of public power*
> *and the people, in close cooperation, can keep alive their sense*
> *of responsibility and work together and effectively in order to*
> *promote the integral development of the country.'* (Vega, 1987)

Since then, the Costa Rican state and the traditional political parties have kept an iron hand on the life of urban and rural communities through political, ideological and organizational control. As community development associations were established throughout the country, the progressive boards started to weaken, eventually disappearing by the mid-1970s.

'Instrumentalization' of the community struggle for housing

The first signs of the growing economic crisis, in the mid-1970s, sparked off various grassroots movements. In urban areas the mobilization of low-income sectors of the population against the increase in the price of public services, demanding housing solutions and higher pay increases, were notable. It is in this economic and social context that numerous housing committees emerged. They were formed by poor households who could not afford to rent or buy a home because they had a low income or no income at all. This situation was compounded by a marked reduction in state investment in housing.[5]

By the beginning of the 1980s there were between 400 and 500 housing committees throughout the country. Initially these were independent groups of households that struggled to gain access to land to build their homes; later, the national political parties gradually penetrated these committees, linking them to the housing fronts they supported. In the early 1980s four housing fronts had been established: the National Patriotic Committee (COPAN), under the direction of a Trotskyist party; the Democratic Housing Front (FDV) and the Costa Rican Housing Front (FCV), both linked to the dominant National Liberation Party (PLN); and the National Housing Front (FNV), with a Communist outlook.

Until the end of 1985, the housing committees and housing fronts frequently undertook mobilizations and protest actions such as the taking of buildings, street closures and invasion of urban land which, on occasion, culminated in fierce confrontations with the police. Nevertheless, the achievements in terms of housing solutions during this time were almost nil. This may have been due to two factors: on the one hand, the Monge Alvarez Administration (1982–1986) was concentrating its efforts on achieving the necessary macroeconomic stability, under the tutelage of the IMF and, on the other hand, the largest housing fronts, with the stronger lobbying capacity (FDV and FCV) and close to the governing party, played a role in containing the movement in exchange for some political 'prebends'.[6]

The start of a new government under the same party (PLN), this time led by Oscar Arias Sánchez, brought about a radical change in the operations of housing committees and fronts. On the basis of an electoral agreement with the housing fronts,[7] except with FNV, the rest of the housing organizations were devoted to the building of houses through aided self-help, thus losing their lobbying character and their capacity to mobilize in order to demand the government kept its promises.

New mental models in social policy: the state, the market and civil society

As in many other capitalist countries, in Costa Rica state intervention in the social realm addressed the structural deficiencies of the capitalist system in providing the bulk of the population with means for their social reproduction. This partly explains why in the 1950s, 1960s and 1970s the Costa Rican state's social intervention increased, thus contributing to the education of the labour force and the improvement of living conditions for large swathes of the population. This social policy was equally crucial for the hegemonic sectors to achieve the necessary political support to foster the economic transformations that took place in these decades.

The scale of social investment undertaken at this time goes a long way to explain how the country reached the 34th position on the Human Development Index (HDI), as well as how the high level of political stability was attained.

From the 1980s onwards, international organizations such as the IMF and the World Bank imposed SAPs on various developing countries that meant radical changes in relation to the previous models of development. In short, SAPs emphasize market relations, the shaping of open economies, and the restructuring of the state to facilitate the free circulation of capital and the transfer of profits to the central countries.

Within this new model of development, the action of the state in the social sphere is understood as one of social assistance and not as one based on rights – with poverty as the (inevitable) social cost of the process of structural adjustment. In other words, it is a new 'socio-economic order' wherein poverty becomes naturalized, and social policy addresses a category of citizens who are considered to be 'weak' and in need of targeted state benefits. In the view of this neoliberal school of thought, the market will take care of ensuring the best and fairest distribution of wealth, individuals will not see their freedom restricted and a citizen dependency on state social policy will not arise.

In Costa Rica, the unfolding of this policy has entailed increasing cutbacks in budget allocations for social organizations and the privatization of some services in health, housing, education, telecommunications and water supply, for example. In housing, there was a shift from a state that in previous decades built housing for wide sectors of the population, especially for lower-income groups, to a state that provides the financial means for families to gain access to land to build on, through loans from private agencies. Thus an essential good such as housing has come to be provided to a great extent by the interests of the real-estate sector. This has contributed to the increase in informal settlements in different parts of the country during the last two decades. This aspect is analysed in greater detail in the following section.

The role of the state and of civil society in housing delivery

The rise of this new political economic current has led Costa Rica towards a profound change in the way social policy is conceived of, and in the role assigned to it. In the specific area of housing, this trend started to become apparent during the Monge administration (1982–1986), when the government declared it had no resources for this sector. Consequently, it was forced to promote 'housing programmes' based on sites and services for low-income households, thus putting an end to a whole period of state delivery of finished housing with the necessary infrastructure and services.[8]

During the Arias Administration (1986–1990), with the support of the housing fronts, a clearly compensatory kind of housing policy, attuned to structural adjustment, was legitimized. Thousands of families were allowed and even encouraged to occupy empty land – either belonging to the state or of very low market value – so that they could gradually build their 'housing solution' with some help from the state, but with practically no kind of planning of settlement development. Within the framework established by this policy, many settlements such as Los Guido, Rincón Grande de Pavas and Los Cuadros were formed: they suffer from serious overcrowding and a lack of infrastructure and basic community services.

During the Calderón Administration (1990–1994) housing policy was weak and kept to the already established framework. It was during the following administration (Figueres, 1994–1998) that a local development programme was formulated, as part of the National Plan Against Poverty. The objective of this programme was to seek solutions to the social problems of 16 communities that were considered to be the most vulnerable. Covering an estimated 300,000 people, the programme intended to look for solutions to the problems that were detected with the active participation of the communities themselves. One of the 'priority' communities selected for the programme was Rincón Grande de Pavas, whose experience is analysed in the following section.

In summary, Costa Rica has changed from being a country with an inclusive and integrative social policy, based on the recognition of social rights, to being a country with an exclusive social policy, which does not allow the problems of the low-income population to be solved. This kind of result is deeply congruent with the social policy that is promoted by structural adjustment. This explains why the majority of the informal settlements established during the period of structural adjustment still exist today. In the light of this retreat of the state, it is necessary to ask, therefore, what are the alternatives, if any, that low-income communities can turn to in order to solve their housing problems.

CASE STUDY: RINCÓN GRANDE DE PAVAS[9]

Origins and development of the area

The area of Rincón Grande de Pavas comprises several settlements which were mostly established during the 1980s and 1990s within the context of SAPs.

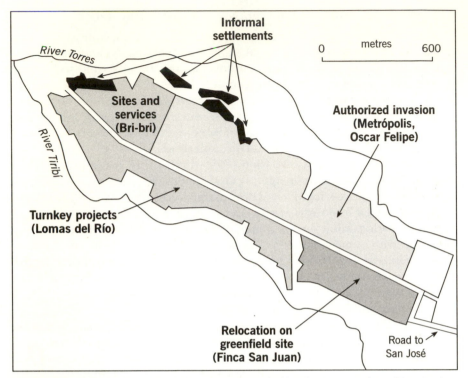

Source: Harry Smith, based on information provided by the Municipality of San José

Figure 8.2 *Map of Rincón Grande de Pavas showing types of settlement according to origin*

Thus, five types of settlement can be differentiated according to their origin (see Figure 8.2):

1   Turnkey projects built by the private sector with state finance.
2   Sites and services.
3   Land invasion agreed between housing fronts and prospective government, followed by a government housing project.
4   Government relocation on unserviced land of households from informal settlements, followed by a government housing project.
5   Informal settlements (*precarios*).

Rincón Grande de Pavas is therefore a heterogeneous area in terms of settlement origin, with different community dynamics in each settlement (see Figure 8.3). This explains the occasional confrontation between settlements as well as with central government institutions. Indeed, each settlement has its own community organizations, which in some cases are legalized and registered with the National Directorate of Community Development Associations, and in others are informal, as for example the housing committees. In Rincón Grande de Pavas examples can be found of the majority of community organizations

Credit: Harry Smith

Figure 8.3 *View of Rincón Grande de Pavas, showing housing provided by central government in the background and squatter settlement in the foreground*

that are common in Costa Rica. These settlements also have things in common, mainly poverty and lack of housing and infrastructure, as well as a series of problems related to crime and other problems. To a large degree, Rincón Grande de Pavas is the joint result of the housing crisis in Costa Rica and the response of successive governments to the problem, based on the provision of houses rather than of serviced housing in a wider sense.

This response, however, has not been uniform throughout the period from 1986 to 1998. A chronology of state–community relations in Rincón Grande de Pavas can be established, with obvious physical and spatial consequences, and reflecting the attitudes and actions of each of the administrations during this period.

Periods in the struggle for housing in Rincón Grande de Pavas

Rincón Grande de Pavas did not immediately reflect the growing social pressure during 1982–1986, resulting from the economic crisis, which was channelled through the housing fronts. The first developments were the result of practices based on two direct state interventions: one built by the private sector, with state finance, whereby complete serviced houses were provided to low- to middle-income households (Lomas del Río); and another consisting of a sites and services project for low-income households (Bri-brí), which was part of the urban development programme financed by the United States Agency for International Development (USAID).

However, the increasing power to negotiate enjoyed by housing committees, which was achieved through the channelling of their demands through
the housing fronts, resulted in the 'authorized' invasion of part of Rincón
Grande de Pavas by organizations linked to the FDV. By means of political
negotiation with the candidate who eventually won the 1986 general elections,
these community groups gained access to land, as well as the promise of a
subsequent rapid intervention by central government in order to provide them
with housing and infrastructure (Metrópolis and Oscar Felipe projects). The
new (1986–1990) government was able to start the construction project by
using the new instruments it created for the delivery of housing nationwide,
such as the Special Housing Commission (which used emergency funds), and
later the national housing finance system. The government's strategy was based
on targeted state benefits, with parallel strategies of community leader co-
option and support to the private sector. Co-option led to the loss of power by
the main housing fronts, thus averting what the government saw as a danger
of destabilization (Chaves and Alfaro, 1990; Chávez et al, 1989; Lara and
Molina, 1997; Molina, 1990).

The policy of targeted state benefits intensified nationally during the
Calderón administration (1990–1994), by means of a policy of 'social compensation' subsidies addressing the lower-income sectors of the population. In
housing, this resulted in the housing subsidy changing from a zero-rated loan
to a one-off grant. However, in Rincón Grande de Pavas government policy
was expressed through the relocation of squatters from informal settlements
in other parts of the metropolitan area to a completely uncleared and unserviced area of land (Finca San Juan), with the intention of subsequently building
infrastructure and housing using the housing grant. In consequence, the
problem of the unfinished project in Metrópolis was compounded by the
creation of a new neighbouring informal settlement, which generated tensions
and confrontation between the two communities.

The inefficacy and slowness of the government's response to the problems
created in Finca San Juan led community groups to attempt to solve these
themselves, thus initiating a period of community self-management within
housing committees in this settlement. Through self-management, part of the
community was able to solve its infrastructure and services problems temporarily. On the other hand, however, there were also a number of cases of 'illegal'
practices among leaders, such as charging quotas as well as selling plots.

Successive state interventions during this period thus created one of the
largest concentrations of poverty in the metropolitan area, with severe housing
and infrastructure problems. In addition, these interventions encouraged new
land invasions on the fringes of the settlements and in open spaces, thus
exacerbating the problem.

The Figueres administration (1994–1998) was faced with a conflict-ridden
urban area with severe deficiencies, with multiple community organizations
and strong leaderships. The new administration's initial reaction was to repress
the community leaders, accusing them of corruption, especially in the case of
Finca San Juan. Subsequently Rincón Grande de Pavas was included as one of
the priority areas in the National Plan Against Poverty. This plan adopted the

strategy of integrating housing and social policy, with a view to achieving integrated community development. In each of the 16 priority areas the government designated a different agency to coordinate the development process. In Rincón Grande de Pavas this role was assigned to PROFAC, the Community Self-management Strengthening Project, a joint initiative of the Costa Rican government, Danish International Development Agency (Danida) and UNCHS.

The other important organization in this process was the Municipality of San José, whose recently created planning department had embarked on the preparation of a land-use plan for Rincón Grande de Pavas as its first project. The municipality was seen by PROFAC as the agency that ought to continue the process of integrated community development once PROFAC pulled out. For the first time, central government addressed the problems in Rincón Grande de Pavas at a settlement-wide level, and for the first time the municipality was given a relevant role in this area.

The role of community in the search for housing solutions: the enabling paradigm of PROFAC

PROFAC started a process based on its experience gained since 1991, aimed at putting into practice the United Nations' enablement paradigm (United Nations, 1987). Its approach was based on the implementation of two basic concepts: community participation and self-management, and the enabling state (Valverde, 1996). The first stage of the process was a rapid appraisal – undertaken jointly with the Municipality of San José – leading to an inventory of community and institutional resources and of their organization and operation. Once these were identified, PROFAC started a process of mediation and coordination whereby two spaces for networking and negotiation were established: one including 90 per cent of the identified CBOs (the Community Representation – *Instancia Comunal*), and one incorporating the 36 institutions that were working in Rincón Grande de Pavas (the Inter-institutional Network – *Red Interinstitucional*). The aim of this process was 'strengthening institutional work in relation to the real needs of the population, and enabling the articulation of demand on the basis of the strengthening of community organizations with a self-management outlook' (Cuevas, 1997).

Through the Community Representation a participatory appraisal process was undertaken, with the participation of around 600 members of the community, the result of which was the preparation of the Local Development Plan of Rincón Grande de Pavas: 1998–2005 (see Figures 8.4 and 8.5). During this process the members of the Community Representation, who were mostly established leaders from the various communities in Rincón Grande de Pavas, were trained in leadership and negotiation skills, for example. This process yielded several results: the approval of the local development plan by the Community Representation in September 1997; the election of a management board for the Community Representation in October 1997, whose objective was to oversee the implementation of the plan and to represent Rincón Grande de Pavas as a whole in negotiations with the authorities; and the construction of a local resource centre for the community.

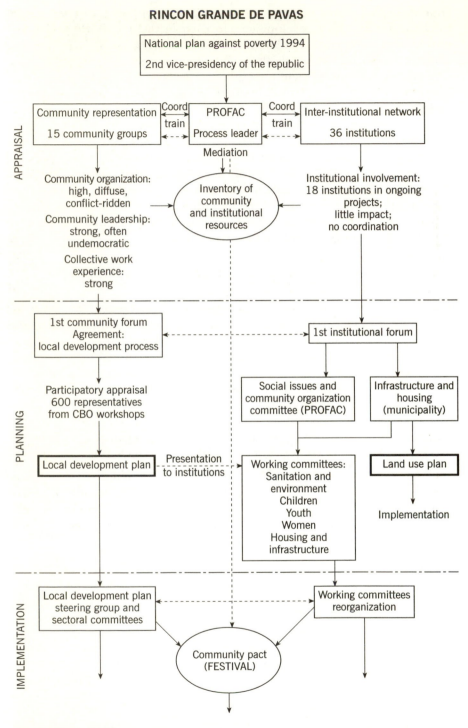

Source: Harry Smith

Figure 8.4 *Participatory process in Rincón Grande de Pavas*

Credit: Harry Smith

Figure 8.5 *Workshop with members of the community and institutions during the preparation of the Rincón Grande de Pavas Local Development Plan*

The Inter-institutional Network was organized initially around two committees, one dealing with infrastructure and housing under the leadership of the municipality, the other addressing a wide range of social and community organization issues, led by PROFAC. The first produced the Rincón Grande de Pavas land-use plan and coordinated the channelling of funds for construction works. These included the building of housing in Metrópolis and Finca San Juan and a secondary school and the widening and improvement of the only access road. The second committee coordinated the implementation of various social programmes in areas such as youth and crime.

The process of creating new spaces for discussion and negotiation, as well as their articulation, encountered strong constraints. One problem was that each of the participating agencies did not give its representatives in the Inter-institutional Network the decision-making capacity that was necessary for the network to become a decision-making body rather than a mere channel for coordination. In addition, no provision was made to guarantee the continuity of the network. Another problem was that the Municipality of San José did not take the lead in the network as was expected by PROFAC, and withdrew from the process when it considered it had fulfilled its mission and it had reached the limit of the expertise and resources it could make available. PROFAC's role was discontinued in 1999 because the Government/Danida/UNCHS project was reaching an end.

The problems encountered by the Community Representation were of a different kind, the main initial stumbling block being the differences and confrontations between community leaders. Despite the initial campaign of the Figueres Government to debunk the leaders of housing groups, PROFAC's strategy was to work with the existing leaders and to train them in more democratic and open ways of community organization. Although it can be argued that an implicit objective of the work with the Community Representation was to reduce conflict, and thereby contribute to the maintenance of an apparent social stability, it is also true that the Community Representation gained strength in its capacity to negotiate with state organizations, and eventually came to be seen as a way to gain access to the state by some of the community leaders that had not participated initially.

The consolidation of the Community Representation, nevertheless, was threatened during the 1998 elections when its members took the precaution to sign 'letters of commitment' with each of the two presidential candidates, whereby these candidates expressed their will to support the implementation of the local development plan. However, the outcome was different. On the one hand, fund allocations were slowed down or halted when the new government came to power, not only through government decisions but also because of other events, such as the discovery of corruption in the management of social funds under the previous government. The change that most worried the members of the Community Representation, however, was the loss of legitimacy in the eyes of a new central government whose approach was different to that of the previous government, and whose aim was to develop a new form of relationship between central government, local government and community organizations, which in principle did not contemplate the participation of the Community Representation.

Therefore, the effect of elections and government changes every four years on the situation of communities with housing, infrastructure and services needs, continues to be strong even when the links between central government politicians and local communities have been weakened. The strategy of clearly supporting a specific party option that allowed the housing fronts to gain important concessions from the new government in 1986, and which entailed gains or losses for the housing committees in the 1990 and 1994 elections – depending on whether they had supported the winning party or not – was abandoned in 1998 in Rincón Grande de Pavas by the Community Representation with the purpose of ensuring support regardless of the party that won the elections. This strategy failed, thus highlighting the growing separation between a state that resorts to the communities only when it needs to go through the motions of representative democracy, and CBOs, whose struggle to keep open the spaces of negotiation with the state is constant.

THE ROLE OF COMMUNITIES IN SUSTAINABLE URBAN DEVELOPMENT IN COSTA RICA

The new model of capitalist accumulation has become established in Costa Rica with certain distinctive characteristics. The state is increasingly relinquishing its role as an active guarantor of the welfare of a large proportion of the population, based on universalist principles. It is taking on a reduced social role, based on the implementation of programmes based on targeted state benefits that do not contribute to the resolution of the problems of poverty, which are becoming intensified as a consequence of the structural adjustment process. In other words, it is increasingly confined to enabling the process of accumulation through the market, while trying to preserve its legitimacy through more targeted state benefits.

One of Costa Rica's specific traits is the low level of decentralization and of recognition of citizen participation by state institutions, despite a strong civil society. This phenomenon is partly explained by the strong institutional-ization of the Costa Rican community movement by central government and by the political parties' and different governments' use of the needs and demands of low income groups for their own ends. This has produced an historic relationship between community organizations and the Costa Rican state that is based on clientelism. A similar situation exists in the unionized labour and peasant sectors.

The increase in unmet social needs and the nature of the 'social policies' of adjustment – which are not based on the recognition of social rights but on the neoliberal concept of 'helping the weakest' – have led to state policy becoming more manipulative in the 1980s and 1990s, during the process of structural adjustment. This tendency is evident in the housing and community development policies of this period.

Only recently (1994–1998) has there been a particular attempt by the state to accept community participation, an example of which is the development process in Rincón Grande de Pavas. However, this process has met with difficul-ties, both in its operation and in its continuity. The first problem has been due to the persistent resistance of state institutions to recognize the autonomous partic-ipation of the community and its organizations, as well as to a lack of delegation of power within the state institutions themselves. The second problem has been due to the continuing manipulation of community issues by political parties, and to the growing rift between these parties and the communities.

In addition, the attitude of community leaders in Rincón Grande de Pavas towards political parties in the 1998 elections suggests that there is a rising feeling of disenchantment with the political apparatus that feeds into the state. Nevertheless, this kind of process does not seem to be seriously affecting the legitimacy the Costa Rican political system enjoys.

If the housing problems of the 'weak' sectors of the population are to be addressed in a sustainable way, the foundations must be found for the estab-lishment of ways to support stable and durable institutions in civil society and their influence on state politics. Sustainability will thus be increasingly in the hands of communities themselves and will depend on their capacity for self-management, rather than in the hands of people and organizations that are interested in maintaining subordination of community organizations and social movements. Some steps necessary to accomplish this would be:

1   The promotion of autonomous processes of organization, with a capacity to channel social demands and to build spaces of negotiation with state

institutions which enable new forms of community development management.

2   The promotion of decentralization processes that fully recognize the role of community organizations in local development.
3   The strengthening of the level of political awareness in the community.
4   The fostering of processes of articulation and coordination of community initiatives at a regional level.

At the local level, and in particular with reference to the case of Rincón Grande de Pavas, some recommendations for improving the prospects of community development would be:

1   To implement the local development plan and to extend its scope to address the issue of job creation so as to improve household incomes.
2   To propose alternative education and employment opportunities for youth, so as to ensure access to greater resources for households in the medium and longer term.
3   To strengthen the opportunities for integration and self-management at the community level.

An important positive lesson emerging from the experience in Rincón Grande de Pavas is how a local development plan, prepared through a participatory process, can become an instrument that provides the community with an identity, raises its self-esteem, helps to focus community efforts and becomes a mechanism for negotiation and community improvement.

Other communities might benefit from the working method followed by PROFAC, which in some aspects proved to be appropriate, especially in so far as it created spaces of negotiation at community and institutional levels, and from the methodology that resulted from this experience. Of particular relevance to other parts of the world, however, is the negotiating power community organizations can achieve through joint efforts and collaboration around a concerted strategy.

In this sense, community development must be (re)conceptualized within the framework of a different project of society, taking as its starting point the concrete daily needs of those who have less and giving them the capacity to develop their own local solutions to their problems. As Touraine states: 'today we must achieve a difficult mutation if we want to be actors within a mutating world' (1997).

9 Community-based Organizations and the Struggle for Land and Housing in South Africa: Urban Social Movements in Transition

Paul Jenkins

Urban Social Movements and Housing in South Africa

This chapter looks at the role of urban social movements in the struggle of lower-income groups in South Africa for access to land and housing. It undertakes this through a review of the development of these movements in the last half century, with a more in-depth description of some of the most recent experience. In particular the chapter looks at the relationship between the social movements and the political sphere. The description of the evolution of urban social movements around housing issues is then analysed in some depth from different political positions. This analysis raises issues of the relationship between civil society and the state which go beyond the South African experience, and are of broad relevance.

Early Social Movements on Shelter Issues in South Africa

Urban development and housing have been highly politicized issues in South Africa since at least the beginning of the 20th century, when the burgeoning urban population began to be separated by race through an application of cordons sanitaires, justified mainly on account of public health.[1] This led to the state's increasing involvement in housing and urban development at a local level through provision of special urban housing areas for certain racial groups.[2] While this initiative remained mainly locally prioritized and financed the impact was limited, as the privileged white urban residents, who wanted some form of physical segregation to match rapidly growing social and economic segregation (already expressed primarily in racial terms), were reluctant to fund this adequately through local taxes.

As a result, while a number of racially segregated 'locations' were developed – and this was more prevalent where the target population was also taxed[3] – the growing depopulation of rural areas after 1923 led to rapidly rising gaps between demand and formal housing supply. By the time of the Second World War the gap between the state's intention vis-à-vis the growing urban lower-income groups (ie control of labour and urban influx) and its capacity to deliver (through direct state provision of housing in special townships) was enormous. This gave rise to widespread informal alternatives, including squatting on unoccupied fringe land; overcrowding in formal townships and workers' hostels; as well as the construction of illegal extensions and backyard shacks in and around these.

The massive migration from rural to urban areas before and during the Second World War was a result of both strong push and pull factors. Evicted from their land – on what had been allocated as 'white' farms – and driven out of overcrowded, drought-stricken native reserves, thousands of Africans migrated to the cities hoping for a better life. Between 1936 and 1946 the African population of Johannesburg doubled, partly as the Pass laws were relaxed due to the need of industry for labour. However, state house construction ground to a halt in 1943–1944, and as a result local government allowed subletting in township houses. This in turn led to rising rents and increasingly the African population resorted to squatting. The squatters' movement – lasting from 1944 to 1947 – was one of the most important struggles of the urban African population at the time.[4] Of these the Sofasonke movement was the most successful (see Box 9.1).

The need to combat the rise of squatting was one of the rallying calls by the ultra-right conservative Nationalist Party, which successfully exploited the concept *swaart vegaar* ('black threat') in the 1948 elections, winning a large majority. The Nationalist platform was based on a commitment to a policy of separate racial development institutionalized through racial specification of all the population into four racial groups,[5] and the creation of a myriad of discriminatory legislation on this basis to favour the dominant 'white' electorate, especially the lower-income section which saw the (also generally lower income) 'non-whites' as a threat. Implementing this policy of massive state intrusion required an enlarged state apparatus, and this was used as an opportunity to promote the Afrikaans-speaking white population – a kind of Afrikaans-affirmative action.[6] It was also only possible due to a buoyant economy, based mainly on the high gold price, and through acquiescence of the more typically liberal English-speaking population, who also of course benefited from segregation.

The impact of apartheid on urban lower-income groups of all races was enormous, as the state implemented the Pass Laws and Group Areas Acts – the latter defining what urban areas would be open for use for different racial groups. The opportunity to remove areas of racial intermingling as well as proximity was allied to the desire to remove what were seen as slums, upgrade

---

BOX 9.1 SOFASONKE

In March 1944 James Mpanza led a large group of followers across the open veld near Orlando municipal 'location' (in what is now Soweto) to occupy vacant land and set up camp with hessian shelters. Within weeks the community comprised some 8000 people, and had risen to 20,000 by 1946. Known as 'peeler' (as he had 'peeled' land from the state), Mpanza was a charismatic man whose late conversion to religion (while in jail on murder charges) underpinned his Sofasonke – 'We shall all die together' – movement. Families joining had to swear allegiance and also pay a membership fee, as well as pay for a site and weekly administration. In return Mpanza offered protection, with strict laws enforced by his 'police'. The area became a no-go area for officialdom and was attractive as a place to escape the myriad laws of state control. The authorities attempted negotiation initially, but by 1946 tried to have Mpanza legally removed to his 'homeland' in Natal Province. Mpzanza fought the legal battle up to the Appeal Court and won, and it was only when a massive new housing programme was started in 1948 that his power began to wane – despite the fact that he amassed a vast personal fortune through his activities.

Although a belated state housing programme undermined the squatters' movement by 1950,[7] it took force to push people in to the new townships, as squatting was for many, in fact, a better option – it was cheaper, nearer to work places and offered some protection against officialdom. As another squatter leader said in 1947, 'The government is like a man who has a cornfield which is invaded by birds. He chases the birds from one part of the field and they alight in another part...we squatters are birds.'[8] The state won in the end – not primarily because it provided an alternative, although this doubtless contributed – but, probably, due to the fact that the isolated nature of the squatters' activities was never consolidated in a wider movement than that of Sofasonke. Mpanza had actually requested the Communist Party of South Africa (CPSA) – which had revived in the early 1940s – to assist, but the CPSA had refused to do so politically, although it ran soup kitchens in squatter camps. Hence an opportunity to widen and politicize the struggle for housing and land was passed by.

---

inner-city land uses (for higher rate income) and disenfranchise the remaining 'non-white' electorate (in the Cape Province).[9] Actual segregation was implemented some time after the legislation was promulgated, however, due partly to (limited) liberal opposition focused mainly at local government level, as well as to the need to create a state apparatus to implement such wide social engineering and physically create the alternatives.[10]

The result was a massive relocation of lower-income groups across urban spaces over a period of some 30 years (only stopping in 1980). The impact was of course highly differentiated, with white groups benefiting with cheap access to well located, and usually well serviced, land and housing well below market value, and the other racial groups being forcibly relocated far from existing, often more central, locations to peripheral areas with substandard housing and very limited services, communities being irrevocably fractured in the process. In general the values paid for compensation were limited and went to the (usually white) landowners of the previous housing, most of which was privately rented. The result inevitably was an enormous state investment, as the predominant option was direct state provision of rented housing. The state initially retained complete control over housing supply with the express intent of using this as a means of urbanization control – through constricting supply and applying rigorous controls to movement it hoped to direct demand to the areas it set aside for these groups – such as in the independent 'homelands'.[11]

Racial segregation was thus achieved to a great degree through widespread enforced community dislocation and individual and household hardship, and the creation of an underclass clearly differentiated in racial terms in vast townships of 'matchbox' houses. In later years (1980s) this changed as the state could not afford to underwrite such massive investment as the economy stalled, and in addition it reacted to the private sector lobby to stabilize a skilled working class and create a middle class of 'non-white' people – necessary as the economic basis changed from predominantly mining to manufacturing and services. The physical separation of the new class-differentiated 'non-white' racial groups, however, remained substantially intact in terms of their limited access to the best located residential areas and amenities, such as commercial and recreational locations.

GROWING POLITICAL RESISTANCE AND THE RE-EMERGENCE OF SOCIAL MOVEMENTS

The racial segregation process in the 1950s and 1960s did not go unresisted, although the paramount power of the state was reinforced through draconian legislation enacted to repress wider political resistance. Allied to the complacency of the wider white electorate this meant that most resistance was fragmented and quickly crushed. Widely reported examples of resistance generally focus on the older, more established inner city urban areas which were destined for forced relocation as 'black spots'[12] such as District Six in Cape Town (see Box 9.2) subsequently popularized in cultural forms such as novels, theatre, musicals and art. Although these relocations were just a drop in the ocean of relocation (and the unrecounted continual harassment of African urban migrants who had no legal rights of residence), they became potent emblems. They were not in themselves successful in resisting the power of the state, but in as much as they entered popular culture and imagery they definitely contributed to more successful resistance later.

Ironically, more successful resistance to the state over squatting came about due to the increase in repressive measures. With the banning of political opposition – the African National Congress (ANC) and the Pan-African Congress (PAC) – the nature of political opposition changed to one of military infiltration and strategic attacks from neighbouring countries, allied to publicity and diplomacy campaigns throughout the world, later resulting in economic and other sanctions. The ensuing political vacuum in majority opposition led to the resurgence of resistance from a younger cohort of the disadvantaged, expressed in 1976 through the Soweto Uprising, starting with resistance to the state's differ-

Box 9.2 District Six

District Six in Cape Town received its name in 1867 when it became the last of six districts created by the Municipal Amendment Act of that year. It housed a lower-income population with close links to the port and was looked on as a marginal space by the authorities. This was reinforced in 1901 when bubonic plague broke out in the city and the police forced tenants from the area out to an emergency camp, although most moved back later. Although doubtless a criminal element was attracted to the informal spaces provided by the area, there was also a strong sense of community, further strengthened in the apartheid era with the regime's attempts to remove what it considered a 'black spot' of mixed race residence.

In 1966, under the Group Areas Act, the area was declared a white area although it took 15 years to fully relocate the 55,000 residents and raze the area. Although it was the focus of much adverse publicity, the central government was essentially supported by the local authority, which was attracted to the higher rates it would be able to apply in the rehabilitated centrally located area, as well as the private sector landlords who were compensated for their properties. The majority of the tenant residents, however, were forcibly relocated to new state rental housing in townships all over the Cape Flats, as far as 30 kilometres from the once nearby city centre. In the words of Fuad Petersen, 'When we were evicted from District Six we lost more than our home. We lost neighbours and friends whom we could rely on in times of sickness or other misfortune' (Isaacs, 1989).

Although the best publicized, District Six was but one of many such forced removals in Cape Town, with others such as Lansdowne and Claremont villages rapidly being redeveloped as gentrified town houses or large commercial centres. One of the largest squatter camps in the city was at Windermere, near Maitland, where various 'non-white' groups cohabited. By 1960 the camp had been forcibly dismantled with the various racial groups separated, including households, as men were allocated places in single sex hostels and families sent back to the Eastern Cape. However, like the birds in the cornfield, squatting soon resurfaced, such as at Modderdam, Crossroads and KTC (see Figure 9.1).

In Modderdam 'coloured' families were issued with eviction notices and promised land nearby, whereas African families were told that they would be screened for the 'Section 10'[13] residence rights and 'illegal' residents sent back to the Eastern Cape. Despite promises of solidarity most of the coloured residents dismantled their dwellings and moved, and on 8 August 1977 a front-end loader arrived, escorted by police, who gave the remaining residents 15 minutes before demolition began, only to stop 10 minutes later when the loader became stuck in mud. The next day demolition continued and violence was only averted by the intervention of the squatter leadership. Over the next few days 10,000 residents moved. However, the vast majority did so to live with families in the established African townships, or to go to other squatter camps such as Crossroads (Silk, 1981).

ential education programme.[14] This led in turn to greater forms of repression, driving another wave of opposition into exile or underground.

The political cadres who went underground were a potent force in raising political consciousness surrounding social issues. This consciousness was expressed in many ways, but perhaps most effectively through the wider politi-

Credit: Paul Jenkins

Figure 9.1 *View of a typical squatter settlement in Cape Town – New Rest*

cal campaign to make the townships ungovernable. This was initially through continued squatting and other informal action concerning housing and urban development, including resistance to forced relocations. In time it expanded to involve deliberate boycotts of state rents and service charges, and eventually to violence in driving out the state from the townships themselves, for instance, through burning down the state administrative offices in townships. There is no doubt that the ability to organize civil society within the townships to defy the state in such a way was due to the political training of activists, but also to its acceptance by the wider community and deliberate (if belated) support by the main political opposition in exile, the ANC. An example of this growing resistance was the fate of Crossroads squatter camp in Cape Town (see Box 9.3).

Despite its successful resistance over more than a decade, the eventual demise of the squatters' movement in Crossroads has been seen as due to (Isaacs, 1989):

1   The lack of politicization of the squatter communities, leading some to opt for alternatives and thus undermining unity.
2   Reliance on crucial support from groups whose class interests were essentially not in common with those of the squatters and hence failure in negotiation on key issues.
3   Repeated corruption and eventually co-option with the state within the leadership, whose rule was often imposed by force.
4   The lack of any clear political backing from broader political forces opposing the regime, other than the loose links to the UDF, thus losing the political potential that the movement represented.

BOX 9.3 CROSSROADS[15]

Crossroads was first occupied in 1975, this being permitted by the government initially in order to register and control squatting. By April 1975, however, about 7000 blacks lived in some 1030 shacks. A strong women's committee mobilized around the possible forced relocations, as the prospect was one of most women being sent back to Eastern Cape. Untypically at the time this group requested and received support from white liberal organizations and churches in the form of advice, funds and legal assistance. In 1976 the government applied to obtain a court order for clearance of the then 10,000 residents. However, the Supreme Court ruled in favour of creating an 'emergency camp' with no immediate threat of removal. This entailed the government having to supply basic services, which it had refused to do previously as it campaigned for removal on the basis of the settlements being a health hazard. This legal status protected Crossroads when the regime demolished other squatter areas such as Modderdam, many of whose residents moved to Crossroads. By the end of 1977 the number of residents had risen to 20,000.

The sense of permanence led to a number of community-led activities being developed, including school building and the creation of committees to deal with security issues, dispute resolution and fund raising. A joint committee later spearheaded resistance to removals, with continued support from outside the community, and increasing national and international media coverage. This was intensified during 1977 and 1978 when troops entered the settlement various times to root out 'criminal elements' and 'terrorists'. Eventually, after lengthy negotiation the government offered to build a New Crossroads in a nearby area and this was accepted by the joint committee.

This led to a survey of residents to be undertaken by the government and the joint committee members. The position of power over who would be included in the new settlement (where only 1662 houses were planned) led to leadership struggles and corruption in both the community leadership and government officials. The community became split between those destined for the New Crossroads and those who hoped to remain in the old area. During this period more and more people came to the area as urban unrest surged, with between 40,000 and 80,000 people resident by the mid-1980s. Suddenly in 1983, the government announced its intention to rehouse all 'legal' squatters in a new town called Khayelitsha, some 20 kilometres away, instead of in the original planned site. Around this time the UDF was formed – a loose federation of some 500 organizations of women, youth, church and community, and other bodies opposed to apartheid. This allowed a broader front of opposition for the squatters' movement.

The new government plan led to renewed battles for leadership and control over access to resources, won by Johnson Ngxobongwana, who had been a leader in the area since 1976. His group eventually established its control, apparently with police connivance, over both the new and old Crossroads communities, where they collected funds. The UDF found itself supporting this group in the absence of any other at local level, despite its violent credentials. In time, however, the Cape Youth Congress (CAYCO), with a strong affiliation to the UDF, developed as an alternative. However, the 'comrades' of CAYCO, as they called themselves, organized enforced boycotts, which alienated some of the population who turned to the 'fathers' under Ngxobongwana, leading to escalating violence in the area, which the police did nothing to stop. In December 1985 the authorities offered the 'old' Crossroads leaders control of a two million Rand housing project – if they assisted in clearing the new 'illegals' from part of the area. The ensuing violence led to thousands fleeing to new satellite camps nearby. This so-called 'black on black' violence, which culminated in some 57 being killed in three weeks in May and June, was then used by the apartheid regime to justify forced intervention. In mid-1986 the original and spin-off camps were destroyed by the older leadership with backing from the security forces, while retaining their rights to administer the new housing area.

This being said, the experience gained lived on in the minds of people, strengthening the fuller development of political consciousness. Perhaps again the crucial failure was the lack of politicization at a broader level, either as an initiative from the squatters or from the broader political opposition.

It could be argued that, while the resistance in the 1960s against forced relocation (as epitomized by District Six) had its importance in defining cultural concepts – or mental modes – on which the political cadres later built (and organized political opposition later still), the transition from community level resistance and protest to a wider urban social movement happened in the 1970s and 1980s around areas such as Crossroads.[16] However, the political potential of resistance to the apartheid regime at community and township level – generally entitled the 'civic movement' in South Africa – was not consolidated, as can be seen below.

POLITICIZATION, NEGOTIATION AND DECLINE

Rather ironically, the UDF, which gave some political credence to the wider development of the civic movement, was quickly sidelined with the unbanning of the political opposition in 1990. This quite probably was a major factor in the subsequent decline of the civic movement. However, before this happened there was a period of increased politicization within the civic movement, and a related high profile negotiation role on key social and political issues. To understand this requires some explanation of the general political dynamics of the transition period. During this period the political hierarchies returning from exile quickly consolidated their position with the older leadership released from long-term imprisonment and, in the case of the ANC, the UDF was disbanded as a political entity, the key politicians being absorbed into the newly consolidated political elites. The attention of the political opposition changed to one of negotiation for state power as opposed to regime overthrow, and this entailed a different strategy. In fact the ANC underwent successive transformations from a liberation movement to a political party and on into government between 1980 and 1994. During this time the space for civil society has been constantly reshaped and is still in a state of flux.

Political context and national housing policy negotiation

In the late 1980s and early 1990s – the transition phase – the political opposition wanted to keep up pressure on the apartheid state, and township 'ungovernability' was maintained as a political lever. However, at the same time the main opposition alliance – between the ANC, the Council of South African Trade Unions (COSATU) and the South African Communist Party (SACP) – began to promote a series of policy formulation activities for the new order. In housing and urban development, as in other fields (eg local government restructuring), these entailed the creation of forums with corporate representation from the government, opposition parties, organized labour, private sector, NGOs and the civic movement. In the housing sector the government quickly pulled out, realizing that it would be boxed in to agreements it did not want to endorse, and that it could in fact drive the process to a great extent from outside. As a result it sidelined the National Housing Forum to a great extent by requiring it to develop the operational mechanisms for a new housing subsidy which it announced in the year prior to elections, and hence much of the initial wide-ranging approach to housing and urban development in a reconstructive sense was never followed through.[17]

Essentially, as argued elsewhere (Jenkins, 1999a), the nature of the neo-corporatist negotiations which these forums represented, led to non-representative positions being put forward and essentially different inter-pretation of key agreements.[18] In terms of the latter the specific different understandings of the agreement (the Botshabelo Accord) signed on housing policy by the different negotiating parties at national level, was soon made clear when, after the new government took power, the private sector made a number of key qualifications concerning its participation in the new policy – effectively holding the government to ransom to take more risk before re-engaging with the sector. In this, fractions of capital were to some extent in disagreement – construction capital wanting high state (and accompanying private sector) investment as soon as possible; finance capital wanting the state to underwrite more risk and to limit its role for lower-income groups.

The upshot of the policy negotiations was a predominant focus during the next six years (up to 1999) on one policy mechanism, the capital subsidy mechanism (so much so this was often referred to as 'the policy'). Partly in response to lobbying by the NGOs and civic movement, this stressed a commu-nity role in delivery. This position grew naturally out of the development path for housing delivery as experienced by these bodies in practice – usually in opposition, or absence, of the state. It also gelled with the COSATU-backed development approach of 'people centred' development, as expressed in the resolutions of its 1993 special conference. This latter had been taken up by the ANC as the basis for an election manifesto – the Reconstruction and Development Programme (RDP) – in a hurried consultative process immedi-ately prior to elections in April 1994 (Marais, 1998).

The resulting housing programmes are analysed in more detail elsewhere (see Jenkins, 1999b) but, in brief, have led to a stress on the provision of 'housing opportunities'[19] through joint state and private sector inputs, despite the initial stress on collective activity. The tendency has been to provide limited additional finance and hence basic sites and services with core housing in peripheral locations. In addition little or no research into housing demand has been undertaken and hence the appropriateness of the housing opportunities has not been assessed. Despite the growing pace of delivery the overall gap between supply and demand is apparently increasing, and latest tendencies to effectively augment supply through raising subsidies are already encountering overall fiscal barriers at the macroeconomic level. The swing from a commu-nity-led development approach to one favouring faster, private–public sector delivery has thus sidelined the initiatives of much of the civic movement.

While in all probability not all positions of the opposition parties, organized labour, private sector and NGOs were adequately represented in the negotiation process, generally speaking these sectors had created structures to enable internal discussion and some degree of consensus. However, the relative balance between their positions did tend to lead to a 'lowest common denominator' rather than a 'highest common factor'. More importantly for this chapter, there were no mechanisms for the civic movement to undertake this process and come to the negotiating table with clear mandates.

The rapidly changing role of the civic movement

The civic movement, as recognized by the forum at the time, was a loose collection of quite widely differing coordinating institutions. In 1992 there was an attempt to create an 'umbrella' coordinating structure for all of these to represent the wider bodies, resulting in the South African National Civic Organization (SANCO). Independent regional coordinating structures of civics such as CAST (Civic Associations of the Southern Transvaal), became SANCO regional bodies, with SANCO branches at community level (varying from small groups to whole townships) subdivided into block and/or street committees. SANCO adopted a unitary, centralized and hierarchical structure, and in some regions this was not accepted by various existing groups, particularly in the Western Cape.[20] The politicization of the civic movement and the attempt to create hegemony round SANCO as a basis for policy negotiation in fact probably led to a decline in the movement.

SANCO's strong hierarchical structure tended to operate predominantly top-down in terms of the desire to control action, membership and – above all – access to resources, rather than function effectively as a representative structure for the rank and file to discuss, reach consensus and make their interests heard at the higher negotiating levels (these included local town/city and provincial negotiating forums and the drafting of the Local Government Transition Act, as well as negotiations in the National Housing Forum). The strong hierarchical structure was seen by many civic structures on the ground (and other coordinating structures) as imposed, and the level of unitary organization was not consolidated. This often led to a split in interest between the local level and provincial or national-level bodies. The organization's weak structure, membership, voting rights and responsibilities vis-à-vis various levels encouraged this. Different levels of the organization effectively had different roles, the local level dealing with local concerns (eg disputes and development projects), and higher levels dealing with organization building, policy, lobbying and funding. This led to leadership struggles, also related to resource control, and contributed to splinter groups forming, especially at local level. While this fragmentation militated against the wider coordination role, it did, however, allow considerable flexibility in the face of local diversity.

After some initial success in influencing policy (especially concerning local government restructuring), this level of activity was not consolidated, despite attempts to maintain a separate autonomous political position – for example, through the development of alternative policies.[21] Two major reasons are put forward for this: the loss of leadership through the absorption of the organization into the ANC alliance[22] and hence government; and resource mobilization constraints. Concerning the former, while some leaders were taken into national government in 1994, local government restructuring in 1995–1996 took a heavier toll, initially via non-statutory appointments in the 'pre-interim' stage and thereafter as elected representatives in the 'interim' stage. As the organization's policy position was that officials could not also hold government office, this led to significant loss of leadership. Both the move of some leadership into government and the leadership struggles related to the choice of candidates for the election under the alliance led to a degree of collapse of the organization at branch level. Over and above this, after the elections fewer people were prepared to undertake the unpaid work involved in the organization – especially as those who had been nominated or were elected were paid. Eventually, in 1997 SANCO changed its policy concerning the continued role of officials after election. This seems to have helped in beginning to rebuild the organization after the local government elections (Seekings, 1998).

Limited funds were raised by the SANCO membership system which was never well developed and there was also limited accountability concerning the use of these funds. From the mid-1980s civic coordinating structures had received substantial funding from foreign donors (for example from the European Union, but also from the Swedish Labour movement, Holland and even USAID). This stopped after the elections, partly due to the objectives of funding (ie the anti-apartheid struggle) and partly due to accountability problems. In the light of poor membership funding and loss of foreign funding support, SANCO turned to corporate sponsorship in the early 1990s, especially related to housing and urban development projects. There was a fine line between these funds and corruption, however, as well as the fact that the sponsors expected results via-à-vis community level support in return. The funding crisis and leadership crisis were linked and these reinforced the problems of organization in the transitional period, with a resurgence of voluntary activity only in the recent period.

The organizational crisis at higher levels concerning policy and resources is in practice also reflected in a different crisis at local level. Whereas in the early to mid-1990s civics played pivotal roles in almost all development projects – to a great extent based on their continued power of veto – this has been challenged by various other development actors. The challenges have come from the private sector, which has alleged that civics block and hold up development,[23] and similarly through resistance from the newly elected government, which also stressed the unrepresentativity of many civics. From 1995, the role of the civics in development projects at the local level decreased, because of the participation of other actors and because development projects were no longer formally required to achieve negotiated pacts with the civics as 'representative' of the community. Some projects (especially larger ones) have set up structures that are independent from the civics to channel community participation, to which they channel resources.

The role of SANCO vis-à-vis government is currently being reassessed. The close links with government created by the election of SANCO leaders has not necessarily brought about a significant advance in its claimed autonomous 'watchdog' role, as many seem to downgrade their links with the organization in their new function. Despite this the ANC's proposal at one stage to form ward committees for local councillors to relate to communities was strongly resisted by SANCO, which sees this as its 'political space'. This proposal was dropped, but there '... seems to be a widespread recognition that the ANC and SANCO need to clarify their respective roles in the post-election context' (Seekings, 1998). This has led to one strand of SANCO proposing to contest local government elections on its own ticket and recent power struggles within the national leadership.

ANALYTICAL VIEWPOINTS

This section reviews analytical positions of the civic movement's relationship to the state in South Africa, both in terms of future options and the underlying theoretical positions which underpin these. It is at this level of analysis that parallels can be eventually drawn with experiences in other urban social movements.

The fundamental options for the movement are seen by Seekings (1998) as:

- remaining fully independent from government, entailing the loss of existing elected councillors as leaders and developing a new set of leaders distinct from the ANC. Seekings calls this the 'civil society' model, where the civic movement channels growing protest at the neoliberalist tendencies of the government;[24]
- retaining a certain independence from the ANC through exercising an independent voice within the government as a lobbying group, perhaps even putting up candidates for election – the 'political society' model; or
- seeking community empowerment through business deals and joint ventures, such as through SANCO Investment Holdings, set up in 1996 – the 'economic society' model.[25]

The first assumes that state policies will not provide for the majority and that these will be open to reactivating protest, the third relies on investment opportunities and financial skills unlikely to be available within the organization as it stands, while the second, however, assumes real power lies with the state. This seems to be the dominant position currently within the leadership and organizational revitalization seems to focus on this, including allowing SANCO officials to take office. In the end, however, the crucial issue is how the organization relates to its rank and file.

The main theoretical grounding of the principal opposition party, the ANC, was for a long time a mixture of nationalist, socialist and communist ideology – this being rather generally defined to maintain a 'wide church' liberation movement. In none of these ideologies was there any clear role for an urban social movement based on issues related mainly to social 'reproduction' (eg housing, health, education and welfare), as all focused on the need to gain state power as the first step to enacting changes concerning social 'production' (ie economic control). In some specific cases the role of the civic movement was specifically queried by radical political theorists; in others it was looked on as a convenient focal point in the 'war of positions' in Gramscian terms. Representing the former position, Blade Nzimande and Mpumelo Sikhosana turned to Marx to argue that civil society and the state are inseparable and the question of democratization cannot be separated from the question of contestation and seizure of state power (Nzimande and Sikhosana, 1995). They therefore criticized viewpoints of other left-wing writers such as that of 'associational socialism', put forward by Mark Swilling, for whom the concept of an autonomous civil society is seen essentially as a counter to state power (see below).

Nzimande and Sikhosana's argument rests fundamentally on a conception of the hegemony of state power, which has to be seized to permit democratization. They theoretically define civil society as inseparable from the state and hence see no separate role for social movements other than the support of the primary struggle and effective working within the state. They thus criticize the tendency (especially after the unbanning of political opposition such as the ANC in February 1990) to separate 'civic' and 'political' issues within the liberation movement, which they see as undermining the building of mass organizations as the basis for political change. Nzimande and Sikhosana's argument assumes class formation and class action being expressed through the political system. They identify the 'need for the creation of organs of (proletarian) state power (or 'people's power') that are simultaneously autonomous mass social formations able to act independently of the state' – that is similar to soviets. This they see as urgent '...as the only means of ensuring a national democracy as well as for laying the foundations for a rapid advance towards socialism'. Concerning the civic movement they agree with Mashamba that mass organizations created 'alternative structures of power, organs of people's power' – 'people's communes'.[26] The ANC and its allied organizations were thus seen as the people's vanguard organizations in the struggle for seizure of the supreme controlling power of the state – the national democratic revolution.

In this context the development of coordinating civic structures was understood as a vehicle to undertake negotiation with the state in the post-1990 transitional period (ie through institutional forums), while still maintaining the autonomy of the struggle. However, while the mass democratic movements – represented, for example, through the UDF – began to define their own autonomy in this period, both in relation to the regime and also the recently unbanned organs of the national liberation movement, this was rapidly terminated. The disappearance of the UDF led to the growing distinction between political and mass organizations – later conceptualized as state and civil society. Nzimande and Sikhosana thus see the change in discourse from 'organs of people's power' to 'social movements' within an autonomous 'civil society' as a very serious theoretical and intellectual retreat, with the implication of separating the vanguard from its mass base. In their analysis, the concentration, in the final event, of negotiation on taking over state power led effectively to an undermining of the potential mass impact on more fundamental negotiations.

Swilling published several papers in the early 1990s concerning the civics as urban social movements and has more recently reiterated his position, retroactively analysing the experience of the service organizations (later NGOs) that grew up to work with the civics and trade unions during this period (Swilling, 1999). Essentially he argues that during the mid-1980s the stress of non-participation with the apartheid regime, yet growing mass movement around social issues, led to two main positions: one (described above) of insisting that the struggle focus on the seizure of state power and hence the urban social movements needed to be co-opted by the political movement; and the other that (as trade unions had managed successfully) it was necessary to begin negotiation on collective consumption at the same time as mobilizing political opposition, the two being linked. This latter position became increasingly accepted by development activists (although not within the main political movement), recognizing that urban struggles were distinct from the national political and economic struggles, although closely allied to these.

This position springs fundamentally from a questioning of traditional revolutionary theory, whereby it is necessary to seize power. In southern Europe and Latin America in the 1970s, eastern Europe in the 1980s and Africa in the 1990s, a new form of 'non-revolutionary regime transition' developed. In these, powerful economic elites realize that political power can be democratized without putting the basic structure of economic power at risk and are prepared to negotiate. In counterpart, opponents of the regime prefer to also negotiate rather than risk failure or prolongation of struggle. To this can be added that the role of the state in many countries has changed in terms of its role vis-à-vis the power of ruling elites. Economic power in reality often exists outside of the nation-state and hence 'seizing power' in the nation-state does not lead necessarily to the possibility of fundamental transformations within the territory, except in isolation – the examples of which have been highly unfruitful. In this situation the struggle for social reproduction or collective consumption is often as critical as that for economic and political power, and it is in this terrain that urban social movements operate.

Concerning regeneration of the civic movement, Swilling considers that SANCO 'betrayed...local accountability and creative responsibility' (Swilling, 1999), doubly so when its officers continued while taking political office. The two preconditions that made it possible to build the wider movement were: a body of effective grassroots organizers (from local mutual aid societies, the student movement and trade unions); and the support of service organizations – now NGOs. He advocates a need for trade unions in particular to encourage the reactivation of grassroots mobilization and organization building, and the reinforcement of the (actually dwindling) role for NGOs in this respect. He suggests that a key role would be played by local councillors in stimulating these activities, assisting with providing a funding base for support activities. In his opinion the demise of SANCO as a force both nationally and locally 'clears the way for a return to loosely connected networks of local associations, rather than a hierarchical centrally controlled structure' (Swilling, 1999).

The resurgence of non-aligned squatter movements, and the growing strength of community-based movements such as the South African Homeless People's Federation,[27] are signs that the urban social movements on land and housing issues in South Africa are far from finished. It remains to be seen whether these develop independently of political parties, or to what extent they are co-opted by these. It may be that the current ruling coalition (of the ANC, COSATU and SACP) will not endure, in which case the parties that withdraw from the alliance may well ally themselves with the civic movement. This could thus develop either along the lines that Nzimande and Sikhosana promote, of mass movements under the direction of a political vanguard, or that promoted by Swilling, of autonomous negotiation on social issues, supported by trade unions. It is possible, but unlikely, that local government councillors will adopt independent positions from the dominant political parties, unless they are elected on an independent basis with social movement support in future. It is quite probable that the ANC-led government will continue its policies focusing on state-promoted economic growth in close collaboration with the private sector, and hence consider its relationship with civil society as subordinate to this. This position is reinforced by the global constraints on economic growth – and indeed on more radical political action, such as through greater redistribution policies. It is in this area that the existing concepts defining relationships between civil society and the state are weakest – what is the transnational role of civil society and how is this effected in the fast globalizing world of today? This issue is returned to in Chapter 11.

CONCLUSION

With reference to the civic movement around land and housing issues in South Africa, there are two main attitudes to urban social movements: in one these are seen as lacking transformatory power unless they align to class-based political movements (which generally involves their subordination), allowing them to participate in the seizure of state power and its subsequent democratization; and in the other there is a view of both a social and a political role for urban social movements in negotiation with the state which permits the balancing of local needs with action for wider and deeper change. The rise and decline of the urban social movements around land and housing issues in South Africa demonstrate some of the pitfalls of broadening social movements and political subordination, and the demands of these movements seem to need action as they have been to a great extent sidelined in this process. There still exists, however, a strong consciousness of mobilization and struggle which can be the basis for a rejuvenation of the wider social movement. Whether this can achieve fundamental transformation within the global macroeconomic constraints facing the new state is a crucial question, the answer to which realistically does not lie in South Africa alone.

10 RENEGOTIATING PLACES: THE EXPERIENCE OF LOW-DEMAND HOUSING IN SALFORD, ENGLAND

Cliff Hague

INTRODUCTION

During the 1980s and 1990s there were important changes in the mental models and institutional forms for the provision and management of housing in British cities. This chapter discusses these changes through a case study of one local authority. Although the case study is pitched at a local scale, it illustrates impacts of wider economic restructuring and changing relationships between the state, the market and civil society.

In the UK, and indeed in most of northern Europe, public housing and town planning developed in the 20th century around the premise that housing and land were scarce resources for which competition was intense. The market was strong in two senses. Firstly, in British and northern European societies markets were the dominant mechanism for allocating resources and shaping politics. Secondly, the presumption was that within markets for commodities, and especially within the markets in land and housing, demand would normally exceed supply. Provision of public housing was undertaken, along with regulation of the private renting sector, on the assumption that market demand would otherwise be so strong as to exclude low-income households from access to adequate housing. The role of the public sector was therefore to restrain or supplement the land and property markets in a way that allocation of the resource was seen to be fair and 'in the public interest'. The statutory codes that govern planning and housing, the practices that officials and elected members followed, and the professionalism and related beliefs of the professionals were all fashioned around the idea of a strong public body operating in a situation of strong but manageable market demand. Indeed, it was the very power and centrality of this relationship that so excluded civil society from the professional discourses for so long.

This chapter explores the organizational forms and mental models that developed in the UK in the postwar period in relation to urban housing, locating these within a framework that can be theorized as Fordism. It then goes on to demonstrate how these models and forms were restructured in the 1980s and 1990s, developing the ideas further through an illustrative case study. The case study is concerned with a situation where one of the consequences of restructuring has been a serious decline in demand for housing within a locality. It is argued that the risk of low demand is not only a concomitant feature of economic restructuring and the consequent retreat of the state, but also poses very deep problems which have then refashioned the specific institutional forms of housing provision and allocation.

There is a need to understand the forms that structural economic change takes in the urban system, and how institutions, professional practices and civil society adapt to such change. There are also direct concerns about policy responses and the way change affects everyday life. In essence the argument is that the late 20th century extension of market power through globalization created a new dynamism and flexibility in housing markets which coincided with a weakening of the power of the state to exercise its compensatory and regulative functions. The changes also repositioned the relation between civil society and the state, although the outcomes are complex. New spaces for negotiation have been created, but the increased fragmentation within civil society is such that the outcomes of the negotiations are very uneven.

LOCAL AUTHORITIES AND HOUSING IN THE UNITED KINGDOM

At the start of the 20th century about 90 per cent of British households lived in housing rented from private landlords. The Housing of the Working Classes Act 1890 provided the legislative basis for the development of local authority housing. However, there was no obligation on councils to build and no subsidies from central government. The level of local authority building under this Act was consequently low (25,000 in England and Wales, 3000 in Scotland). By 1914 only around one per cent of the population was housed in this tenure. The First World War made the problems of overcrowded and unsanitary housing worse. House building virtually ceased in this period, and a shortage of housing developed, especially in industrial areas where the essential shipbuilding, engineering or munitions workers were concentrated. Pressure on housing caused rents to rise and this led to increased political activism and tenants' campaigns including rent strikes. This was a potential threat to the war effort and the government solution was the passing of the Rent and Mortgage Interest (War Restrictions) Act 1915, which fixed rents at the level they had been in 1914. This was the first significant state interference in the UK's free market in housing. It made the future subsidizing of housing by central government virtually inevitable.

When the war ended, the government faced strong demand for housing. The Prime Minister, Lloyd George, promised that he would provide 'habitation fit for the heroes who have won the war.' This led, for example, to the passing of The Housing and Town Planning Act 1919, which introduced the principle of state subsidies for housing. Local authorities were obliged to estimate the levels of housing shortage in their districts. Central government met all the costs of building housing, except for a local government contribution of the sum raised by putting an extra penny (four fifths of a penny in Scotland) on the rates (the local property tax). This Act also extended rent control.

The interwar years set the parameters for the development of the British housing system through to the 1980s. Two tenures increased in significance – public renting and owner occupation – while the third, private renting, declined. The public sector housing was overwhelmingly built and managed by local authorities, with a voluntary sector social housing movement (so common in much of northern Europe) only really developing to any significant size from the 1970s. While the emphasis on the extent to which local authorities should lead the housing programme varied between different governments in the years that followed, there was a political consensus on their overall importance in housing provision. From the 1950s until about 1970 comprehensive redevelopment within the urban areas was an important factor in changing the tenure balance. Typically private rented and owner-occupied houses were demolished and replaced by council houses.

The public sector reached its zenith in 1979 – 6.5 million dwellings, almost a third of all houses. In Scotland public sector housing was more significant still – by 1976 the public sector comprised over 54 per cent and was increasing. In Great Britain about half the population were owner occupiers. Private renting was down to 13 per cent and housing associations were of negligible significance.

This brief history shows how a distinctive institutional form developed. The notion of Fordism usefully encapsulates the key elements. There was an accommodation between the market and the state. The market provision of new houses increasingly came to be dominated by national and international companies building large volumes of standardized houses for those who were able to pay a market price for them. The state, through local councils, provided the houses (also built in bulk, mainly on contract by private companies and increasingly using industrialized building systems) for those unable to afford a full market rent. The spaces of negotiation between the state and the market largely concerned the balance of state subsidies between the two sectors, and the scale of the building programmes. The spaces were largely filled by politicians who played 'the numbers game', seeking to outbid each other in the number of houses they promised to build.

There were important mental models in all this, especially in respect of local authority housing. Elected members of local authorities, especially those from the Labour Party, tended to see council housing as an equitable, even socialist form of tenure, because it allowed for allocation on the basis of need rather than ability to pay. Even those antipathetic to socialism accepted the idea of council housing being a form of provision for the needy. In other words, it was perceived that demand exceeded supply with respect to council housing, and so a key task for those providing and letting such property was to devise rational and legitimate mechanisms to allocate tenancies. This meant systems of allocating points to provide a relative weighting for different categories of need (eg medical need and overcrowding) and merit (eg residing in the local area, or spending time on the list of those seeking local authority housing).

It also followed that those granted a tenancy should be grateful and treat the house with respect. Paternalism was a key element in the mental model associated with council housing, and the role of civil society was to stand patiently as a member of a waiting list, until such time as sufficient 'points' were accumulated to merit the offer of a tenancy. There were periods and places when tenants became more organized and demanding (see Hague, 1990) but until the 1970s these were the exception, not the rule. The 1950s and 1960s were the golden age of the professional in local government. Bureaucracies grew with the welfare state, and representative democracy was firmly in place. The power of the state vis-à-vis both the market and civil society was at its zenith.

ECONOMIC RESTRUCTURING AND ITS IMPACTS ON THE BRITISH HOUSING SYSTEM

The oil crisis of 1973–1974, perhaps more than any other single event, triggered a fundamental change in the form of the housing system. As interest rates and unemployment escalated, the state was powerless to employ the Keynesian demand management methods that had served so well over previous decades. The fiscal crisis was acute. In 1976 the IMF agreed a major loan to the UK, but on condition that cuts were made in public spending. At constant prices an average cut of £475 million a year was made in total spending on council housing in each of the four years 1975–1976 to 1978–1979. The government undertook a major review of its housing policy in 1977, and clearly signalled a change of direction:

> 'Housing policies have come to a turning point and are due for reappraisal...the priority given to housing has to be weighed against the claims of other important services and against the need for resources to regenerate our industrial base...' (Scottish Development Department, 1977)

Thus the cuts in public spending meant that the organizational forms of public sector housing were changing, and spaces for negotiation between local and central government over the scale of investment were being narrowed. The mental models of council housing were also changing. Even in Scotland the traditional emphasis on public sector housing was being overtaken by consumer changes to favour owner occupation. The allocations and management of council housing would also have to take on board a more diverse set of tenants, not just the traditional family with children. In particular, local authorities would get the primary responsibility for housing the homeless, and housing authorities would need to better coordinate their activities with social work departments in local government. Taken together these trends, noted in the Labour government's review of housing in 1977, implied a very important shift in the mental model of council housing. As those able to afford to do so became consumers of owner-occupied housing, so the tenants of council housing would increasingly constitute a more marginalized social group. There was also some suggestion that the traditional paternalism might also need to be rethought, with new scope for tenant participation and new rights and freedoms for tenants.

The Conservatives' victory in the 1979 election brought an ideological zeal to the direction of change that had been evident since the oil crisis. There was a commitment to reduce public spending and borrowing so as to cut taxes. In the housing sphere this was reflected in a desire to expand owner occupation and reduce state housing. Thus the housing minister in 1987 said:

> *'I can see no arguments for generalized new build by councils, now or in the future...The next great push after the right to buy should be to get rid of the state as a big landlord and bring housing back to the community.'* (William Waldegrave quoted in Malpass, 1990)

Since 1979 we have seen:

- an increase in owner occupation from 55 to 67 per cent of all households (though a slower rate of increase since 1990);
- a reduction of private renting continuing until 1990, since when there has been an increase for the first time since 1919;
- increased housing association activity (though starting from a very low base); and
- a steep decline in council housing, from nearly a third of all households to only a fifth, the first such reduction since the First World War.

One consequence of these changes (which have parallels in other aspects of social policy) has been to shift the UK away from the European housing pattern where renting is the norm and social housing a significant sector, and towards the American pattern of private ownership and a residual public housing category. These trends were achieved by two processes: differences in rates of building (and demolition) across tenures, and transfer of properties from public renting to other tenures.

From 1980 council tenants gained the right to buy their houses at prices that were discounted to take account of length of residence. Some councils had sold houses before that, but now the 1980 Housing Act obliged councils to sell, whether they wanted to or not. The discounts made it attractive to buy, especially as other policies were pushing up council rents. The maximum discount was 50 per cent at first, though this was increased to 70 per cent under the 1986 Housing and Planning Act. Over 1.6 million houses were sold to sitting tenants between 1980 and 1996, equivalent to a quarter of the 1980 stock of houses owned by the public sector. In contrast only 250,000 council houses were built in this period and most of those were pre-1985.

Two outcomes are widely recognized from these policies. Firstly, housing has increasingly become a commodity, something that exists not just to meet a human need but as a market good which is exchanged for a price subject to market fluctuations. Secondly, council housing has become a residual sector, housing a socially excluded group of the population. The proportion of council tenant households containing no earners was 11 per cent in 1962, 44 per cent by 1982 and 66 per cent by the mid-1990s.

As politics caught up with the global economic changes that first became evident in the mid-1970s, local authorities' role as housing providers has been drastically diminished, while owner occupation, housing association tenancy and even private renting have increased. The discretion of local authorities to determine how to manage the houses they own has also been curtailed. Not only do all council tenants have an automatic right to buy their house, often with substantial discounts, but the scope of councils to borrow money to carry out repairs and improvements to their property has also been restricted through legislation.

Linked to these changes has been the dramatic restructuring of the mental models associated with council housing. Instead of being sought after, it has become a tenure of last resort: a tenure that is widely perceived to be stigmatized. This itself alters the relation between the landlord and the tenants. Furthermore an institutional form which embedded the idea of collective and community linkages, through having a shared landlord, was replaced by an institutional form which defined individual households within housing markets as the dominant mode of civil society. At the same time the local authorities have had to come to terms with the idea that their tenants can claim some rights. Indeed, there was a clear attempt by the Conservative governments between 1979 and 1997 to build a model of consumerism as defining civil society's relation to housing across all tenures.

This summary is necessarily abbreviated. It oversimplifies some aspects of the process of change and only probes a few of the more obvious outcomes. In being pitched primarily at the national level it also fails to probe some of the spatial differences through which these wider trends have been mediated. Thus a fuller understanding of the institutional effects of neoliberalism in housing within the context of global economic restructuring is more effectively researched through a local case study.

THE GROWTH OF LOW-DEMAND HOUSING MARKETS

The first real signs that some local authority properties were difficult to let began to be acknowledged in the early 1970s. For example, in 1970 the Scottish Housing Advisory Committee produced *Council House Communities*, a report which spoke of unpopular housing areas with unlet and vandalized houses. Typically these were either in the slum clearance estates from the 1930s or in the new system-built blocks which were often located on or beyond the edge of the city and lacked social facilities. Escalating fuel prices after the 1973 oil crisis added problems of heating and dampness to the list of factors making for unpopular house types.

The Conservative government in the 1980s saw tenure as the prime problem. Houses were unpopular because they were council houses managed by bureaucrats at the behest of Labour politicians. The flagship 'right to buy' policy did indeed prove attractive to tenants in stable, popular estates, typically those where houses were in traditional designs (that is two-storey houses with their own gardens front and back) and enjoyed access to a good range of local facilities. The stock that remained in local authority ownership was disproportionately in non-traditional designs (such as high-rise flats) and unpopular by virtue of reputation or location. There were a range of government initiatives which sought to change tenures in these difficult areas or house types; for example, funds were made available to improve properties which would then be sold by a developer.

Pawson et al (1997) showed that there could be serious problems in housing association lettings which reflected demand and not just poor management. Power and Mumford (1999) have provided graphic descriptions of the problems of low demand in mixed tenure and owner occupied areas. Lowe et al (1998) have talked of 'abandonment'. Significantly, Bramley (1998) suggested that there was, in effect, a north–south divide in terms of housing need, with the north having a relatively affordable private market, surplus social lettings and low household growth. This notion of a north–south divide implies that the problems are more rooted in structural economic change than in local management practices or deficiencies in the stock of housing.

In summary, one of the consequences of the increased marketization of British housing has been the emergence of serious imbalances both between and within tenures and between and within regions. The emergence of low demand as a problem within the owner-occupied sector seriously subverts the mental models that have been constructed for that sector. If the tenure imbalance and the residualization of council housing reflects the outcomes of policy and politics on the mental models of housing provision, the regional imbalances appear to be more direct consequences of global restructuring within regional economies.

The Experience of Low-demand Housing in Salford

Economic restructuring in Salford

We now turn to a case study of the city of Salford to analyse the local impacts of some of these changes. Salford is a significant part of the second largest city-region in the UK – the Manchester conurbation. In the early 1960s 125,000 people lived in 'old Salford', the inner city, mainly in terraced two-storey houses built in the 19th century. Although good quality housing was in short supply, there was economic stability. Unemployment in those days was just one per cent. The docks at the Salford end of the Manchester Ship Canal were one of the country's busiest ports. Adjacent to them was the huge Trafford Park industrial estate, which at its peak employed some 75,000 people (Robson, 1988). There was lots of manufacturing, often mixed in cheek by jowl with the housing, a steel works in Irlam and major coal mines operating nearby (see Figure 10.1).

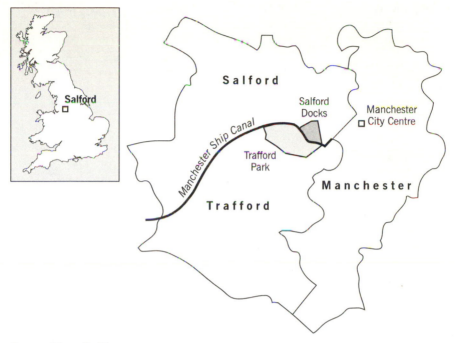

Source: Harry Smith

Figure 10.1 *Map of the Salford area*

So, old Salford was a place where people lived who worked in the docks, steel works, coal mines and manufacturing industries on the west of the Manchester conurbation, a 'dirty old town'. Civil society was linked to the market and the state through a number of networks. At the workplace trade unions were important means of protecting collective and individual interests. People left school, went into employment as labourers, artisans or typists, and got married at 19 or 20 (Carr, 1998). Mothers helped daughters and sons-in-law to get a house by having a word with the local rent collector, while also getting their name down on the council waiting list. Those with savings might have been able to put down a deposit on a small, pre-1919 terraced house. The job, the partner and the house were then expected to last for life.

Globalization of economies exposed much of the economic base of this pre-1980s Salford to fierce competition. By 1980 unemployment in Salford was 14 per cent, as labour-intensive production in traditional primary and manufacturing sectors moved to lower-cost locations within the new international division of labour. Technological change creating larger vessels and fewer dockers, together with changed trading patterns following the UK's entry into the European Economic Community in 1972, saw a serious run down of the port activities. The docks closed in 1984. The steelworks had already closed and so had most of the South Lancashire coalfield. There was a similar story in manufacturing with notable closures and rationalizations in major local employers. Overall Salford lost 26,885 jobs in manufacturing between 1975 and 1991 (Salford Partnership, 1998a).

Table 10.1 *Percentage employment change by sector (1971–1986)*

Sector	Great Britain	North-west
Metal manufacturing and chemicals	−38	−48
Metal goods, engineering and vehicles	−37	−45
Energy and water supply	−34	−42
Other manufacturing	−30	−46
Transport and communications	−16	−34
Retail	7	−1
Warehousing and hotels	33	26
Education, health and other services	34	15
Banking, insurance and finance	62	36

Source: Robson, 1988

The pattern of change was similar throughout the UK, but hit hardest in areas like the north-west of England including Salford, where primary and manufacturing jobs were especially significant. The north-west lost a higher proportion of its jobs than the national average even within the same industrial sectors (see Table 10.1). Robson (1988) summarized the spatial consequences as 'self-reinforcing to create a decision-making, information-rich, affluent South and a routinized, low-skill, impoverished North.'

The effects in Salford of these long term and far reaching changes in the regional economy of the north-west of England were devastating[1] – 'When we lost the manufacturing base, the whole thing collapsed' (Carr, 1998). Although unemployment has been falling since 1993, there are still significant unemployment levels in the area of pre-1974 Salford.[2] Almost one in four of the unemployed have been out of work for over a year (Salford Partnership, 1998b). Global restructuring has reshaped the lives of the people and deconstructed the networks linking individuals horizontally into civil society and vertically to the market and to the local council.

Substantial proportions of Salford citizens qualify for special state subsidies targeted at poor households.[3] Thus one consequence of the restructuring has been to create a serious fissure within the population. Substantial numbers have been excluded from full involvement in the labour market, and have been put in a relationship of dependency on the state or on illicit forms of income generation. But, as Table 10.1 shows, the change has not just been about the loss of jobs, for in some service sectors there has been an important growth of jobs. There have also been important changes in the nature of work itself, with the growth of part-time working, self-employment and short contracts. This panoply of change is widely recognized as creating a new flexibility in labour markets and in production, which stands in marked contrast to the scale and predictability of Fordism.

The consequences of such dramatic changes extend well beyond the workplace. As discussed earlier, they are reflected in significant changes in the state–market relationship. They affect housing markets and refashion the culture and expectations within civil society. In the days of full employment and large employers it was the shortage of housing that dominated the agenda of Salford's council. Salford now has a serious surplus of housing. The local authority is ranked at number seven in the table of largest surplus social lettings in England in 1997, with a surplus flow per annum of 18.6 lettings per 1000 households (Bramley, 1997). The change from the form of housing provision and allocation which dominated until the 1980s is dramatic. The chapter now explains this transition.

Slum clearance and the municipalization of housing

Before the 1974 reorganization of local government extended its boundaries, the old Salford council had to grapple with an impossible land budget as it sought to address housing need. The city had no land available for new housing development within its boundaries, and the land that was not industrial was mainly covered by densely packed streets of terraced houses, with little open space and few facilities. The housing problems were exacerbated by demographic growth. Urban containment dominated the planning policies of surrounding authorities where land was potentially available. High density redevelopment was Salford's only option, and the Salford local authority grasped it. The bulldozers worked their way through the worst inner city properties, and new high-rise council-owned flats replaced the slums that were owned by their occupiers or by private landlords. Local government reorganization in 1974 changed the land supply position, and roughly coincided with the switch from high-rise to low-rise council housing developments, as the unpopularity and costs of high-rise housing began to be recognized by both central and local government.

Through the 1960s and well into the 1970s housing provision in Salford came to be increasingly dominated by the development and allocation of properties by the local authority. The 'points system' assessed need, people went on to a waiting list, or were rehoused when comprehensive redevelopment cleared away their house. It was believed that municipalization offered better conditions than the slums, and so houses provided by the council would be sought after and allocated by the council on criteria of need, not willingness to pay. Thus rents were generally low and there were few differentials in rent levels between different types of property. In these circumstances, officials perceived no need to involve tenants or even to seek their views – if you got a council house you were lucky and should be grateful. Local councillors would be the channel for some negotiation by their constituents over access to such scarce housing. The elected representatives might then present the needs of their constituents, either individually or as a group, as the situation required. Meanwhile, the council itself would negotiate with central government over technical matters such as centrally determined housing-cost yardsticks and over loans to carry out the new building. Thus a strong local authority was engaged in a large construction programme of standardized units, very much on the Fordist model. Properties were allocated by rigid, bureaucratically determined criteria of need. The private market in housing dwindled as slums were compulsorily purchased by the council, demolished and replaced by new council flats. All of this was to change very quickly.

Disposal of local authority houses

The relationships between central and local government, and between the state and the market, changed dramatically with the advent of the Thatcher government in 1979. The tenants' right to buy their council houses was not negotiable, nor was the ending of new council house building. The financial squeeze on local authorities made it difficult to even maintain the existing stock of houses of which the councils were landlords. Councils and tenants alike were pointed to the market as the way to solve housing problems, though, as we have seen, by the early 1980s the regional economy of the north-west of England was in some disarray.

By the early 1980s Salford's population was about 240,000, although the inner city was now below the 70,000 mark (City of Salford, 1998), because of reduced densities through redevelopment and the voluntary migration of people seeking private housing. The council owned almost 40,000 houses, there was still a waiting list for council houses and most of the properties owned by the council were fully let. The main indicator that made Salford's housing department aware of low demand was transfer requests from people wanting to move out of non-standard house types such as maisonettes, high-rise and deck-access schemes.[4] Such properties were mostly located in the inner areas, the pre-1974 Salford, and had been built in the 1960s and 1970s. The tenants' right to buy, the flagship housing policy of the Thatcher government, did not have much effect in Salford, especially in these areas and house types: the scale of unemployment in such areas, combined with the unpopularity of the house types, probably inhibited potential purchasers.

Salford's response to the realization that there were unpopular house types and areas within its stock was the disposal of unpopular properties to the private sector. This was part of a wider strategy that was most evident in the redevelopment of the docks to create the Salford Quays development of offices and executive flats. The council's aim was to diversify the housing stock and tenure options available within the city, and so to stem the further loss of population and jobs. Disposal of properties also reduced the council's liability in respect of repairs and maintenance. Council homes refurbished by private house-builders came on to the market during the mid-1980s property boom, targeting first-time buyers, who were mostly young professionals coming from outside the area (Carr, 1998). Houses 'sold like hot cakes' and soon doubled in selling price.

This policy was a very significant and controversial change of direction for the council, which was solidly Labour-controlled. After 60 years of increasing the numbers of council houses Salford was now disposing of stock to private developers. After structuring policy around the idea that a house only had a use value and was a collective asset for the citizens, Salford was now looking to the commodification of housing and the incentives it provided for individual and private capital accumulation. Salford's pragmatic approach, as opposed to the ideological opposition to market liberalism in the neighbouring city of Manchester, was backed by central government with important allocations of funds for urban regeneration.

Thus in the 1980s the emergence of a surplus within the local authority housing stock was a factor in fostering a withdrawal of the state from part of the housing stock. New organizational forms were developed to link the council to private house builders, with central government grants and incentives playing a key 'lubricating' role. The national policy imposed from central government sought to bypass local authorities and their traditional role as housing providers. A direct link between the market and civil society was forged through mechanisms like the 'right to buy' and 'refurbishment for sale', but the conception of civil society that underpinned this was of people as atomized consumers. Thus in the 1980s the mental model of council housing was changing within the Salford City Council, though the process of change was uneven. The mentality built through years of housing shortage and municipalization did not disappear overnight, and the new measures which the council adopted could have been interpreted as a means to stabilize the situation, rather than as a vehicle to carry change through to a new conclusion.

The 1990s – flexible lettings

In the 1990s further important changes were made in the perception of local authority housing. The all-pervasiveness of consumerism would itself be sufficient explanation of the residualization of council housing. In the UK of the 1990s, any form of housing provision not delivered as a commodity would appear dated and stigmatized, a necessary second best to market provision. The growth of social exclusion as one consequence of economic restructuring is embedded in geography as well as tenure. The better off moved out and into owner occupation.[5]

The city council was still landlord to a series of badly designed 1960s estates, where open layouts provided opportunities for crimes against property and parked vehicles and the non-traditional house types were unpopular. These areas were tackled vigorously by the council through successful bidding into a range of central government urban and housing funds in the early 1990s. Security systems were installed, with closed circuit television (CCTV), fencing and defensible space, manageable garden areas and concierge systems in some of the high-rise blocks. Three and four storey maisonettes were 'topped' to create traditional two storey houses with pitched roofs.

More significant than the physical improvements, there was a change in the approach to letting properties. Not only had the state retreated, but it also had embraced the workings of the market within its own practices. According to Mitchell (1998), it was in 1993 or 1994 when it became clear that within the council stock there were properties for which there was no demand. This realization necessarily implied a deconstruction of the mental models that underpinned the allocation of tenancies, and forced a restructuring of organizational forms within the housing department. The council created more flexible lettings schemes and began to market properties through advertising in the local press. A senior housing officer in Salford explains:

> *'Our points system means less and less. We have designated flexible lettings areas... 42 per cent of our council housing stock has been taken out of the normal letting process. You don't have to go on the normal waiting list to get a tenancy in these areas; housing officers are free to deal with whoever is interested.'*
> (Townsend, 1998)

To tackle the symptoms of low demand, the perception of council housing must be changed not only within the bureaucracy, but also within the local civil society:

> *'The public perception is still that council houses are only for the unemployed and that you have to be in the queue for a year. We are advertising tenancies, with a free phone number to get over the message that the council is an option for renting, and that you don't have to be a single mother to qualify. We are using people from the private sector to train our staff in telephone skills. Advertising is a big part of our role now. We are not getting a huge return, but it is here to stay.'* (Townsend, 1998)

Thus low demand within a market society effectively abolished the idea of council housing as a collective resource to be allocated on the basis of 'rationally' determined need. The social fragmentation, working practices and culture of flexible labour markets also influenced the way in which housing was reorganized. Flexible letting means that there is an increasing divergence between the profiles of the old and new tenants. Many of Salford's tenants first got their council house when their terraced house was cleared in the 1960s or 1970s. Increasingly these people will be dying or requiring a different type of accommodation. New tenants are younger, single, mobile and not wanting a tenancy for life (Townsend, 1998).

Economic change has altered the pattern of household formation, and the provision of local authority housing has had to change to compete with other housing providers, including private landlords, housing associations (who provide 'not for profit' houses to rent) and adjacent local authorities who themselves face the same problems of filling their houses. Townsend (1998) explains that Salford responded by offering furnished tenancies and supported tenancies for the young and single, and by spending more on empty properties so as to increase their attraction and facilitate letting, among other strategies to maximize the council's share of a declining market.

Another Salford housing official, Molloy (1998) makes similar points, saying 'we have moved from allocation on need to simply letting the property'. He says the council makes 17,500 offers a year but only one in four of these is taken up. He reports that many applicants drop out when they hear it is the council who are letting the house. The council is adopting marketing strategies including show houses, but has to surmount deeply ingrained perceptions of council housing both among the general public and within the housing department itself.

Mitchell (1998) explains how the council is marketing properties in an era of flexible housing markets:

> *'We have tried to identify and market to potential new client groups – for example gay couples, through targeting the Pink Press. We have very aggressive marketing now. We advertise and offer incentives and try to decorate properties for new tenants. We offer furnishing and white goods (ie fridges and washing machines or similar domestic appliances) and will give a £150 decorating voucher. In the past tenants were content to be tenants of the council for life. Now we find that many of the new tenants we are able to attract move out again after six months. So a lot of our concern is focused on turnover and the staffing inputs that generates. Only those with no other choice will take and stay long term in a local authority tenancy. Increasingly people have choice and exercise it.'*[6]

It is clear that the organizational form of local authority housing in Salford has changed greatly through the advent of flexible letting. Although 'there is still a culture of property in the housing department, rather than a sense of customers', 'very aggressive marketing' is now part and parcel of the work of the housing department. The offer of white goods mirrors one of the sales techniques used by house builders in marketing new properties to first-time house buyers. The pressure is on housing officers to fill unlet houses and flats, and to avoid the termination of tenancies and consequent need to re-let. Such changes have implications for the spaces of negotiation between tenants and the landlord. There is less scrutiny of prospective tenants than was the case when demand exceeded supply. In addition, tenants and prospective tenants have new powers in situations of low demand. It is relatively easy to be allocated a council house (or to get a new let from another landlord), and this means that the threat of losing a tenancy as a consequence of antisocial behaviour or other misdemeanours is less draconian in its implications than in high-demand housing areas and times.

Low demand, owner occupation and negative equity

The impacts of restructuring are not confined to the local authority housing. The economic changes and their social consequences have resulted in low demand in the markets for private housing in Salford and similar northern de-industrialized urban areas. In particular the bottom end of the owner occupied market, mainly comprising terraced houses built before 1919 (see Figure 10.2), or houses that were purchased from the council under the right to buy, have been badly hit by the collapse in house prices that took place in the early 1990s, creating widespread problems of negative equity for houseowners.[7]

The experience of falling property prices, so contradictory to the 1980s mantra about the unqualified benefits of owner occupation, set new parameters within which people formed aspirations and made housing choices. A

Credit: Cliff Hague

Figure 10.2 *Unoccupied private sector housing in Salford, built in the 19th century*

change in work, relationships and perceptions has occurred. Carr (1998) argues that 1990s first-time buyers are different from their predecessors in the 1980s. After the early 1990s recession young people had heard tales of negative equity and repossessions, and many hedged their bets by renting instead of buying. They created a new demand for rented property from reliable tenants, a message which investors began to pick up and respond to.

Carr says that buying picked up again after 1996, but:

> *'The new cohort of people entering the housing market for the first time want mobility. They know they are in flexible labour markets, where there can be changes in job specifications and contracts are often short-term. This generation are people who have seen prices fall and know about the problems of selling, so they opt for renting and mobility. We are seeing the emergence of a very flexible housing market.'*

The very dynamism of this new housing market creates new opportunities and carries new risks. Not only was the market for renting growing in the early 1990s because of a new caution among households who might previously have been buyers, but the expansion of student numbers also created a new sector of demand for cheap rented housing. The revival of private renting had been one of the aims in Conservative government policy. Housing benefit had been structured in such a way as to create incentives to private landlordism.[8]

Negative equity then inflated the stock for renting, as owners who could not sell became 'reluctant landlords'.

As with the public housing sector, the new flexibility in housing markets created new practices. Lenders repossess the houses when an owner cannot afford to pay the mortgage. In parts of Salford such repossessed terraced houses are bought and sold at auctions (or reputedly in pubs!) for around £3000 a house. The new purchasers then rent the houses to people on housing benefit for rents that yield a return on the capital investment. If the tenants cause problems to the property, the main people to suffer are local owner-occupiers, as prices fall still further, and the pool of property available for cheap acquisition and renting for a rent guaranteed through housing benefit is further increased. There are suggestions that links have developed between financiers, speculators, local criminals, property companies and those offering commercial security services to residents.

Civil society in areas of low-demand housing

The nature of the negotiation between the council, as landlord, and its tenants, as part of civil society, is complex and the emergence of low-demand housing areas is producing significant changes. There have always been tenants who make difficult neighbours, but housing managers in a situation of scarcity could impose countervailing pressures and sanctions. Permanent unemployment and the spread of hard drugs have exacerbated the difficulties of life among the socially excluded and their neighbours. Women from a council housing estate in Salford pinpointed the economic problems of the neighbourhood:

> *'Older workers have been made redundant and the younger ones have no jobs. Some jobs that people can get don't pay well. So people get into a rut and don't have the skills to get out of it.'*

These same women[9] described everyday life in such circumstances as being badly affected by crime. They reported car crime, violence against property and muggings of old people as favourite activities among young delinquents. In their opinion, 'Car crime is for the hell of it, but theft is to feed drug-taking habits. Those taking drugs used to be 16–20 year olds, but now it is 10–15 year olds.'

The women saw that the traditional mental model of council housing, with its associated organizational forms to allocate tenancies on the basis of a bureaucratic assessment of need, had been a factor in weakening the bonds within civil society. They blamed councils for dividing communities by refusing to allocate local houses to the second generation, and thus sending families away from their links.

These women had responded to the problems of their area by forming a community organization to represent their views to officialdom. The core of the group was made up of people who had lived in the area since the houses were built; though some had been there before the slum clearance had taken place. They saw themselves as the remnants of 'a good community'; those left after many had opted to move out.

However, it would be reductionism to fully equate civil society with formal community organizations. Neighbourhoods can have a number of informal structures that steer everyday life, though they may not be readily visible. In much of inner Salford there is a strong community tradition of not giving evidence to the police. This is known as a 'no grassing' culture, and together with fear of intimidation, it makes convictions difficult to obtain. One interviewee argued that self-policing of neighbourhoods through local criminals was a vital factor in determining the stability of an area. When this network was broken, the area declined and drugs became a major problem.

Perceptions of self-policing and 'no grassing' are themselves mental models of a form of community solidarity, though they have probably failed to keep pace with the fragmentation of community that has occurred.

RENEGOTIATING PLACES

The change in the form of provision of housing in Salford over a generation is immense. The spread of the market, its penetration into the form of local authority housing provision and management is notable. But the case study shows that in particular places 'the market' has some very specific features and consequences. In Salford, as in many other towns and cities in the north of England, economic restructuring has led to social and spatial fragmentation, in which public sector housing and the old terraced houses in the private sector serve only a residual sector of the population who are unable to exercise choice elsewhere in the housing market. The details would vary between Salford and other places, but the overall picture is that local economies have been restructured through forces that stretch far beyond the locality itself. As societies have fragmented and social polarization has increased so the contrasts in housing markets between places and the disparities in housing experiences between people have also widened.

It appears that housing markets have been restructured, partly through political interventions in the phase of neoliberalism, but more fundamentally through the cumulative impact of much wider processes of economic, social and cultural restructuring. The instability of the labour market and the exclusion of large numbers of people from the serious prospect of rewarding legal work have altered housing demand not just quantitatively, but also qualitatively. People have had to renegotiate their place in these new structures – whether by moving out, exercising the right to buy, getting on the 'housing ladder' of owner occupation, becoming a 'reluctant landlord', not 'grassing' on criminal neighbours, or through taking the opportunity to sell 'security services' to frightened residents. In a situation of quantitative housing surplus but qualitative housing shortage, people manipulate the resources available to them to broker the best 'deal' they can. In these situations there is always somewhere, and some groups, at the bottom of the list.

The dramatic changes have also obliged local government to renegotiate its own way of working. In part these changes have been imposed by central government, notably in a series of restrictions on local government finance.

Table 10.2 *Organizations, mental models and negotiation in changing housing markets*

	Fordism	Flexible housing markets
The housing market – key organizational forms	Decline in small 'landlordism' through compulsory purchase and slum clearance	Emergence of 'reluctant landlords'
		Repossessions, auctions and new 'landlordism'
The housing market – key mental models	'Safe as houses' – property as safe investment	Negative equity – house ownership as risk as well as opportunity
	'Ladder' of owner occupation that first-time buyers need	House purchase delayed in favour of renting and mobility
Local authority housing – key organizational forms	Municipalization through clearance of unfit private housing and new-build local authority housing	Disposal of property through right to buy , 'refurbishment for sale' and demolition
	Needs assessment allocation mechanisms – points and waiting lists	Flexible lettings, marketing and furnished tenancies
	Local authorities as monopoly landlords	Competition among social landlords, and from private landlords
Local authority housing – key mental models	Housing as a collective resource that is scarce and must be allocated 'rationally'	Housing stock is surplus, with properties and neighbourhoods that are difficult to let. Marketing skills of the private sector are needed to fill the properties
	Paternalism towards tenants	Tenants as customers
	Local authority as main housing provider	Private house builders as partners
Civil society – key mental models	Community based on shared experiences and limited choice	Individualism and consumerism
	Stability	Instability
	Council housing as a tenure for life	Council housing as a temporary option at best
Civil society – key forms of negotiation	Local councillors to press a case for rehousing	Community organizations to press needs to council
	Informal family-based contacts with rent collectors to gain access to tenancies in the private sector	Housing benefit entitlement as a key means of gaining access to properties in the public or the private sector for those on low income

But the experience of Salford shows how important a factor the market has been in bringing about change. Ironically it has been the extreme weakness of the housing market that has forced such a significant change in the local authority's housing policies and practices. In disposing of properties, demolishing houses, marketing tenancies, and reassessing practices in respect of evictions, probationary tenancies and other facets of housing management, the council is renegotiating the role that it plays and its relation to its tenants and to the other housing providers.

While necessarily oversimplified, Table 10.2 attempts to summarize the main features in the transition from housing provision under Fordism to housing in flexible housing markets, based on the case study.

In summary, low demand for housing is an important issue confronting policy makers in parts of the UK that have undergone de-industrialization and market liberalization in the last two decades of the 20th century. It exposes the extent to which planning and housing systems have been premised on the idea that the market is sufficiently strong to require regulation and even direct state provision of goods and services to ensure equity and meet needs. The scale and depth of restructuring has negated such assumptions and forced a renegotiation of attitudes and practices among politicians, professionals and the public. In that process the experience of place has both been dramatically changed, and also become more fragmented, more commodified and more significant.

PART 3

ANALYSIS AND CONCLUSIONS: STRENGTHENING THE CHANGING ROLE OF CIVIL SOCIETY

11 RELATIONSHIPS BETWEEN THE STATE AND CIVIL SOCIETY AND THEIR IMPORTANCE FOR SUSTAINABLE DEVELOPMENT

Paul Jenkins

INTRODUCTION

The objective of this chapter is to draw on the country case studies presented in the previous eight chapters, using the analytical framework identified in Chapter 2, as a means to identify:

- the relationships between the state, market and civil society;
- the local and global context for these; and
- the institutional structure (mental models and organization).

Based on this analysis an overview of the relationships between the state and civil society is sketched in order to complement the current predominant focus on those between state and market. This leads to an investigation of the intermediary role of urban social movements and subsequently to general recommendations on the role of civil society in sustainable urban development.

The analysis will be structured round three implicit questions:

1   What are the relative roles and interests of the state, market and civil society in the countries studied, and how are these changing?
2   How do institutions (mental models and organizational forms) promote or constrain the greater legitimacy of the state and a greater responsiveness to civil society through providing spaces for negotiation?
3   How can local institutions act within a global perspective and how can global forces adjust to local needs?

OVERVIEW OF THE CASE STUDIES

Mozambique

The Mozambican situation describes a nation-state where local forms of governance have been dominated by the central state since the beginning of the colonial period – some 100 years ago – but which is now embarking on a new era. However, whether new, legally but not financially, autonomous local governments will be able to resist the pressures of the still relatively strong central government (albeit weakened from 15 years of structural adjustment) is open to question. More importantly, will local government be able to deal with the demands of global and regional market forces – which are re-entering the national and local economy – as well as be more responsive to local communities' needs? This is particularly important due to the weak level of organizational capacity within communities after decades of repression and the continuing low level of negotiation between the state and civil society, leading to a perceived level of illegitimacy of the state.

The relationship between the state and the market in Mozambique has been a stormy one over the past 25 years, changing from the colonial situation where a corporatist state intervened heavily in the national and local economy, although subordinated to regional and global market forces, to one where the central state dominated economic activity with market forces extremely limited at all levels. The failure of this attempt at economic self-reliance, due to global and regional pressures as well as the social and economic isolation of the majority of citizens from the state, was followed by a rapid restructuring of the state in parallel with an opening to market activity. The weakened state has attempted to regulate global and regional market forces vis-à-vis national economic agents, but has been limited in this due to external pressure and weak national economic response. The resulting 'wild west' market economy has grown rapidly in the last few years, but only in restricted sectors and with low labour engagement. The majority of the urban population therefore still do not have access to the formal economy and the state has not provided any real context for more adequate local economic development.

Concerning state relations with civil society, only in the past decade or so have independent vertical organizations in civil society begun to develop, and these have not focused on urban development in any significant way. Urban development has traditionally been a low priority for central government both before and after independence, and while this is of greater interest to local government, local elites dominate access to social and economic facilities, with increasing marginalization of the poor majority. International agencies have had some impact on the central state and may continue to do so at local government level, where they have latterly supported the activities of NGOs. However, the scale of these activities in relation to the impact of global and regional economic forces is very limited. Physical urban development and human resources remain highly underdeveloped in parallel with the local urban economy. The result of current trends is likely to be more inefficient and more inequitable urban areas.

Despite this general context, the fact that communities have actually managed so much of their own affairs fairly independent of the state or formal market is, perhaps, the key to a more sustainable form of urban development. To date this 'informal' urban deveopment is based on mental models and organizational forms that are generally modified from traditional rural situations. While these have served well so far in the light of relative protection from market forces, they are in danger of fragmentation in the current economic context. As such there is an urgent need to modify and strengthen the horizontal forms of civil society, at the same time as build vertical spaces for negotiation with the state, to allow both resolution of immediate urban problems as well as a more sustainable basis for future urban development in the medium term. Some of the other case studies illustrate ways in which this could be developed.

Pakistan

Pakistan represents a country with a much more established and complex form of government, with decentralization to established federal and metropolitan levels, but one where state legitimacy is equally queried by the majority of the urban population. Despite its level of establishment, the state has very poor levels of coordination, definition of powers and capacity to act. In addition, there is a very weak sense of government service and public morality, leading to high levels of corruption. This affects all areas of life including social services such as transport and productive activities such as industry, as illustrated in the two case studies.

The nature of the legal system tends to support this status quo for the benefit of the social and economic elite and the bureaucracy rather than wider society. There is a close relationship between the state and key economic agents, which exert strong political pressure given the newly industrializing status of the country. However, this relationship is not explicit and the level of accountability between the state and society is thus undermined. In this situation the state both intervenes to restrict market forces (as in transport services), and withdraws to allow market forces free reign (as in industry). The nature of this dualistic position is presumably grounded on the balance between demands of dominant market sectors and important social sectors.

The acceptance of the situation of state corruption by the majority is (as in Mozambique) underpinned by a mental model with a low level of expectation of the state within civil society. Thus, while communities at times mobilize at local level around issues such as industrial pollution, there do not seem to exist many channels for vertical negotiation with the state to make a significant impact. The intermediate role of NGOs or social companies, such as in the example of public transport in Faisalabad, may represent a way to circumvent the actual political economic reality of the current state regime. However, the unique nature of this quasi-state body, based almost entirely on an elite of non-corrupt government employees and acceptance of its almost paternal authority, militates against its replication in a wider way. In addition, it is not clear how this innovation can benefit the majority of the urban poor, and indeed the local impact of macroeconomic changes may well threaten its continuity.

Recent steps taken by the military government in Pakistan appear to offer a way to challenge this institutional status quo of self-serving government at all levels. It remains to be seen, however, if the 'accountability courts' and independent tribunals can break the deadlock. Of crucial importance here is the attitude of the population and its interest and capacity to take direct action. Thus, despite these recent changes within the state (self-imposed, though in the case of industrial pollution brought on by international regulation), it has been suggested that there is a need for international support to strengthen the role of intermediaries between the state and the community. These intermediaries could adopt NGO-type structures, for example, and their role would be to promote higher levels of perception and organization in the regulation of activities such as industry and public transport. While this may be a necessary first step in introducing new mental models, the sustainability of the approach must be based on a genuine strengthening of the role of civil society to negotiate with the state more adequately. In addition, in the present political context it does not seem likely that any state-promoted form of community self-development can have any major impact. Again other case studies illustrate models of how civil society has engaged with the state in different situations.

China

Despite its superficial similarity to Mozambique in terms of its socialist political orientation, China is less like the Mozambican case study than the previous Pakistani one. This is mainly due to the nature and level of state capacity and its dominant role in development, continuing even today despite market reforms. There has been a very long tradition of state paternalism and control in China, linked to relatively effective redistribution and state capacity at various levels, which existed long before socialism. This allowed the widespread control of production and its location, limiting urban development to 'manageable' proportions, which in turn allowed a concentration of resources in urban productive activities and social distribution of differential benefits through state-controlled economic units.

While the opening to market processes remains tightly controlled by the state, as does urban development in the formal sector, the impact of market forces has also allowed ambiguities to be exploited by a growing informal sector – for instance on the urban fringes and inner urban areas. Here the long tradition of passive acceptance of state control of production and reproduction has been bypassed by dynamic forms of socio-economic interchange based on a mix of market and traditional structures. This form of local economic engagement has proved ideal for the demand for more flexible labour, and hence is implicitly accepted by the state, which still retains control of the formal economic system. It remains to be seen, however, how the deeper penetration of global market forces will be controlled by the state and how this will affect the wider population in China, such as in widening urban–rural disparities.

Concerning relations between the state and civil society, it is unclear whether the urban village model developing in the peri-urban areas of Beijing is a transitional and isolated phenomenon, or whether it is the model for wider application in the future. State restructuring and market reform are still in fairly early stages for China in general, but already there are signs of growing social problems of wider rural–urban migration and underemployment. The revitalization and modification of traditional power structures in the urban villages can be seen as the result of weak autonomous associational structures in civil society (horizontal and vertical) due to years of repression, such as in Mozambique. However, the degree of social acceptance of the new forms of social control is unclear, as these seem to be coercive, based on powerful individuals. It will thus be of interest to see how these embryonic structures within civil society develop and how they develop relationships with the state, which is itself in a process of changing relations with the market.

Philippines

Unlike various other case studies in the book, in Manila there is a clear definition of relationships and powers between national, metropolitan, local and neighbourhood forms of governance. However, implementation in practice has its difficulties. In governance terms these are related to the nature of metropolitan authority vis-à-vis fairly autonomous local governments, as well as the stability of national government support for the neighbourhood level. In terms of urban development, another issue is the nature of the national legal system with weak regulatory powers, for example, over land use and transport planning. In general, however, the nested institutional relationships, while complex, allow negotiation by local government and communities, albeit limited, on more fundamental issues of national policy. In this respect market forces have stronger lobbying powers, especially at a local level, as their interests can fit well with the revenue-earning interests of the local state.

While recently threatened in terms of the national resource base, the neighbourhood *barangays* seem to represent a stable focal point for both community self-development and social control – reminiscent of the *Grupos Dinamizadores* in Mozambique. However, unlike in Mozambique, the barangays have a clearer institutional and legal context within which to work and access to resources and political leverage, although this is highly dependent on central and local government respectively. The *barangays* developed from traditional social structures (such as is embryonic in Chinese urban villages), but were transformed by the state as a means for low-level administration. While the case study does not elaborate on this, it would appear that in general the wider population accept the role of the *barangays* as being representative, despite their reliance on a rather elite leadership. Certainly, the space for self-development within neighbourhoods afforded by state support for *barangays* has raised levels of self-reliance and fostered direct action. The system does, however, rely on political patronage.

It is at the wider political and economic level that the mental models and organizational context for community-led development would appear to be limited in this case study, as the *barangay* system is constrained to the extent in which it can raise issues such as those affecting environmental management, land use and transport at city level, which in turn is influenced by national policy.

Here the strong influence of the mental model of individual freedom over land use has led to a weak regulatory role for the state vis-à-vis the market and individual, preferentially benefiting the higher-income groups, as in land access and transport. Thus, despite the usefulness of the model in relationships between the local and metropolitan levels of government, the degree of independent negotiation that the *barangay* system can allow is limited at national levels. Hence, while this is a useful model for structuring relations between the state and civil society, the lack of autonomy limits the extension of bargaining power to change the basic 'rules of engagement' established by the state.

Costa Rica

The state in Costa Rica displays characteristics rather more similar to those of the UK than some of the other case studies in developing and transitional economies, although its form of interaction with civil society is rather different. Costa Rica has a relatively long tradition of a highly centralized state with weak local government and few intermediate levels. Despite frequent changes of political leadership the overall regime of social democratic welfare has dominated in the last 50 years, providing a high level of stability for international and national economic activity. This, however, has been fundamentally challenged by the changes in macroeconomic structure, to a great extent induced by global economic changes, with an undermining of the social welfare approach and greater decentralization of the state promoted by market forces and international agencies.

One of the means for obtaining political economic stability in the past has been the continuing ability of the central state to dominate negotiation with civil society. Whether with trade unions, peasant movements or urban-based community organizations, and their consolidated fronts, the state has managed to co-opt these through complex systems of patronage and clientelism. The most recent manifestation of this was during the period of macroeconomic stabilization and subsequent economic restructuring, when the resulting socio-economic crises led to broad social mobilization. In this transitional period, it is probable that the social movements created had a more effective bargaining position than before or since, through the state-sponsored system of community development. In addition, despite the overall level of stability achieved, the result has, however, been growing instability in social redistribution at local level.

Generally speaking, the adoption of an official community development approach by the state to social and welfare issues has stood the state in good stead throughout the last four decades, and it has received international support and acclaim. However, it is within this context that the state is renegotiating a new approach in the face of global economic pressure, with a change from welfare based on rights to a definition of inevitable poverty which needs to be contained, and which is to be serviced through market mechanisms. In parallel, the labour market is being forced to become more flexible, with the creation of intermediate non-state structures to provide non-unionized labour protection. In this trend towards deregulated labour markets, Costa Rica is not dissimilar to more developed welfare states, including that of China.

Other means by which the state has initiated this new approach includes the promotion of greater decentralization within government and a devolved role for civil society within the new approach based on targeted state benefits. This includes new forms of state support for organizations within civil society through capacity building. However, to what extent this will create a new model of partnership between state and civil society at local level is queried as the relationship between local government and civil society has been traditionally weak. In addition, it is not clear to what extent this model can provide a channel for greater negotiation between communities and the state at a general level, as opposed to another form of co-option and channelling political opposition, especially as the role of the state vis-à-vis the market is changing so markedly. Thus, again, while the model seems to work for the relationship between the central state and civil society, it is proving less effective at local government level and has little impact at supranational level, where the stresses increasingly originate.

South Africa

Probably the most conflict-ridden situation between the state and civil society in the case study chapters is represented in South Africa. Here paternalism and control were used to socially, economically and politically segregate society on the basis of race to permit the preferential benefit for one group, which otherwise might have been subject to different class or indigenous nationalist pressures. While this process began under a relatively decentralized political system, it was highly centralized during the apartheid era, when a corporatist state structure maintained its position through ongoing negotiation with key economic agents (not unlike in Costa Rica, but within a very different social context). The result of this subjugation was widespread social exclusion and a relatively low level of engagement in the economy by the poorly skilled majority – legacies which now constrain South Africa's repositioning in the global economy.

The situation of political and economic hegemony by a state–market partnership was radically threatened through political opposition, including a very strong protest role within civil society, which was in itself based on a long tradition of community-based alternatives. These alternatives were often (as in China and Mozambique) based on traditional social structures, and were sometimes coercive. However, they permitted the development of an alternative mental model to one of relative resignation to state domination that pervades other countries such as Pakistan. The essential difference in South Africa was the alliance of these community-level actions to political opposition in broader urban social movements, as also happened in Costa Rica. As in Central America this relationship proved difficult, as it was open to co-option.

In South Africa, however, it can be argued that the level of co-option was limited before the new political dispensation, and continued so afterwards – mainly due to the fact that the urban social movement was not well consolidated. Hence there is still the opportunity to consolidate this level of activity within civil society. This is relevant due to the fact that the new state has substantially continued to implement essentially corporatist structures in the face of global economic and political forces (as well as federal opposition). There is thus growing dissatisfaction with the relative inability of the new central state to change the social and economic status quo – to a great extent due to these external pressures. However, to what extent the resources exist within civil society to do this without the support of strong vertical associations such as trade unions or opposition political parties remains to be seen. Nevertheless the model of autonomous urban social movements is strongest in this case study, with the capacity to operate from a local to national level.

United Kingdom

As a 'developed' country, it might be thought that the UK represents potentially a different analytical outcome from the other case studies. However, on the contrary, despite the contextual differences, many of the same forces are at work, with not dissimilar reactions. As in all the other case studies the forces of economic globalization have impacted heavily on the capacity of the nation-state – and eventually the local state – to control its relationship with the economy and society. Despite the vast resource differences there are thus parallels to be drawn and lessons to be learned.

The state in the UK has been increasingly centralized over the past 25 years, substituting strong local government and changing its relationships with civil society and the economy. In addition, from a position of hegemony in paternalistic control in the public interest through forms of Fordism – permitting strong management of markets and redistribution based on socially rational principles – the state has been weakened in both regulatory and redistributive power through the pressures of global market forces and political neoliberalism. Restructuring the state and market relations has led to a subsumption of the state's redistribution within the market – such as in housing allocation in the face of low demand.

While this process has created more flexible and dynamic markets, potentially providing greater individual choice, it has also created regional and class inequalities with the social and economic exclusion of large social groups from the dominant formal economy, who tend to become concentrated in certain regions and urban areas. While not repressed as such, the context for community organization around social reproductive issues was predominantly subordinated to the negotiation between the state and the market via trade unions and representative democratic institutions.

During the economic restructuring this was seen as insufficient and direct action by organized groups within civil society at community and other levels grew in importance. However, with the fragmentation of communities (both geographic and communities of interest) through the commodification of housing, the impact of this movement has been muted, although apparent. The ensuing social and economic exclusion has recently been taken up again by government as it represents a growing political issue. Whether the new approaches promoted by the state to reduce exclusion can change the structural context or not is open to question, and these can be seen as attempts by the state to co-opt or head off political opposition, as in Costa Rica. However, there is the possibility that civil society can develop its own momentum within this context, as happened in Costa Rica and South Africa in transitional periods – and has in fact happened on other broad social issues worldwide, as elaborated on below.

General observations from the case studies

There are very marked differences in the case studies of the relationships between the state, market and civil society, reflecting historic development, the actual political economy, and the institutional capacities within each sector. In general, however, the move to a weakening of the role of the state is evident, with a growth of market dominance in many sectors. In parallel there are changes in civil society which affect communities, often expressed as a growing individualism, which is more frequently constraining than supportive of relationships between the state and civil society. To a great extent this is seen as due to the globalization of market forces, with the result that communities are prone to additional stresses and fragmentation.

Concerning the relations between the state and civil society, three main situations are illustrated in the case studies:

1   Limited community relationships with the state (Mozambique, Pakistan and China).
2   Community action in urban development promoted by the state (Costa Rica, Philippines, at times South Africa, and latterly UK).
3   Independent community action negotiating with the state (South Africa and at times Costa Rica).

Despite the trend for economic forces to threaten community cohesion, there is, on the other hand, a wide range of organizational forms within civil society which challenge this, although these are not often consolidated beyond the local or intermediate level. This is partly due to the prevailing mental models whereby many communities and organizations within civil society withdraw from negotiating with the state, as this negotiation does not in itself produce results since the state is itself increasingly constrained by global forces beyond its control. It is noticeable that in various circumstances it is the traditional vertical power structure within civil society which has been the basis for community-level activity, as, for example, in China, the Philippines and at times South Africa. In contrast in Mozambique it is modified forms of traditional horizontal structures which dominate, while in Pakistan, Costa Rica, the more recent period in South Africa and the UK there seems to be a reliance on formal (modern, vertical) political structures.

The attributes of the models developed for negotiation between state and civil society in the case studies can be summarized as is shown in Table 11.1.

The most effective proactive models would appear to be those where the state invests in community development, such as in the Philippines and Costa Rica; however, there are distinct limits to the wider effectiveness of these as

Table 11.1 *Attributes of negotiation between state and civil society in the case studies*

	Traditional horizontal structures	*Traditional vertical structures*	*Modern vertical structures*
Weak relationship	**Mozambique** Adapted kinship structures survive in the urban areas after traditional vertical structures of governance used in the colonial period were substituted by state-sponsored neighbourhood level organizations, which were then discontinued during the retraction of state activities associated with structural adjustment	**China** Traditional village-based governance structures reactivated in new role in urban setting, outside of state control, but providing form of socio-economic organization as well as political basis for (limited) negotiation with the state. The 'strongman' leadership, however, seems to act in coercive ways	**Pakistan; UK** Representative democratic systems of local government, supported or paralleled by trade unions (in the UK) provide the only route for communities to engage with the state. However, these are open to marginalization (UK) and corruption (Pakistan), and are seen by many as being ineffective
State-induced relationship		**Philippines; pre-transition South Africa** Traditional governance structures deliberately reactivated in urban setting in Philippines as basis for local-level organization, subordinated and linked into local government systems. In South Africa, local 'warlords' provide protection from the state in squatter areas and later negotiate with the state vis-à-vis urban consolidation, albeit in a coercive manner	**Costa Rica; recent UK** The welfare state approach changes in the current period of 'slimmed down' government to promote activity within civil society organizations as an alternative to state and market supply of services. However this can imply a relinquishing of state responsibility for lower-income, less politically influential citizens
Independent relationship			**Transitional periods Costa Rica; South Africa** Independent urban social movements developed before and during periods of political transition, playing an important political role alongside other forms of vertical structures within civil society (eg political opposition and organized labour). However, these were generally co-opted by the state or opposition parties prior to changes in the political basis and were not consolidated thereafter

the state negotiates with other interest groups (increasingly including international capital). In these situations at times more autonomous models have arisen, such as the urban social movements in Costa Rica and South Africa. Given the trends of economic globalization outlined above, withdrawal of the state, and the tendency to fragmentation within civil society, the capacity for organizations within civil society to organize and create mutually beneficial relationships with the state and economic forces is growing more important. So too is the capacity to take this one step further to permit independent negotiation where mutual benefit is not identified.

Relating this to the wider political economic context, today's governments cannot ignore the needs of significant parts of the urban population in any sustainable future, even if this is what the dictates of a global market economy require. As such, in situations where inadequate means or levels of negotiation between civil society and the state occur, independent social movements will continue to rise from community direct action, and demand negotiation with the state on social issues such as urban development. However, the fact that negotiation on these issues cannot necessarily be resolved within nation–states in the current global economic context, highlights the need for the creation of mechanisms to transcend national borders. Social movements can also, however, transcend these boundaries, as has happened for global issues such as women's liberation, civil rights and environmental movements. The next part of this chapter therefore looks at these 'new social movements' and what can be learnt from them in creating a more sustainable urban future.

THE ROLE OF NEW SOCIAL MOVEMENTS IN SUSTAINABLE URBAN DEVELOPMENT

What are new social movements?

In many cities across the world local-level interest groups unite to improve their physical environment. When community-based organizations organize in broad-based associations they can form a social movement which has influence far beyond that of the individual organizations. However, defining what constitutes an 'urban social movement' is not so easy, as aims and consciousness, as well as scales and methods of operation, can all be combined in various ways in different political, economic, social and cultural contexts.

Manuel Castells defines urban social movements as social entities working collectively to attain the following goals: raising the standard of collective consumption, furthering community culture and reaching for political self-management, thereby changing 'urban meaning' or mental models. By influencing the conception of 'urban meaning', urban social movements can bring about fundamental structural social change (Castells, 1983). Examples of major urban social movements across the world given by Castells include peace and civil rights movements, women's liberation, ecological groups and regional separatist movements. These essentially cut across class lines and work with high levels of autonomy from the state and have at times achieved significant global impact.

These social movements are generally labelled as new – why is this? Part of the definition of 'new' social movements has been the distinction of these from 'traditional' social movements, such as organized labour and peasant movements. These latter draw on wide constituencies, but essentially develop conflict along the lines of social class. New social movements, however, encompass protest across social classes, lobbying and pressurizing government agencies over development and social issues, and tend to be organized on an ad hoc basis (Saschikonye, 1995). In other words, while the objective of the former – perhaps more aptly called 'political' movements – is the capture of state power, the latter are issue-based and often content to influence policy, or resolve specific circumstances. The recent growth of new social movements is thus seen as being linked to failures (and perceived failures) of state regimes to reflect the demands of wide constituencies, and hence often tend to be developed as alternatives to the existing political process.

To what extent are these social movements truly global? Schuurman (1989) argues that in the developing world the role of the state and the objectives of urban social movements vis-à-vis the state concerning collective consumption are qualitatively as well as quantitatively different from those in the post-industrial developed world, and this needs to be reflected in the definition of the term. He proposes a wider definition of an urban social movement, with particular reference to the developing world, as a social organization with a territorially based identity, which strives for emancipation by way of collective action – emancipation being seen as 'liberation from hierarchical dependency relations... [these being those] in which the power structure is such that one of the actors has a dominant role and extracts more value from the interaction than the other actor(s), which leads to marginalization processes' (Schuurman, 1989).[1] This definition thus does not insist on societal reform as an aim, as does that of Castells, but does not exclude this. However, as McCarney (1996) indicates, urban social movements in the developing world increasingly aspire to change policy as well as local circumstances.

Urban social movements in the developing world thus tend to be formed round basic issues of survival and struggles to gain access to the basics of collective consumption, and less around broader issues such as state power and the basic underlying economic structures.[2] The capacity of these movements to effect fundamental change is thus questioned by those who see this as the prerogative of the state. As we have seen in the Costa Rica and South Africa case studies, the dilemma for many social movements is whether to become involved in the institutionalized political process and remain key agents of transformation within this, or assert autonomy and pressure from without – which may permit under-represented sections of society a voice not possible within the political process, but may not effect fundamental change.

Referring to the developed world, Canel (1997) indicates that new social movement theorists explain the emergence of these movements in a context of structural transformations and significant cultural and political change related to late capitalism.[3] There have been two basic approaches within this theoretical context. One approach stresses that the changing role of the state in the context of late capitalism has become contradictory as it attempts to ensure both the continuation of the conditions for capital accumulation and, at the same time, political hegemony and legitimacy while widening the scope of democratic governance. The state thus broadens its role in both economic and social regulation, but in the process becomes a central source of inequality and power differentials. In this context the inability of formal political parties and trade unions, for example, to articulate multiple demands of widening numbers of interest groups leads to the emergence of new collective actors. New social movements are thus seen as broadening political articulation by social agents, while maintaining relative autonomy from the political system *per se*.

The other main approach focuses on the crisis of 'meaning' that the increasing 'intrusion' of the state and market into society has created, with new social movements being seen as defending lifestyles. This stresses the cultural orientations of social relations – that is the set of cultural models which guide social practice – with hegemony over these being contested and negotiated by different social groups. In this analysis, conflict in post-industrial societies focuses on the production of 'meaning' – as opposed to the means of production (industry-based societies) or civil and political rights (commerce-based societies). The transformation to the post-industrial context has brought new roles for the state – for example, the bureaucratization and massification of social life – and the establishment of mass culture. New social movements thus focus on collective control over the redefinition of social roles and consumption – for example, around issues such as gender, ethnicity, age, neighbourhood, environment and peace. In this view, social movements are not seen as essentially based on economic issues, but rather on ideological, cultural and political issues. Changes in societal type in this approach are thus seen as taking place within the political system, with a central role for the state, in contrast to the former approach (Canel, 1997).

What can be the role of new social movements in sustainable urban development?

Summarizing, in broad terms we can distinguish the general consciousness and aims of new social movements as:

- raising standards of collective consumption;
- furthering community culture, changing 'meaning' and definition of social roles; and
- effecting societal change through new socio-political agents, representing a wider range of interest groups, without necessarily participating in the formal political system;

with the proviso that in the developing world their actions may be more issue based, oriented to resolving ad hoc circumstances with possible intentions to influence policy, rather than focused on societal change *per se*. However, if the aims of the social movement correspond closely to more general aims of improving collective consumption, there is a strong likelihood of it becoming co-opted by a class-based political movement (such as organized labour or political parties), or it may be co-opted by the state itself.

The case studies identified constraints on relations between civil society and the state in challenging the actions of nation-states when co-opted by the state, and the difficulties in widening the impact of urban social movements autonomously from the state or established political agents. It also identified the problems associated with the local, or national, focus for action of these movements. What permits a movement to transcend these boundaries and achieve a broader impact? This is partly the organizational structure which can be created, which is essentially locally based but 'networked', as opposed to any hierarchical system, but is also the definition of meaning and mental models.

Concerning organizational constraints, a critical factor in determining the potential for urban social movements has been identified as the resources it can mobilize – funds, human resources, facilities (eg offices, equipment) and legitimacy.[4] In fact, as noted by Sachikonye (1995), the growth of some social movements is tied to state resources such as public sector investment in tertiary education which increases the number of intelligentsia, or capital investment growth which increases formal employment and permits wider unionization.[5] At times, mobilizing basic resources can become the dominant aim of the movement to even survive. This, however, does not mean that urban social movements cannot emerge in resource-starved environments; on the contrary, in these situations human resources can at times be mobilized much more successfully due to higher degrees of legitimacy within these movements compared to the state.

Perhaps the most important issue in the growth of wider organizational forms within civil society is the form of collective 'consciousness' – or the mental models – that shape perceptions and record experience. An urban social movement generally arises from activities across a wide number of territorially-based organizations which have some form of collective feature, thus permitting a collective consciousness to be created. However, as the urban social movement begins to confront its opponents – often the state – there comes a crucial period when it has to operate in non-territorially defined ways. It is at this point that many urban social movements in the developing world fail in making a wider impact, either because they do not mobilize sufficient resources to transcend the local space; they do not maintain adequate legitimacy as they do this, or they become co-opted by other institutions. Despite these difficulties, when large numbers of the population of a community, town, region, state, or even at a global level, begin to conceive of common needs, truly powerful changes can occur, as can be seen concerning the civil rights, environmental, gender and regional separatist issues mentioned above.

In general there would appear to be considerable scope for social movements to develop in the realm of urban development. As we have seen above, the relative withdrawal of the state and 'marketization' of many factors of urban development has led to fragmentation of community capacity, but also increased the need, and space for operation of this. Key to developing beyond the isolated community-level activity is the establishment of mental models which stimulate collective action, and the strengthening of organizational forms. A crucial aspect here is access to resources. To achieve this may mean an incipient social movement allying itself with the state, or with other stronger more 'traditional' structures, such as opposition political parties, trade unions and the church. In this the social movements run the risk of being submerged or co-opted and not being able to negotiate fundamental issues which may be beyond the scope of the nation-state anyway.

On the other hand, in recent times effective global social movements based on strong mental models in dealing with social and cultural issues have developed and had a significant impact. Perhaps what is needed is to learn something from these global movements about their development and operation, and to apply this to the urban development sector. In as much as sustainability has been a mental model championed within this context, the social organizational base for sustainable urban development would appear to have the cultural basis partially in place. Clearer understanding of the pros and cons of the relationship of urban social movements to other institutions, especially the state, is an essential part of this.

This section has focused on the relationships between the state and civil society, which is a dominant theme of this book. As noted in a wider overview of urban research undertaken across the major regions of the world (McCarney et al in Stren, 1995), this relationship is the basis for new forms of 'governance', which is perhaps the most important issue in sustainable urban development. The dominant message is that new forms of governance through new relationships between the state and civil society need to be formed to permit more sustainable urban futures. These will evolve and be negotiated in different ways in different places. In addition, the strengthening of organizational forms within civil society will permit stronger links and negotiation between economic forces – predominantly market oriented – and civil society, and through these two linkages, civil society can condition the links between the state and the market, as illustrated in Figure 11.1.

CONCLUSIONS

This chapter set out to examine the relationships between the state, the market and civil society and what form of institutions (mental models and organizations) operated in the case studies. In this it has focused more specifically on the nexus between the state and civil society, and has reinforced this with a short review of the potential for new social movements to contribute to sustainable urban development – whether autonomously or in cooperation with the state and economic forces. The third main theme of the chapter is the relationship between local and global, and here again the potential for social movements to transcend the local to the national level – and beyond to have global influence – has been discussed.

It is argued that there is a need for new relationships between the state, the market and civil society at the international, or global, level, as well as at the local and national level. The globalization of market forces requires this. As

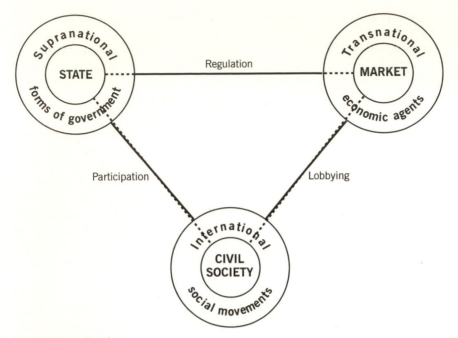

Source: Harry Smith

Figure 11.1 *Links between state, market and civil society*

noted in Chapter 2, we are living in a period where the economy (driven increasingly by global market forces) is not regulated adequately by the state or social forces, and is creating widespread social and political imbalances across the world. As noted by Karl Polanyi many years ago, the economy needs to be embedded in, and controlled by, society, or else severe disequilibria are created, such as has happened in the past at times of rapid social, political and economic change.[6] Rather than the market creating equilibrium, it is society and its organizations which do – and the state is essentially meant to be a socially representative organism. The fact that the state (or specific groups who dominate state power, including the state bureaucracies) often does not adequately represent the wider society is evidenced in the need for wider forms of governance and broader relations between the state and civil society that has been stressed above.

Hence there is a need for a reconstitution of socially responsive state power to counteract that which is essentially subordinating itself to the new global market forces. This cannot take place within one nation-state – or arguably even within any macro-regional power bloc – but requires a broader acceptance. The model for such supranational governance of the past half century – the UN and its various related organizations – has never developed this role effectively as it is hamstrung by the actions of individual nations', whether economic or by political veto. These organizations essentially reflect the realpolitik of the immediate post-Second World War period, which is demonstrably outdated in today's fast changing economic and political context.

How could some broader form of supranational state power develop? There would appear to be three options: it could be promoted by existing nation-states, or power blocs of these; by transnational economic agents; or by international social institutions. The first option is indeed on the agenda, as noted in Chapter 2, but it is difficult to see nation-states – which have managed to squabble over supranational regulation so effectively for the past 50 years – resolving this themselves. The second option is also on the agenda, as, although resistant to global economic controls, transnational economic agents do encounter the difficulties of operating across such wide political and social disparities, and potentially can gain from more stability. That they will act as promoters of broad social equity is, however, not likely without regulation. Lastly, new social movements have already shown their potential in changing mental models, institutions and actions of economic and state actors, although there are many areas where their efforts have not been successful as yet.

In conclusion, it is suggested that a combination of the three main forces reviewed above is needed to create new forms of socially relevant urban development across the world, benefiting from new economic opportunities and not resisting these *per se*. While the slow movement to macro-regional power blocs is perhaps a step in the right direction, as is the negotiation between these and transnational economic agents, there is also a need for counterpart movements within civil society, at macro-regional and international level, to build on (and support) urban social movements which develop at local and national level. In this way local institutions can more effectively begin to act within a global perspective, as well as ensuring that global forces begin to take on board local needs. Only when appropriate mental models and organizational forms within civil society at all levels are created and strengthened will it be possible to be more positive of creating a sustainable urban future across the globe.

12 CIVIL SOCIETY AND NEW SOCIAL MOVEMENTS

Michael Carley and Harry Smith

This book has highlighted the importance of innovation in urban management at the local level, and demonstrated the important role civil society can, and must, play in urban development, globally and locally. At the outset, the importance of urban management to nothing less than the future of the planet was stressed – given that, by the middle of this century, almost three quarters of the world's population will live in cities.

Major challenges to urban management were considered including population growth, urban poverty and poor living conditions, land take-up and urban sprawl, traffic congestion, pollution and the need for ecologically benign ways of living. It is also clear that, at the beginning of the 21st century, democracy and capitalism face many destabilizing influences, both from competing political systems and capitalism's built-in contradictions – ecological, social, economic and cultural. The old Right–Left ideological conflicts of the 20th century have largely receded but old tensions still exist and new ones have surfaced, inherent in:

- competing aspirations for both material advancement based on excessive, inefficient resource consumption and pollution, and fuelled by the spread of consumerist lifestyles, and wider environmental well-being through the century;
- inequality between North and South and rich and poor internationally, and within countries and city-regions;
- the failure of the economic agenda of trade and capital liberalization, and privatization of enterprise, to grapple with the social dislocations inherent in the workings of the market economy; and
- the inability of political and market systems to take a long-term view of human prospects.

Looking optimistically, the main hope for achieving a new pattern of genuinely sustainable development in the 21st century is recognition that while there must be limits on processes of unmanaged economic growth, there are no constraints on the creative powers of human beings to achieve quality of life within these limits. The mobilization of human creativity is the real task of sustainable development. As human society has evolved in the face of major environmental, economic and technological changes in the past so it will continue to do so. The crucial question is, how are human societies constituted today and how do they achieve the new balance in the face of changes such as globalization, information technology and genetic modification technologies?

CIVIL SOCIETY AND SOCIAL DECISION MAKING

This book has argued that, from an institutional perspective, the resolution of these challenges could not come about without two factors: higher levels of what was called horizontal and vertical integration of policy and practice, and enhanced democratic participation. Such improved integration is the key to sustainable development in the city-region of the 21st century: integration between economic vitality and quality of life; between the needs of the local and the global; between long-term sustainability and short-term politics; between bottom-up, local innovation and top-down, national urban policy; and in terms of genuine integration of key players in political decision making, including local communities. As this book has stressed, integration is especially important between sectors: state/government, market/business/economy, and civil society/community/households; and between spatial levels of action: neighbourhood or village, city, urban region, national and international.

A recurrent theme running through the book argues that civil society, through democratic participation, should be brought much more fully into the processes of decision making and urban management. Without this, sustainable development will not be achieved, despite all the rhetoric in general support of the concept. As stated in Chapter 1, the definition of sustainable development stresses that it is a political process of mediation between economic, social and environment objectives, and between the objectives of government, business and civil society. Mediation implies an equality of bargaining power, and the institutionalization of roles of the three sectors. Building essential linkages between sectors and spatial levels of action has been described as action networking and is discussed below.

Chapter 2 developed an analytical framework for understanding the institutional basis for a more active role for civil society in relation to the state and the market, and for explicitly distinguishing between the various interests of state, market and civil society. Institutions were then defined as both the organizational forms and the mental models that underpin the structure of society, economics and politics. The former include organizations that foster negotiation and mediation in vertical relationships, such as the relationship of lobby groups, trade unions or NGOs to government and business; and those that foster mainly horizontal linkage, such as religious organizations and kinship systems.

Mental models, on the other hand, are based on sets of mainly socially determined values and preconceptions, for example, about property rights, the role of public interest in social decision making and the nature of representative democracy or the welfare state. These models have substantial influence on the shape and functioning of both physical and social aspects of urban systems. An important point is that mental models may vary from North to South, from country to country – even of a similar level of economic prosperity – and between rich and poor in any society. However, prosperous sectors of different societies may increasingly share a common, consumerist mental model, which views action by government as relevant only insofar as it supports market operation to benefit individual consumers as opposed to the long-term interests of society as a whole. Globalization and international marketing efforts attempt to foster the harmonization of mental models, to create a more uniform set of consumer aspirations. However, this trend also faces resistance from many organizations in civil society, including NGOs and religious groups.

FROM THE LOCAL TO THE GLOBAL

Finally, with regard to many civil society initiatives, the importance of local action within a global context was stressed. This must be the main route to shifting political action in civil society from the current condition of mainly isolated, local initiatives, easily ignored by the power structure and vulnerable to manipulation and co-option, toward the idea of what were defined as new social movements. The ultimate objective of these many diverse movements must be to embed civil society in governance systems worldwide, as proposed in the previous chapter. Governance was defined as government working in partnership with business and civil society. The first step of this process, from a community point of view, is often for government to assist with providing resources for community capacity building and community development.

The case studies in Costa Rica, the Philippines and Faisalabad in Pakistan, although not without limitations, are examples of state investment in community development. These represent a form of institutionalization where civil society and the state have addressed development jointly, though not necessarily on equal terms. Institutionalization can lead to a degree of local empowerment, that is, devolution of authority over local planning, assessment of service quality and some financial resources from 'city hall' to local areas. This is quite different from participation that is intended to create an appearance of empowerment, without actually doing so.

This is not to argue that community groups, or NGOs, need always look for cooperation with the state, but that independent action becomes more sustainable if processes of community governance are institutionalized within the operation of the state. As the last chapter noted, many urban social movements can well face a dilemma of whether to cooperate with the state, at the risk of being co-opted by it, or to retain autonomy, but at the risk of being ineffectual in the face of the entrenched power structure. There is no right or easy answer except to note that for organizations in civil society, multiple development strategies are likely to be more robust than a single strategy, however straightforward that may appear.

NEW MENTAL MODELS

Embedding civil society in governance is important as mental models of the role of government in society have shifted in the 1990s towards individualism, consumerism and governmental restraint or withdrawal in areas of intervention seen to be more efficiently carried out by market mechanisms. However, as Carley and Christie (2000) note, markets may be necessary, but they are hardly sufficient for quality of life in a modern society, which requires an element of community life to offset the growing and debilitating effects of mass consumerism in developed societies.

In this context, community is not only defined as locally based, but also as coalitions of interest groups, which can operate at all levels from the local to the global. These interest groups can use new technology to foster their own development and to engage in action networking around the world, to create both organizations and new mental models. A fundamental task for these new mental models is to be able to critique the prevailing economic dogma, while recognizing the many advantages of market mechanisms and the powerful, and reasonable, consumer aspirations of the vast majority of the world's population.

New organizations and new mental models can come together in new social movements. As argued in Chapter 2 the overall objective of these is for society to guide the activity of the state, and for the market to be held socially accountable. This objective, so simply stated, suggests a substantial global project for the 21st century. This book does not pretend to have all, or even any answers, but in conclusion it is suggested that there are two tasks that need to be taken forward in the coming decade if this overall objective is to have a chance of achievement. These are embedding local action in city governance, and thus, indirectly, in national and international governance; and using action networks to build new social movements.

BOTTOM-UP INNOVATION AND LOCAL GOVERNANCE – LESSONS FROM UK EXPERIENCE

This book has stressed that sustainable development is about empowerment – experience the world over tells us that unless people participate on an institutional basis in shaping solutions to the challenges of development they are not committed to them. To achieve empowerment, it is necessary to overcome what is often called democratic deficit, which describes citizens' alienation from decision processes and the resultant cynicism about governance and democracy. Practically, this requires that government must begin to share responsibility and power over city-planning processes and urban service delivery functions with the residents of the neighbourhoods of the city. To achieve this, one option is reform of local planning systems for integration of town planning and Agenda 21 concerns at the neighbourhood level.

There is a temporal dimension to this empowerment, which means moving from the short-term to the long-term involvement of citizens in governance.

Recurrent failure to achieve sustainable urban development derives in part from a mistaken assumption in policy processes that deep-seated urban problems can be resolved by temporary or 'catalyst' initiatives. Such temporary initiatives may be useful to focus resources and energies, but they are seldom sufficient. Residents are less interested in temporary palliatives or one-off opportunities for participation that do not lead to a tangible outcome, and more concerned to achieve better management and maintenance of their houses and environment, for all time (Carley, 1999).

Indeed, the energies that go into temporary initiatives can divert attention from a real need for innovation and to make steady, incremental improvements in mainstream policies and practices in local government, as well as to institutionalize the role of community in that process. In this sense, community capacity building becomes a fundamental task of urban development, which itself implies steady improvements in quality of life on issues affecting all neighbourhoods and at the city level, for example, in the provision of high-quality public transport and reductions in air pollution. Community development is essentially management, participation and investments that result in steady and long-lasting improvements in the economic, social and environmental prospects for residents and their neighbourhoods, which are democratically determined, accord with residents' needs and aspirations, and which are also likely to benefit their children and grandchildren.

To overcome democratic deficit, we need to think beyond existing mechanisms of decentralization, to what really needs to happen to allow continuity in sustainable urban development. Looking at the case of the UK, the authors think neighbourhoods need to be put back on the map, which will be a challenge to the typical organizational culture of local government. Decentralization of power to local residents will only really work when it is not temporary or a special case, but when it is a uniform policy throughout the local authority, to rich and poor neighbourhoods alike, so that a 'culture of decentralization' takes hold.

Over the 'long haul' required for sustainable urban development, a reformed local planning process could provide a major opportunity to integrate traditional planning with area regeneration and Agenda 21 requirements. This could be done in a way that would meet local aspirations and provide residents with an opportunity for regular participation in shaping the future of their community. Plans that they had a hand in preparing would be more comprehensible, and there would be more commitment to implementation. Rather than residents needing to relate to one agency in the power structure after another, in a kind of wearying journey from housing to environmental services to transport to planning and so on, the local planning process could serve as a 'one-stop' focus point for integrated, future action. The case of the *barangays* in Metro Manila provides a good example of how this process could begin, and the *barangays* themselves will hopefully develop their functions and competences in future.

Democratized local planning could provide the opportunity for people to be regularly involved in a whole variety of issues such as housing condition reviews, environmental assessments of the neighbourhood and environmental improvement schemes; designation of sites for new-build housing and for business and industry; development of local parks, play areas and recreation facilities; promotion of the vitality of local shops; consideration of transport proposals for bus routing, pedestrians, cyclists, cars and any other relevant matter of local concern.

In this way, local vision could be built into development planning. Local people would participate in a process of mutual learning with planners about the future, the role of their neighbourhood in the city-region, and the planning process itself. Statutory requirements, where they exist, need not suffer, and plans and planners might even become more popular. It is worth noting that participation rates in local planning processes are in the order of 5 per cent of the population in the UK, compared with up to 70 per cent in other northern European countries, indicating the scope for additional involvement even in a country with a sophisticated, albeit non-participatory, planning system. This new model of local, communicative planning in the UK context requires what has been described as a 'new professionalism' on the part of planners – 'on tap rather than on top'.

This participatory notion of planning implies that local people have the opportunity to become involved from the beginning in development objectives for the neighbourhood, rather than being presented with a professional *fait accompli* laden with technical terms, as is now the case. Where area regeneration was required, these objectives would be embedded in the statutory plan, and reviewed periodically for their achievement. Statutory recognition can also help to 'bend' main programmes in local government toward the achievement of local development and Agenda 21 objectives.

As some of the preceding chapters illustrate, this strengthening of local government and the institutionalization of local community cooperation in planning is limited in scope in certain contexts, and difficult to achieve in others, due to different degrees of centralization and to the weaknesses of local government and civil society. Bottom-up innovation is more likely in these cases to be achievable directly through new forms of organization in civil society. In any case, in both the developed and developing worlds, a strengthening of local communities' involvement in planning and developing their own neighbourhoods requires the use of appropriate methods and techniques.

PARTICIPATORY PLANNING TECHNIQUES

Many approaches and techniques have been developed during the second half of the 20th century, both in the developed and developing worlds, that can be drawn on to achieve this continuing involvement of local communities from the beginning.

In the developed world, the backlash against post-war comprehensive redevelopments and top-down mass housing projects led to reappraisals of planning systems in the UK and US, and to the adoption of reforms to the system as well as alternative approaches. These gave rise to approaches such as advocacy planning, community-focused agencies such as Planning Aid, attempts to bring the planning process closer to the neighbourhood through community design centres, and specific tools for participatory goal setting and prioritization such as Planning for Real. After a period of great activity during the 1960s and 1970s, the evolution of participatory approaches in the developed world slowed down during the more market-centred 1980s, but in the 1990s these approaches began to come to the fore again (Rydin, 1999).

Participatory methods and techniques have also evolved in various fields in the developing world, and lessons learnt there are now feeding into approaches in developed countries. The need for the poor to question the reasons for their plight and to gain an understanding of the factors that have to be addressed, that is to achieve *concientização* (conscientization), was advocated by Freire in Brazil in the 1960s and 1970s, thus stressing the importance of education and mobilization for full participation in development (Freire, 1972 and 1974). Another source of participatory approaches was in agro-ecological research, where the recognition of the value of local knowledge led to the development of rapid appraisal techniques – initially in rural areas and eventually also in urban areas – which later became participatory appraisal techniques (Chambers, 1994). In addition, participation has been a keystone of many community development and self-help housing programmes and projects in the developing world, under both international agencies and government agencies, with an increasing stress on participation not only in information gathering and through labour inputs, but also through community self-management and participation in decision making (Mitlin and Thompson, 1995).

New tools for community participation are constantly being developed, and there is currently a wide-ranging toolbox from which the most appropriate can be chosen. Recent useful compilations of participatory tools are Hamdi and Goethert (1997), Srinivasan (1990), Wates (2000) and Wilcox (1994). These tools range from inexpensive activities such as informal walks to costly ones such as information technology (IT)-based community profiling; from information gathering activities such as interactive displays to decision-making forums; and from one-off events such as exhibitions to ongoing networking.

Indeed, a crucial aspect of these participatory activities is whether they form part of a more continuous process or are simply one-off exercises. Occasional activities such as activity weeks or community workshops can be worthwhile means for community participation, but it is through continuous activities that participation can become inbuilt into planning and development, permitting fuller engagement of civil society in these processes. Design assistance teams and neighbourhood planning offices are two examples of such continuous activities. However, over and above these, it is increasingly apparent that an overarching process of networking is essential to promote and achieve participation.

It is also important that participatory activities and capacity building are a complement to, but not a substitute for, the empowerment of local communities through the institutionalization of their role in urban governance. This requires genuine devolution of authority to local communities. In the UK, for example, there is a move towards what is called 'neighbourhood management' within the context of a national community planning initiative and a national strategy for neighbourhood renewal (Cabinet Office, 2000). Neighbourhood management, if it is to be effective politically and socially, must involve devolution of control over planning of the neighbourhood, quality of service delivery from senior levels of government and, in some cases, direct management of public resources.

ACTION NETWORKS AND NEW SOCIAL MOVEMENTS

The neighbourhood movement in the UK may or may not succeed in altering what has been traditionally a top-down political culture and structure of government, which exists not only nationally but also in terms of the relationship of local city governments to the communities they serve (Carley et al, 2000). One problem is that while some neighbourhoods are self-organized internally, there is little in the way of a network of neighbourhoods to push their role in the national political arena. Even at the city level, there is often little linkage of one neighbourhood to another, despite many common interests. What is needed at all levels, from local to global, is networking.

The role of networks in successful urban development has been noted in the literature on self-help housing in the developing world (Turner and Fitcher, 1972; Turner, 1996), in relation to planning in the UK context (Healey, 1979, 1997), and in regime theory (Stoker, 1995). From different viewpoints and across different disciplines, there is substantial agreement on the positive effect the existence of networks has on the outcome of housing projects at any scale, planning strategies and the coordination of social action.

In this vein, a vital innovation, flagged up in Chapter 1, is the development of action networks. These are flexible, non-hierarchical, democratic and consensus-seeking partnerships between different interests, spanning sectors, localities, regions, whole countries and even the globe. In the face of dynamic, complex, interconnected problems, action networks foster flexible, experimental organizations spanning communities and scientific disciplines, bridging policy compartments and social sectors. These organizational forms are capable of rapid learning, using all available knowledge – including local or indigenous skills and knowledge, not just those deemed expert or scientific.

Action networks are based on the ideal of equal partnership between government, business and civil society, and foster consensus and increased levels of trust between them in attempting to address major conflicts of interest between environmental, economic and social goals. They work within flexible initiatives, with a continual process of problem specification, action, feedback and revision of policy (Carley and Christie, 2000).

Global action networks are engaging in campaigning, in mutual learning and multidisciplinary research, and in experiments in voluntary self-regulation. They can be seen as efforts to 'civilize' globalization processes, develop patterns of sustainable urban management and more transparent governance of the international economy. Some examples of these diverse networks are the Society for Promotion of Area Resources (SPARC) in India; the work of

Homeless International around the world; Jubilee 2000, the campaign for the cancellation of international debt; and the parallel NGO summits at recent major international conferences such as Habitat II at Istanbul in 1996.[1]

The action network could become a still stronger element in the process of strengthening the role of civil society and local action in governance directly through political action and indirectly through awareness raising, consensus building and mutual learning between communities and countries. For this to happen governments and the business sector are required to enable more direct forms of participatory democracy, which will clearly be an uphill struggle. Only action networking between communities engaged in self-development, and in alliance with other organizations in civil society, including campaigning and development NGOs, churches and trade unions, could generate the necessary social movements to allow this important shift in the institutions of governance, and the mental models implied. The concept of community, and its realization, also provides a platform for the development of self-awareness, and social awareness, of the limitations of individualistic consumerism as a principle for the organization of society.

Empowerment could well begin in the neighbourhood, addressing local development issues, which is the appropriate level of concern for many people. The aggregation of neighbourhood action toward sustainability will in turn give rise to sustainable cities, and these to sustainable city-regions, and so on. Neighbourhood action will also clearly suggest where city and national policies and practices conflict with sustainability principles and ought therefore to be altered.

The empowerment of civil society through action networks can support the blossoming of the required new social movements, as these networks can provide the necessary links between community level initiatives. As noted in the previous chapter, social movements often emerge around resource mobilization, but can also require access to resources in order to flourish. In this sense, action networks do not only provide access to these but also, in so doing, are themselves a vital resource. Thus action networks can play a similar and complementary role in the promotion and support of new social movements to that played by trade unions, political parties, universities and the church in the past.

Another crucial element in initiating these new social movements is the shifting of mental models. In this respect, it is hoped that this book will have contributed to the understanding of the current and potential roles of civil society in sustainable urban development and to the questioning of existing mental models and the suggestion of new ones. These need to underpin a process of urban development more firmly anchored in the needs and aspirations of civil society, in which research and practice directly support community self-development around the world.

NOTES

PREFACE

1   CEHS is the international part of the School of Planning and Housing within Edinburgh College of Art/Heriot-Watt University. It is one of a small number of UK-based higher educational institutions specializing in planning and housing issues in the developing and rapidly urbanizing world. The School of Planning & Housing, as well as offering planning and housing degrees at undergraduate and postgraduate level, is also an important centre for research, both academic and funded. The areas of specialism within the School are planning, housing, urban regeneration, and international planning and housing, each of which have research and teaching teams which link recent research and teaching, to the mutual benefit of both. This book is based on participation within the International Research and Teaching Team, and draws primarily on research of staff and students within CEHS.

CHAPTER 2

1   Key proponents of NIE built on the pioneering work of Ronald Coase's study *The Nature of the Firm* (1937) and *The Problem of Social Cost* (1960). Douglass C North, in particular, widened the scope of this analysis through his *Structure and Change in Economic History* (1981) and *Institutional Change and Economic Performance* (1990). Robert Bates stresses the political aspect of the new institutionalism in *Markets and States in Tropical Africa* (1981); *Essays on the Political Economy of Tropical Africa* (1987) and *Beyond the Miracle of the Market* (1989). The latter two writers have been (indirectly) very influential in the development policy of the World Bank – see *World Development Reports 1986, 1987, 1991, 1994* (as noted in Leys, 1996). NIE is seen as 'new' in that it is different from an 'older' form of institutionalism in economics represented by the approach that pointed to the dichotomy between business and industry and between the institutional and technical aspects of an economy – ie societal reactions to, and constraints on, innovation and new technology.

2   NIE retains the assumption of scarcity, and hence competition, that underpinned the neoclassical theoretical axiom of choice, but rejects the assumption that the market represents the impersonal exchange of goods by means of voluntary transactions on an equal basis between large numbers of autonomous, fully informed entities with profit-maximizing motivations, who are able to engage freely. On the contrary, NIE stresses that in reality information is seldom complete and economic

agents are influenced by different ideas (or mental models). According to North (1995) these are in part culturally derived (ie produced through the intergenerational transfer of knowledge, values and norms which vary radically among different ethnic groups and societies) and partly acquired through experience (ie which is 'local' to the particular environment). Consequently, there is immense variation in mental models, and indeed in formal educational models.

There are thus a series of transactional costs that are not recognized in the neoclassical model. The costs of transacting arise as information is costly and asymmetrically held by parties in exchange. It also includes the costs of determining price and enforcing agreements. It is the means of reducing informational and transactional costs and uncertainties that NIE argues leads to the importance of 'institutions'. Institutions in this sense are not only organizations but also traditions, rules and 'habits of thought' – an often used example of such an institution is that of property rights. Institutions are composed of formal rules (laws and relations), and informal constraints (conventions, norms of behaviour and self-imposed codes of conduct) – the latter legitimizing the former. Institutions also include the enforcement mechanisms for both. The importance of mental models, which are at least partly culturally derived, is thus recognized in NIE and this leads to the recognition that markets are only one type of social device for defining the terms of transactions. This aspect of NIE is stressed when looking at the means by which 'social dilemmas' are transcended – ie where 'rational' economic choices by individuals lead to outcomes that are socially unacceptable – echoing the concern of classical economics to reconcile private passions and public interests.

3   Recent Latin American experiences in 'participatory open councils' (*cabildos abiertos*) and in 'participatory budgeting' (*orçamento participativo*) provide examples of civil society engagement in local state decision making and budgeting respectively, thus purportedly effecting a shift from representative to participatory democracy.

CHAPTER 3

1   See Jenkins (1999b) for explanation. Reciprocity refers to mutual (and often socially obligatory) gift giving between kin and friends; and redistribution of the (again often obligatory) payment to central political or religious authorities, which use the receipts for their own maintenance as well as the provision of community services, and emergency stock for individual or communal disaster. Together with market forms of exchange these were identified by Karl Polanyi in two seminal studies (Polanyi, 1944, 1977) as the three main forms of socio-economic interaction. A reciprocal socio-economic system is thus based on symmetrical exchange in relationships, whereas redistribution is based on an institutional pattern of centricity in relationships. Redistribution can either be through the state (eg taxes and welfare), or other social organizations (churches, mutual aid societies etc).

2   The chapter draws on the author's experience as a city planner in Maputo from 1980 to 1985, as well as continued involvement from 1985 to 1993 at policy level, and more recent research work in land and housing concerning Maputo during 1998–1999. For more detail and information on the case studies see Jenkins (1998, 1999a, 1999b).

3   The general situation in Mozambique at the beginning of the 1990s was described as critical by the UN, with an estimated 1.7 million displaced people, who had lost virtually all of their possessions, as well as an estimated 2.85 million affected by

severe shortages of food and other essential items. The total population at the time was estimated at 17–18 million.

4   At a national level the project did, however, have an influence on policy in as much as it was used as a basis for the 'orientations' in the First National Meeting on Cities and Communal *Bairros*, Resolution No 5 'Urbanism'. Throughout the 1980s this short document was the only official statement of urban development guidelines. However, like many of the similar 'orientations' developed at the same time, these were never made explicit official policy, were not legislated, and were open to interpretation.

5   The full context for this discussion actually only surfaced much later, in 1992, when it was initially proposed that part of the upgraded area benefit from a World Bank Urban Rehabilitation Project, which would legalize land rights and allow development of an urban land tax as a basis for reactivated urban renewal. Despite no official reason from City Council executive members being made for refusal of this proposal, it was criticized off the record to the author as consolidating undesirable land use in a key urban area. It is precisely this area that is currently in danger of forced relocation by the City Council to allow northward expansion of the formal urban centre for higher-income groups, as all available land nearby has been already occupied (formally or informally). There is thus an urgent need to consolidate the land rights of the existing population, yet there are few appropriate mechanisms to undertake this, and possibly even less political will. See Jenkins 1998 and 2000.

6   The *Gabinete de Habitacão e Urbanizacão da Região de Maputo* (GUHRM), transformed into the National Housing Directorate (DNH) in 1979.

7   This decision was also based on the fact that with only 25 architects or planners in the whole country (six of whom were Mozambican), it was considered important to concentrate resources on training (Saevfors, 1986).

8   One positive legacy of the project was the continuation of the experimentation with development of an appropriate method of basic sanitation. This initiative continued as a separate pilot project, with technical and financial assistance from various international agencies. The project underwent several phases, with the initial involvement of the Ministry of Health (1980–1983) followed subsequently by construction cooperatives supported by the City Council (1983–1987); production units run by a special United Nations Development Programme (UNDP) assisted project in the National Physical Planning Institute (1988–1995); and more recently privatized units (1996–present). This programme is cited as one of the United Nations Centre for Human Settlements' (UNCHS) global best practices, despite its continued reliance on international agency support.

9   These activities subsequently had an influence on the deliberations of the 'First National Meeting on Urban Planning' in 1982, when guidelines were established for the priority development of basic sites and services schemes to be undertaken at a city level by the city councils, with assistance from the provincial planning delegations.

10 This programme began in an ad hoc way in 1982, but by 1985 some 10,400 plots had been demarcated with minimal state and international NGO resources – the highest rate of land demarcation before or since (Jenkins, 1999b).

11 One of the results of the 1982 First National Meeting on Urban Planning had been the commitment by the National Housing Directorate (later transformed into the National Institute for Physical Planning) to develop structural plans for the main urban areas to guide urban development and norms. A Maputo City Structure Plan was subsequently developed during 1984–1985, with an illustrative Urban District

Development 'Action Plan' to try to link physical, investment and infrastructure planning. Both these plans incorporated the Bairro Laulane residential expansion area.

12 This was the direct experience of the author in his role as chief urban planner, responsible to give a technical appreciation of all land allocations at city level. While the stress in the 1981–1984 period had been on land allocation in new urban areas within the Urbanization Programme, supported by the then City President, who had a high political profile, the change of City President in 1983 brought a new emphasis, as the new City President did not have such a political backing and sought to develop this through land allocation, principally within the already developed urban areas, to high ranking political and government officials.

13 This was never defined or monitored by the government or the World Bank. However, in practice, the objective of reaching lower-middle income groups was probably achieved, due mainly to the widespread plot occupation in the area by lower-income families before and after the project design, and the lack of any effective cost recovery. The fact that most plotholders would have difficulty in affording the project costs, together with the pressure on them to sell given the growing demand in the, as yet informal, land market for serviced residential land by middle- and upper-income groups, would probably have entailed the project eventually benefiting higher-income groups had this been applied.

14 The World Bank's own evaluation of the policy impact of the project on the other hand was 'negligible'. This, however, was extremely narrow and focused only on the issue of reducing state subsidies and implementing cost recovery. The narrow nature of the World Bank evaluation meant that this did not take into account the wider policy context, or associated activities.

15 The overall four-year project was approved in August 1988, becoming effective in February 1989. It included infrastructure rehabilitation; solid waste management; credit lines to support micro-enterprises; housing components; and support for institutional development and project administration in both Maputo and Beira (the second largest city). With a total of US$ 85 million the project thus represented by far the largest single foreign investment in urban infrastructure since independence. Twelve per cent of this amount was later cancelled. The World Bank provided US$ 60 million as a soft loan, with Finland, Spain and Mozambique sharing the majority of the remaining costs. Overall, housing components totalled US$ 23 million, including inner city housing rehabilitation (completion of 249 unfinished housing units and rehabilitation of 990 state rental apartments in the city centres with relocation of occupants to 380 new core house units on five new infill sites); upgrading of existing and provision of new housing expansion areas (1144 and 2493 plots respectively), and also provision of credit for the purchase of 1540 house construction material kits in the infill and expansion areas.

16 Defined in the early 1990s by the World Bank as urban households with cash incomes per family member below 5000 Metical/month at 1989 prices and no access to small subsistence plots in the 'Green Zones'; and peri-urban residents with limited or no access to garden plots, substantial food purchase requirements, and limited potential for cash income earning. In 1993 this included 60–70 per cent of the rural, and 50 per cent of the urban population (World Bank, 1993).

17 Possibly as this would have entailed a different target group and project description, but also in that the World Bank and the central government implementation units were not very concerned about who occupied the land, underlying the fundamental lip service to cost recovery in the project proposal as this was mainly meant to be recovered through cross subsidization of the other housing sub-

component (rehabilitation of inner city apartment blocks). This did not happen as this housing sub-component also achieved limited success – Mozambican Government counterpart funding for the three inner city buildings to be rehabilitated collapsed, leading to only 340 apartments out of the targeted 774 being rehabilitated. In addition most of the existing tenants could not afford the rehabilitated apartment rents and hence these were made available to a completely different target group. The relocation of tenants to the core units was, however, successfully completed, although these were highly subsidized.

18 Grest suggests that with changing state–civil society relations and decentralization of state power to local authority in the urban areas it will be possible for civil society coalitions to be created around local issues and for these coalitions to endorse candidates for election. This position is to some extent supported by Chichava (1997), who argues that more effective and equitable urban management in Mozambique requires the involvement of non-state actors, as well as devolution of power and responsibilities from central government. While Chichava supports the possible involvement of the private and NGO sectors, he also stresses the importance of the GDs in the interface between the state and the population. He is unclear, however, how this might be effected as he does not suggest how they might be more clearly accountable to local communities.

19 This survey was carried out on a random sample of households in a variety of neighbourhoods, developed in three key periods: before independence, after independence but before structural adjustment, and after structural adjustment. The areas surveyed included central city, peri-urban and peripheral areas, planned and unplanned, with a geographical spread across the metropolitan area of Maputo-Matola. Some 25 per cent achieved formal access, 65 per cent informal, and 10 per cent purchased (illegally).

20 Such as the Mozambican Association for Urban Development (AMDU). In general, the projects undertaken by AMDU were to be identified and implemented through the active involvement of local communities. The main areas to be covered by the projects were construction and the rehabilitation of infrastructure; health and environmental health; income generation; and education and skills training. In 1991 AMDU initiated a programme of 'participatory development and urban management' in one peri-urban area in Maputo, later expanding this to neighbouring *bairros*, and by 1996, involving some 3000 families in pre-school construction, resource centre and recreation spaces and health-related urban management projects. From 1994 it has been coordinating its activities with the City Council and has received funding from local enterprise, local and central government sources, embassies, international NGOs and some international agencies. Its impact, however, is still very restricted. See Rosario (1996).

CHAPTER 4

1 The ETPI is a non-profit joint programme of the Federation of Pakistani Chambers of Commerce and Industry (FPCCI) and the Government of the Netherlands, with the cooperation and involvement of all the chambers of commerce and industry and industrial associations. The FPCCI launched ETPI in the middle of 1996 as a five-year programme. It comprises five major components: database development, institutional networking, dissemination and communication, institutional support and training, and demonstration projects. The overall objective is:

'...*to promote the use of environmentally safe technologies for the production of environmentally safe products by Pakistan's manufacturing/industrial sector. This objective will be achieved by adopting measures of pollution abatement, waste management and recycling, chemical recovery, more efficient utilisation of natural and/or economic resources, production and installation of instrumentation and control systems for utilising the more efficient and environmentally safe production technologies.*' (National Environmental Consulting (Pvt) Ltd and Haskoning Consulting Engineers and Architects, 1996)

CHAPTER 5

1 The divisional commissioner is generally a senior officer of the provincial or federal civil service. He is appointed by the provincial government. The commissioner is the administrative head of a revenue division, responsible for an area usually consisting of more than one district, and has wide-ranging responsibilities including civil administration, law and order, and vested judicial powers. In addition, he is ex-officio chairman of the RTA and exercises considerable influence in all aspects of transport.
2 A concessionary fare is allowed to students on stage carriage services, which had a particularly adverse effect on the publicly owned services in Lahore and Faisalabad. Students are charged only a token fare for distances up to 30 km. This concession is not available for FUTS services.

CHAPTER 6

1 To the visitor to contemporary Beijing these developments are only the most recent page of the history which is written in the urban form of the city. Beijing has been China's capital with few interruptions for the past 600 years. Unlike entirely new urban areas produced in the reform period, such as Shenzhen, or cities with relatively short colonial histories such as Shanghai, the legacies of the prevailing urban regimes of the city's history remain visible and tangible in its urban forms. The Forbidden City, temples and parks, *hutongs* (Beijing's lanes), Tiananmen Square, Stalinist housing, Chinese socialist work unit compounds and new high-tech areas and business districts all reflect the social, political and economic history of the city.
2 During this period, the first streets in Beijing were paved, street lighting was introduced and the first sections of the city walls were demolished to make way for German constructed rail lines (Sit, 1995).
3 Based on the author's fieldwork carried out between 1997 and 1998.
4 The main goal of development policy was to maximize economic growth through industrialization, but government policy regarding urban development varied as attitudes shifted within the CCP between Soviet-style policies that advocated the development of cities in order to create and enlarge the urban proletariat, and Maoist policies that sought to break the link between urbanization and industrialization which had previously been a feature of both socialist and capitalist development. During this period 80 per cent of investment in the People's Republic of China (PRC) was in industry and 80 per cent of this was in heavy industry (Lieberthal, 1995).

5 Public participation took the form of ideologically directed voluntarism. Public works were completed using mass participation in voluntary projects, often aimed at providing modern infrastructure in rural areas.

6 Urban form was a result of the interaction of socialist ideology, state control and economic planning. Cities were planned according to the ideals of socialist ideology. Urban planning was one arm of the system of national socio-economic planning. In physical terms, a major emphasis was placed on spatial equity. The size of cities was strictly limited. The state controlled the vast majority of housing, and journey-to-work times between segregated areas of housing and industry was to be limited. The locations of services and shops was planned so as to provide equality of access. Traffic flows were segregated from residential areas. The city centre was to be the focus of state symbolism expressed by features such as Tiananmen Square, the world's largest public square, which was enlarged and embellished after 1949 (Bater, 1980).

7 Regulations for which were established in 1958.

8 The *hukou* system also restricted movement between cities. In order for an urban resident to legally move from one city to another people were required to obtain government approval, for which they would first have to provide a guarantee that they had employment and a place of residence in their destination city.

9 During some periods, particularly the Cultural Revolution, many people travelled extensively – ostensibly for political purposes.

10 During this period land had no value and could not be sold, rented or used as collateral for a loan.

11 French and Hamilton (1979), based on a study of eastern European cities, identified a number of distinct zones in the typical 'socialist city': historic renaissance or medieval core; inner commercial, housing and industrial zones from the capitalist era; a zone of socialist renewal where modern construction is progressively replacing earlier capitalist construction; socialist housing of the 1950s; integrated neighbourhoods and residential districts of the 1960s; isolation belts; industrial zones; and open countryside, forests, hills and tourist facilities.

12 In contrast to the pervasive intervention of the state in urban development, in rural areas development was little changed by the Communist Government and was carried out on a family or local collective-centred basis. The construction of housing in particular was a family-orientated activity (Wang and Murie, 1999).

13 Large cities became increasingly dominant in the urban system. In the 1950s there were only five cities with a population of over one million. In total these cities had a population of ten million or 25 per cent of the total urban population. By 1987 there were 23 cities with over one million population. Their total population was 29.8 million, which equated to 40.3 per cent of total urban population (Kirkby, 1985).

14 See note 11 on French and Hamilton's (1979) work.

15 Land for formal development is usually allocated in large parcels to state-owned development companies, which provide good quality modern infrastructure and then either sell the improved land to secondary developers or construct and lease buildings themselves. Examples of this type of large-scale development in Beijing include Shangdi information base to the north of Beijing's university area and Wangjing New City between the city centre and the airport.

16 Beijing has three types of district. These are the inner city (Shiqu), the urban area which includes the four districts of the core area (Chengqu) and the rural districts which are under the control of the municipal government (Jiaoqu).

17 53.7 per cent are aged between 15 and 35, compared to 32.8 per cent of Beijing natives; 66.1 per cent are male, compared to 51 per cent of Beijing natives (Beijing Municipal Statistical Bureau, 1998).

18 A major contribution to this section of the chapter was gleaned from conversations with Xiang Biao, latterly with the Department of Sociology at Peking University and currently with St Hugh's College Oxford, and also with other Chinese academics and planners, while carrying out fieldwork in Beijing between 1997 and 1998.

19 Details of these initiatives were provided by Huang Yan of the Beijing Municipal Institute of Planning and Design.

CHAPTER 7

1 In a historical perspective, there was a time that a sense of the *barangays* being consolidated as a national movement occurred. But this was during unusual political conditions which ought not to be replicated – the Martial Law period of the Marcos administration. During this time local political leaders were given additional prominence by the regime for purposes of its consolidation of political power.

CHAPTER 8

1 Between 1980 and 1982 real GNP fell 9.2 per cent; official unemployment doubled, increasing from 4.8 to 9.4 per cent; accumulated inflation reached 207 per cent; and wages dropped 30 per cent in real terms (Barahona, 1997a). As a consequence of this, between 1977 and 1983 the level of poverty rose from 25 to 34 per cent (Céspedes and Jiménez, 1995; Barahona, 1997b).

2 According to a survey undertaken by the Clinic in Pavas, 54.1 per cent of the population in Rincón Grande de Pavas is originally from San José, 36.1 per cent is from other Costa Rican provinces, and 9.8 per cent is from other Central American countries (Cordero, 1996).

3 Decentralization, understood as a process of transfer of power and duties from the centralized state apparatus to subnational (local or regional) organizations with relative material, legal and administrative autonomy, is a process that has not yet come about in Costa Rica (Rivera, 1998).

4 'Mobilized worker' is the term used for a worker who has been made redundant by a public sector organization as part of staff reduction policies.

5 According to data from the Ministry of National Planning and Economic Policy (MIDEPLAN), between 1975 and 1986 the percentage of social expenditure allocated to housing averaged 4.9 per cent and never exceeded 60 per cent, while the amounts allocated to education and health during that same period were never lower than 28 per cent and 41 per cent respectively (MIDEPLAN, 1990, cited by Valverde et al, 1993).

6 By prebends or political clientelism we mean the attainment of political favours or material or symbolic goods, in exchange for a controlled political manipulation of protest movements. This kind of practice is also rife in the majority of peasant organizations and trade unions in Costa Rica, leading to their description as 'organizations that are functional to the system' (Trejos and Valverde, 1995).

7 This electoral agreement was signed by the presidential candidate Arias Sánchez and the leaders of the housing fronts. Basically, the agreement was that the housing fronts would support this candidate in the elections in exchange for a commitment

to develop 'housing solutions' for these groups. In Costa Rica, 'housing solution' refers to any kind of response to housing need, such as the granting of a housing subsidy (*bono de vivienda*), a plot or money to build a shack (*rancho*).

8 See Valverde (1983) for an analysis of this new policy.

9 This case study draws on doctoral research undertaken by one of the authors – see Smith (1999).

CHAPTER 9

1 For a description of the historical development of urban housing for lower-income groups in South Africa, see for instance Jenkins (1997), Parnell and Hart (1999) and Wilkinson (1998).

2 Legislated for in the Native (Urban Areas) Act 1923.

3 See the 'Durban model' in Parnell and Hart (1999).

4 The Alexandra bus boycotts (1940–1945) being the other.

5 The racial groups defined by apartheid were 'African', 'Coloured', 'Asian' and 'White'. The terms are used in this chapter only in as much as this is necessary due to differential state policies.

6 In 1949 the central civil service staff numbered some 57,000, rising to 110,000 in 1958 and 139,000 in 1958 (144 per cent in 20 years), the greatest rise being in the period 1950–1960. It later rose to 213,000 in 1967 – a 53 per cent rise in 9 years (Posel, 1999).

7 This was true mainly of Johannesburg, whereas the persistence of squatting in Durban and Cape Town led to the passing of the Prevention of Illegal Squatting Act (1951). In Cape Town the squatter population was as high as 150,000 in 1948 and squatting persisted to the 1960s and (as elsewhere) resurfaced again soon after – partly due to the desire by the apartheid regime not to allow Africans permanent residence rights west of the Fish River in the Eastern Cape, and hence the refusal to provide family accommodation. This led to a further and more rigorous Prevention of Illegal Squatting Act (1977).

8 Chief Monongoaha, quoted in Barker et al (1992).

9 African voters were generally disenfranchised in 1936 in South Africa (they never had any rights in the Transvaal states before Union), with a retention of the vote for the Cape 'Coloureds' until 1956, when this was also abolished.

10 For example, whereas in Cape Town prior to 1962 the local authority had supplied some 15,000 house units, by 1982 it had supplied a further 63,000 units – an average of 3000 per year (peaking at over 8000 in 1979). These figures exclude housing provided for the African population by the Cape Divisional Council outside the municipality limits (Jenkins, 1994).

11 Homelands were areas set aside for the African population, based on eight different ethnic groups (Tswana, Xhosa, Venda, Shangaan, Swazi, Ndebele, Zulu and Southern Sotho), as legislated in the Bantu Authority Act of 1951. These were based on the previous native reserves (created initially in 1913 with only 7 per cent of the overall land area, rising to 13 per cent in 1936).

12 'Black spots' was the name given by the government to areas of 'African' settlement in designated 'white' areas.

13 Section 10 residence rights were established in the Black Urban Areas Act of 1945, giving residence rights in the urban areas to Africans who either were born there, had continuous employment for 10 years (same employer) or continuous residence for 15 years.

14 The Bantu Education Department indicated in 1976 that it would regard Afrikaans as one of the official languages of education. This led to a massive protest by school children, 20,000 from Soweto alone marching in June of that year in protest, with extremely serious police reaction. This protest then mushroomed as the 'Soweto Uprising'.

15 For more information on Crossroads, see Cole (1987), on which this draws.

16 There were many other such acts of resistance in the late 1970s and early to mid-1980s such as housing battles leading to the forming of the Port Elizabeth Black Civic Organization and Soweto Committee of Ten (later Soweto Civic Association), and the rent strikes in Durban (leading to the forming of the Joint Rent Action Group).

17 For example, proposals on issues such as the reconstruction of urban areas and rental housing and densification strategies. For more detail see Jenkins (1999b).

18 Such as agreements on providing housing credit by the private financial sector, who subsequently rigidly interpreted affordability levels despite agreeing formally to engage in lower-level lending.

19 'Housing opportunities' is the term currently used by government to include a variety of housing products – from a basic serviced site with or without a core unit to a redeveloped hostel room or flat in a rehabilitated apartment.

20 For example CAHAC (Cape Areas Housing Action Committee), formed in the 1980s in the Cape Town city area, mainly in so-called 'coloured' areas, and the Western Cape United Squatters Association (WECUSA), active in shack settlements. The Western Cape Civics Association (WCCA), mainly active in older 'black' townships, and the Western Cape Hostel Dwellers Association (WCHDA) did join SANCO.

21 For example, concerning housing, 'Making People-driven Development Work' (1994), SANCO.

22 After long negotiations SANCO agreed to participate in an alliance with ANC, SACP and COSATU.

23 This was the position put forward to the ministerial task team on housing by the construction, finance and local government sectors in 1996, leading to the dropping of the requirement to get community approval for proposed housing projects – see Jenkins (1999a).

24 As advocated by Mzwanele Mayekiso (1996).

25 As advocated by Moses Mayekiso (see Seekings, 1998).

26 Elsewhere Nzimande and Sikhosana (1995) define the difference between social movements and organs of people's power – the latter having working class leadership and the fundamental objective of the revolutionary transformation of society, while the former are issue-based pressure groups often across class lines, and do not necessarily aim for fundamental social transformation, often being reformist and conservative.

27 The federation was created in 1992 with the participation of communities from 40 settlements in South Africa and Namibia, and has established links with a number of similar organizations in other parts of the developing world. The federation is assisted by the NGO People's Dialogue and assists individuals from squatter settlements, backyard shacks and hostels to set up savings programmes that are used for small-scale loans – not only for housing. It has also created a number of Building Information and Training (BIT) centres, some of which receive state support (see Bolnick, 1993 and 1996).

CHAPTER 10

1 Salford is ranked by the DETR as the 31st most deprived local authority district in England and fourth in the north-west. In other words its social problems are bad but by no means unique.

2 Salford as currently construed only dates from the 1974 local government reorganization, when the 'old Salford' of terrace houses was aggrandized by the incorporation of 'the outer areas' – a number of previously self-governing towns such as Irlam to the west.

3 For example, 32 per cent of its households were in receipt of housing benefit, and 22 per cent were getting council tax benefit in January 1997, while one third of all pupils receive free school meals (Salford Partnership, 1998b).

4 Maisonettes are three- or four-storey blocks with two-storey houses one on top of another, or above a flat. Deck-access schemes are blocks of flats where external balconies provided 'streets in the sky' giving access to the front doors of the flats.

5 In the late 1990s the population within the administrative boundary of Salford was down to 228,400, living in 100,000 houses, 32,000 of which were still owned by the city council, although the concentration of council houses in the inner area, the pre-1974 Salford, would be higher.

6 The turnover of tenancies of Salford's local authority houses in 1998 was around 14–15 per cent of the tenancies each year.

7 In the mid-1980s the prices of houses were rising in all parts of the UK, and the idea of home ownership was strongly promoted by government and the house-building industry. In Salford the pre-1919 terraced houses were the only affordable way into owner occupation for many households (Carr, 1998). However, the inflation in the housing market in the south-east of England became so extreme that it led to a downturn in the national economy and by 1991–1992 the collapse of house prices had spread from the south-east of England to reach Salford. Falling values meant that many houses were worth less than the amount which their owners had borrowed to buy them. This is known as negative equity, and it hit the generation of 1980s first-time buyers. Properties purchased under the right to buy also went down in value, though as long as they had had large discounts, owners did not suffer negative equity. However, those who wanted to move found it hard to sell, and the best alternative option became renting, mainly to tenants on housing benefit.

8 Housing benefit is a state contribution towards the cost of house rental for people on low incomes. This state subsidy is means tested and paid directly to the landlord.

9 Their names are not referenced because they were promised anonymity when interviewed.

CHAPTER 11

1 Schuurman also argues that in developing countries many are still engaged in what are essentially non-capitalist forms of production (albeit subordinated in various ways to the dominant capitalist mode); there is a high degree of class heterogeneity; and the disarticulation between production and consumption has been the predominant situation since capitalist penetration, with growing levels in recent times due to urbanization without corresponding capital accumulation. To this can

be added the argument that the role of the state in the developing world is as much focused on controlling the factors of social reproduction as those of production, over much of which it has limited control (Simon, 1992). This puts the state in the developing world in a rather different position vis-à-vis urban social movements when it negotiates between the demands of global economic forces and local social groups.

2   In periods of repression or corruption within political systems, urban social movements are also formed in the developing world around issues of state power, but in an ad hoc way.

3   'New social movement' theory is to a great extent a critique of the reductionism of Marxism concerning the role of the working class in social change and stresses the socio-cultural nature of these movements, which it locates primarily within civil society. It criticizes the theoretical primacy awarded to economic factors of Marxism, with politics and ideology seen as secondary, as well as the assumptions concerning class as the fundamental defining agent for identification (Canel, 1997).

4   'Resource mobilization theory' – in counterpoint to new social movement theory – focuses on these processes of resources, organizational dynamics and political change that create the parameters for larger-scale processes to operate. This theoretical position is very different from that derived from 'relative deprivation' and the functionalist view that collective action arises in the abnormal conditions of rapid social change. An essential difference between new social movement and resource mobilization theories is that the former stresses discontinuity with previous social movements, while the latter sees contemporary social movements as not essentially different from these – or indeed from other types of formal organization (see Canel, 1997).

5   The availability of resources can also lead to the professionalization of social movements and more hierarchical structures being created to achieve more effective institutional change. These, however, have more difficulty in grassroots mobilization.

6   Polanyi was basically an economic historian, although his studies touched on many areas, including anthropology. Polanyi's studies concentrated on: the relation of the economy to society in 'primitive and archaic systems' and the origin, growth and transformation of 19th century capitalism (see Dalton, 1971, for an overview of Polanyi's work).

CHAPTER 12

1   An example of a research network that is close to the contributors to this book is the North–South Research Network, which aims to provide a ground for exchange and mutual learning between researchers who are based in the UK and are focusing on human settlements in the developing world, as well as a research-based resource for government, business and civil society. Wider research networks in this field are the Network-Association of European Researchers on Urbanization in the South (N-AERUS) and the Forum of Researchers on Human Settlements (FRHS), the latter established in the context of the follow up to the Habitat II conference.

REFERENCES

CHAPTER 1

Carley, M and Christie, I (2000) *Managing Sustainable Development*, Earthscan, London

Carley, M and Kirk, K (1998) *Sustainable by 2020? A Strategic Approach to Urban Regeneration for Britain's Cities*, The Policy Press, Bristol

Carley, M and Spapens, P (1998) *Sharing the World: Sustainable Living and Global Equity in the 21st Century*, Earthscan, London

Goldblatt, D (1996) *Social Theory and the Environment*, Polity Press, Cambridge

Mbeki, T (2000) 'The North Does Not Have All the Answers', reprinted in *The Independent*, 2 May

McGee, T G (1992) 'Asia's Growing Urban Rings', *United Nations University – Work in Progress*, vol 13, p9

Mitlin, D and Thompson, J (1994) *Special Issue on Participatory Tools and Methods in Urban Areas*, International Institute for Environment and Development (IIED), RRA Notes, Sustainable Agriculture and Human Settlements Programme, London

Newman, P W G and Kenworthy, J R (1989) *Cities and Automobile Dependence: A Sourcebook*, Gower, Aldershot

Robins, N and Roberts, S (1998) *Consumption in a Sustainable World*, report of workshop held in Kabelvag, Norway, IIED, London

CHAPTER 2

Castells, M (1996) *The Rise of the Network Society – The Information Age: Economy, Society and Culture*, vol I, Blackwell Publishers, Malden, Massachusets and Oxford, UK

Friedmann, J and Douglass, M (1998) Editors' Introduction in Douglass, M and Friedmann, J (eds) *Cities for Citizens: Planning and the Rise of Civil Society in a Global Age*, John Wiley & Sons, Chichester

Harvey, D (1990) *The Condition of Postmodernity: An Enquiry into the Origins of Cultural Change*, Blackwell, Cambridge, Massachusetts and Oxford, UK

Healey, P (1995) 'Discourses of Integration: Making Frameworks for Democratic Urban Planning' in Healey, P, Cameron, S, Davoudi, S, Graham, S and Madani-Pour, A (eds) *Managing Cities: The New Urban Context*, John Wiley & Sons, Chichester

Healey, P (1997) *Collaborative Planning: Shaping Places in Fragmented Societies*, Macmillan Press, Basingstoke

Leys, C (1996) *The Rise and Fall of Development Theory*, James Currey, London
Lloyd, J (2000) in *Scotland on Sunday*, 9 January
North, D C (1995) 'The New Institutional Economics and Third World Development' in Harriss, J, Hunter, J and Lewis, C (eds) *The New Institutional Economics and Third World Development*, Routledge, London
Swyngedouw, E (1986) 'The Socio-spatial Implications of Innovations in Industrial Organization', Working Paper no 20, John Hopkins European Center for Regional Planning and Research, Lille

CHAPTER 3

Abrahamsson, H and Nilsson, A (1995) *Mozambique: The Troubled Transition*, Zed Books, London
Azarya, V (1994) 'Civil Society and Disengagement in Africa' in Harbeson, J W, Rothchild, D and Chazan, N (eds) *Civil Society and the State in Africa*, Boulder, London
Braathen, E and Jørgensen, B V (1998) 'Democracy Without People? Local Government Reform and 1998 Municipal Elections in Mozambique', *Lusotopie*, 1998, pp31–38
Chichava, J A Da C (1997) *Urban Management in Mozambique: With Particular Reference to the Capital City, Maputo*, PhD Thesis, Department of City and Regional Planning, Cardiff
Ekeh, P (1975) 'Colonialism and the Two Publics in Africa: a Theoretical Statement', *Comparative Studies in Society and History*, vol 17, no 1
Grest, J (1997, unpublished draft) 'Maputo City, Mozambique: Global Pressures, Local Responses and the Invention of Civil Society'
Hirschmann, A O (1970) *Exit, Voice and Loyalty: Responses to Decline in Firms, Organizations and States*, Harvard University Press, Cambridge, Mass
Jenkins, P (1990) 'Mozambique' in Mathey, K (ed) *Housing Policies in the Socialist Third World*, Mansell, London
Jenkins, P (1991) *Housing and Living Conditions in two Peri-urban Bairros of Maputo City*, UNDP-UNCHS Project MOZ/86/005, Maputo
Jenkins, P (1998) *National and International Shelter Policy Initiatives in Mozambique: Housing the Urban Poor at the Periphery*, vols 1 and 2, PhD Thesis, Centre for Environment & Human Settlements, School of Planning and Housing, Edinburgh College of Art/Heriot-Watt University, Edinburgh
Jenkins, P (1999a) 'Maputo City: The Historical Roots of Under-development and the Consequences in Urban Form', School of Planning & Housing Paper no 71, Edinburgh
Jenkins, P (1999b) 'Emerging Land and Housing Markets in Maputo City', School of Planning & Housing Paper No 72, Edinburgh
Jenkins, P (2000) 'Urban Management, Urban Poverty and Urban Governance: Planning and Land Management in Maputo, Mozambique', *Environment & Urbanization*, vol 12, no 1, pp137–152
Polanyi, K (1944) *The Great Transformation*, Reinhart and Co, New York
Polanyi, K (1977) *The Livelihood of Man*, Academic Press, New York
Rosario, M (1996) 'Pfuka Bzixile – Wake Up It's Dawn. 1991–1996 Sustainable Development Experience in the Maputo Peri-urban Quarters – Participatory Development and Urban Management', Associação Moçambicana para o Desenvolvimento Urbano AMDU, Maputo

Saevfors, I (1986) *Maxaquene: A Comprehensive Account of the First Upgrading Experience in the New Mozambique*, UNESCO, New York

White, G (ed) (1985) *Revolutionary Socialist Development in the Third World*, Wheatsheaf Books, Brighton

World Bank (1993) *From Emergency to Sustainable Development*, World Bank, Mozambique

CHAPTER 4

Afsah, S, Laplante, B and Wheeler, D (1996) *Controlling Industrial Pollution: A New Paradigm*, Policy Research Working Paper no 1672, Policy Research Department, The World Bank, Washington DC

Cribb, R (1990) The Politics of Pollution Control in Indonesia, *Asian Survey* vol XXX, no 12, pp1123–1135

Dawn (2000) Internet edition, http://DAWN.com, May 15

Environmental Protection Agency Punjab (1993) *Punjab Urban Environmental Project, Project Preparation*, Main Report, vol 1, Environmental Protection Agency Punjab, Lahore

Government of Pakistan (1996) *Economic Survey 1995–1996*, Government of Pakistan, Finance Division, Economic Advisor's Wing, Islamabad

Government of Pakistan/Joint Research Committee – International Union for the Conservation of Nature and Natural Resources (1992) *The Pakistan National Conservation Strategy*, Government of Pakistan/IUCN, Karachi

Government of the Punjab (1973) *Master Plan for Greater Lahore*, Housing and Physical Planning Department, Government of the Punjab, Lahore

Government of the Punjab (1998) *Directory of Registered Factories*, Bureau of Statistics, Government of Punjab, Lahore

Hameed, R and Raemaekers, J (in press) 'Environmental Regulation of Industry in Lahore, Pakistan', *Third World Planning Review*

Hameed, R and Raemaekers, J (1999) *Putting Over the Message: A Programme in Pakistan to Build Capacity for Pollution Abatement Among Industrialists*, Paper presented at the 16th Inter-Schools Conference on Communicating for Development, University of Westminster, London, 11–13 April, 1999

Hartman, R S, Huq, M and Wheeler, D (1997) *Why Paper Mills Clean Up: Determinants of Pollution Abatement in Four Asian Countries*, Working Paper no 1710, Policy Research Department, The World Bank, Washington, DC

Hettige, H, Huq, M, Pargal, S and Wheeler, D (1996) 'Determinants of Pollution Abatement in Developing Countries: Evidence from South and Southeast Asia', *World Development*, vol 24, no 12, pp1891–1904

Huq, M and Wheeler, D (1993) *Pollution Reduction Without Formal Regulation: Evidence from Bangladesh*, Working Paper no 1993–39, Environment Department, The World Bank, Washington, DC

Khator, R (1991) *Environment, Development and Politics in India*, University Press of America, Lanham, New York and London

Lahore Development Authority/World Bank/International Development Agency (1980) *Lahore Urban Development and Traffic Study: Urban Planning, Final Report*, vol 1-A, Lahore Development Authority, Lahore

Ministry of Environment, Local Government and Rural Development (1997) *Pollution and Monitoring Survey of the River Ravi, Annex A to the Main Report*, Draft Report

TA 2276–PAK, Ministry of Environment, Local Government and Rural Development, Government of Pakistan, Islamabad

National Environmental Consulting (Pvt) Ltd and Haskoning Consulting Engineers and Architects (1996) *Environmental Technology Program for Industry, Progress Report, September–November 1996*, FPCCI/Government of the Netherlands, Karachi

Prior, A (in press) 'Bridging the Compliance Gap in Environmental Regulation: Problems in the Theory and Practice of Planning Enforcement', *Planning Theory and Practice*

Qadeer, M A (1983) *Urban Development in the Third World*, Praeger Publishers, New York

World Bank (2000) *Greening Industry: New Roles for Communities, Markets and Governments*, Oxford University Press, Oxford, UK

Younas, M, Afzal, S, Khan, M I, Jaffery, I N H and Farooq, M (1997) 'Forms of Cd, Pb, Zn and Cr in Contaminated Soils of Raiwind, Lahore Pakistan', 8th National Chemistry Conference, 1997, University of the Punjab, Lahore, Pakistan, quoted in Younas, M, Shahzad, F, Afzal, S, Khan, M I and Ali, K (1998) 'Assessment of Cd, Ni, Cu, and Pb Pollution in Lahore, Pakistan', *Environment International*, vol 24, pp761–66

CHAPTER 5

Anjum, G A and Russell, J R E (1997) 'Public Transport Regulation Through a Government Organised NGO: The Faisalabad Experience in Pakistan', *Transport Reviews*, vol 17, no 2, pp105–120

Armstrong-Wright, A (1993) *Public Transport in Third World Cities*, HMSO, London

Armstrong-Wright, A and Thiriez, S (1987) *Bus Services: Reducing Costs, Raising Standards*, World Bank Technical Paper, no 68, The World Bank, Washington, DC

Briggs, D A (1989) 'A Model for the Analysis of Urban Public Transport Operations, Costs and Fares Under Conditions of Highly Fragmented Ownership', *Proceedings of Seminar M*, PTRC, Summer Annual Meeting

Darbera, R (1993) 'Deregulation of Urban Transport in Chile: What Have We Learned in the Decade 1979–1989?', *Transport Reviews*, vol 13, no 1, pp45–59

Faisalabad Divisional Commissioner (1994) Master Plan of Faisalabad, Office of the Divisional Commissioner, Faisalabad

Faisalabad Urban Transport Society (1993) *Constitution of the Faisalabad Urban Transport Society* (FUTS), Faisalabad

Government of Pakistan (1995) *Greater Islamabad/Rawalpindi Area Transportation Study* (GIRATS), Draft final report, Ministry of Communications, Islamabad

Gwilliam, K M (1997) 'Ownership, Organisation and Competition Policy: An International Review', *Proceedings of the Fifth International Conference on Competition and Ownership in Land Passenger Transport*, University of Leeds, Leeds

Hague, C (1997) 'The Road from Istanbul: The Challenge of Habitat II for Planners and Architects', *Proceedings of the 14th Inter-Schools Conference on Global and Local Development: New Agendas, New Partnerships*, School of Planning and Housing, Edinburgh College of Art/Heriot-Watt University, Edinburgh, March

Idris, K M (1996) *A Preliminary Evaluation of Faisalabad Urban Transport Society*, Transport Research Centre, Government of Pakistan, The Planning Commission, Islamabad

Kwakye, E A (1994) 'A Multi-disciplinary Approach to the Urban Transport Problems in Ghana', *Third World Planning Review*, vol 17, no 4, pp421–438.

Roth, G and Diandas, J (1995) 'Alternative Approaches to Improving Route Bus Services in Sri Lanka', paper presented at *4th International Conference on Competition and Ownership in Land Passenger Transport*, Rotorua, New Zealand

Russell, J R E and Anjum, G A (1996) 'Recent Developments in Urban Public Transport in Pakistan', paper presented at *Association of Collegiate Schools of Planning – Association of European Schools of Planning (ACSP–AESOP) Joint International Conference*, Toronto, July

Russell, J R E and Anjum, G A (1997) 'Public Transport and Urban Development in Pakistan', *Transport Reviews*, vol 17, no 1, pp61–80

Russell, J R E and Anjum, G A (1999) 'Optimising Urban Public Transport Regulation in Pakistan? The Faisalabad NGO Model', *Third World Planning Review*, vol 21, no 2, pp63–82

United Nations (1996) *The Habitat Agenda: Goals and Principles, Commitments and Global Plan of Action*, United Nations Conference on Human Settlements – Habitat II, Istanbul, Turkey, 3–14 June

Chapter 6

Bater, J H (1980) *The Soviet City: Ideal and Reality*, Edward Arnold

Beijing Municipal Statistical Bureau (1998) *Beijing Statistical Yearbook 1998*, China Statistical Publishing House, Beijing

Berger, P L and Neuhaus (1977) *To Empower People: The Role of Mediating Structures in Public Policy*, American Enterprise Institution for Public Policy Research, Washington, DC

Burgess, E W (1925) 'The Growth of the City' in Park, R E, Burgess, E W and Mackenzie, R D (eds) *The City*, The University of Chicago Press, Chicago

Castells, M and Sheridan, A (1977) *The Urban Question: A Marxist Approach*, Edward Arnold

Chan, K W (1994) *Cities with Invisible Walls: Reinterpreting Urbanization in Post-1949 China*, Oxford University Press, Hong Kong

Chan, K W (1996) 'Post-Mao China: A Two-Class Urban Society in the Making', *International Journal of Urban and Regional Research*, vol 20, no 1

Davis, D et al (eds) (1995) *Urban Spaces in Contemporary China: The Potential for Autonomy in Post-1949 China*, Cambridge University Press, Cambridge, UK

French, R and Hamilton, F E I (1979) *The Socialist City – Spatial Structure and Urban Policy*, John Wiley & Sons, Chichester, UK

Kirkby, R J R (1985) *Urbanization in China: Town and Country in a Developing Economy 1949–2000 AD*, Croom Helm, London and Sydney

Lewis, O (1976a) *The Children of Sanchez: Autobiography of a Mexican Family*, Penguin

Lewis, O (1976b) *Five Families: Mexican Case Studies in the Culture of Poverty*, Souvenir Press

Lieberthal, K (1995) *Governing China: From Revolution Through Reform*, W W Norton & Company, New York and London

Liu, X and Liang, W (1997) 'Zhejiangcun: Social and Spatial Implications of Informal Urbanisation on the Periphery of Beijing', *Cities*, vol 14, no 2, pp95–108

Ma, L and Hanten, (1981) *Urban Development in Modern China*, Westview Press, Boulder, Colorado

Ma, L and Xiang B (1998) 'Native Place, Migration and the Emergence of Peasant Enclaves in Beijing', *China Quarterly*, 1998, pp546–581

Nee, V (1989) 'A Theory of Market Transition: From Redistributive to Markets in State Socialism', *American Sociological Review*, vol 54

Nee, V (1992) 'Organisational Dynamics of Market Transition: Hybrid Forms, Property Rights and Mixed Economy in China', *Administrative Science Quarterly*, vol 37

Nee, V and Su, S (1996) 'Institutions, Social Ties, and Commitment in China's Corporatist Transformation' in McMillan, J and Naughton, B (eds) *Reforming Asian Socialism: The Growth of Market Institutions*, Michigan Press, Ann Arbour

Parriss, K (1993) 'Local Initiative and National Reform: The Wenzhou Model of Development', *China Quarterly*, no 134

Rowe, W (1986) *Hankow: Commerce and Society in a Chinese City, 1796 to 1889*, University of California Press, US

Russell, J (1971) *China's Economic Development Since 1949 – A 'Maoist' Model of Development*, Edinburgh College of Art Research Paper

Sit (1995) *Beijing, The Nature and Planning of a Chinese Capital City*, John Wiley and Sons, Chichester, UK

Wang, Y P and Murie, A (1999) *Housing Policy and Practice in China*, MacMillan, UK

Xiang, B (1998) 'There is a Zhejiang Village in Beijing (Beijing youge Zhejiangcun)', *Sociology and Social Investigation*, vol 3

Xiaoli, L and Wei, L (1997) 'Zhejiangcun: Social and Spatial Implications of Informal Urbanization on the Periphery of Beijing', *Cities*, vol 14, no 2, pp95–108

CHAPTER 7

Abracosa, R (1996a) *DENR Institutional Strengthening: Managing the Urban Environment*, Department of Environment and Natural Resources, Manila

Abracosa, R (1996b) 'Managing the Urban Environment', presented at the lecture forum on Urban Environmental Management and Sustainable Development, Development Academy of the Philippines, Pasig City

Basaen, I M (1996) 'Capacity 21: Philippine Perspectives and Experiences on Sustainable Development', prepared for a seminar on Urban Environmental Management, Davao City

Bautista, J R (1999) 'Preliminary Outcomes of Fieldwork on Barangays in Metro Manila', unpublished paper

Cabanilla, A R Q (1996) *Towards a Framework Plan for Sustainable Development*, MMDA, Manila

Carley, M (1999) 'Neighbourhoods: Building Blocks of National Sustainable Development', *Town and Country Planning*, vol 68, no 2, February, p59

Carley, M and Spapens, P (1998) *Sharing the World: Sustainable Living and Global Equity in the 21st Century*, Earthscan, London

Carley, M and Kirk, K (1999) *City-wide Urban Regeneration: Lessons from Good Practice*, The Scottish Executive, Edinburgh

Carley, M and Christie, I (2000) *Managing Sustainable Development*, Earthscan, London

Development Academy of the Philippines (1996) *State of the Philippine Ecosystems, and Metro Manila: A Briefer*, DAP, Manila

Frenkel, M (1986) 'The Distribution of Legal Powers in Pluricentral Systems' in Morgan, R (ed) *Regionalism in European Politics*, Policy Studies Institute, London

Furedy, C (1992) 'Garbage: Exploring Non-Conventional Options in Asian Cities', *Environment and Urbanization*, vol 4, no 2, pp42–61

Gozun, E (1994a) 'Community Governance in Urban Environmental Management', *The Urban Environment*, vol 1, no 4, p1

Gozun, E (1994b) 'Business and Community: Waste Minimisation in Metro Manila', *The Urban Environment*, vol 1, no 6, p2

Gozun, E (1996) 'The Situation of the Urban Environment in Metro Manila', paper presented at the Forum on Urban Environmental Management for Sustainable Development, Manila

Hardoy, J E, Mitlin, D and Satterthwaite, D (1992) *Environmental Problems in Third World Cities*, Earthscan, London

Local Government Code (1991), RA 7160 (Code); Implementing Rules and Regulations (IRR), Manila

Owen, S (1995) 'From "Predict and Provide" to "Predict and Prevent": Pricing and Planning in Transport Policy', *Transport Policy*, vol 2, no 1, pp43–49

Republic of the Philippines, (1994) 'An Act Creating the Metro Manila Development Authority', Republic Act 7924, Manila

Sharp, R (1992) 'Organizing for Change: People-Power and the Role of Institutions' in Holmberg, J (ed) *Policies for A Small Planet*, Earthscan, London

Smith, B C (1985) *Decentralisation: The Territorial Dimension of the State*, Allen and Unwin, London

CHAPTER 8

Barahona, M A (1997a) 'El Desarrollo Económico' in Quesada, J R (ed) *Costa Rica Contemporánea: Raíces del Estado de la Nación*, Proyecto Estado de la Nación, San José

Barahona, M A (1997b) 'El Desarrollo Social' in Quesada, J R (ed) *Costa Rica Contemporánea: Raíces del Estado de la Nación*, Proyecto Estado de la Nación, San José

Céspedes, V H and Jiménez, R (1995) *Pobreza en Costa Rica: Concepto, Medición y Evolución*, Academia de Centroamérica, San José

Chaves, E and Alfaro, L A (1990) *La Comisión Especial de Vivienda en el Marco de la Política de Vivienda de Interés Social en la Administración Arias-Sánchez (1986–1990)*, Dissertation, Escuela de Antropología y Sociología, Facultad de Ciencias Sociales, Universidad de Costa Rica, San José

Chávez, E M, Fallas, S P, Sancho, M A, Sancho, C M, Ruíz, M V and Vargas, Y (1989) *La Autoconstrucción Como Alternativa de Solución Para el Problema de Vivienda*, Escuela de Trabajo Social, Facultad de Ciencias Sociales, Universidad de Costa Rica, San José

Cordero, A (1996) 'Sistematización de Diagnósticos de Rincón Grande de Pavas', Equipo Interagencial de Naciones Unidas (Photocopy)

Cuevas, F (1997) 'Estudio de Caso: Rincón Grande de Pavas: Una Experiencia Gobierno Facilitador en la Autogestión Comunitaria', paper, MIVAH/HABITAT/UNDP, San José

Lara, S and Molina, E (1997) 'Participation and Popular Democracy in the Committees for the Struggle for Housing in Costa Rica' in Kaufman, M and Dilla, H (eds) *Community Power and Grassroots Democracy: The Transformation of Social Life*, Zed Books, London and New York

Molina, E (1990) *Repercusiones Político-organizativas del Acuerdo Político Firmado Entre los Frentes de Vivienda y el Estado Durante la Administración Arias Sánchez*, MSc Dissertation, Universidad de Costa Rica, San José

MIDEPLAN (1990) *El Desarrollo Social en el Largo Plazo*, MIDEPLAN, San José

Paz, G (1998) *Una Patria de Propietarios y no de Proletarios*, EUNA, Heredia

Rivera, R (1998) *La Descentralización Real en Costa Rica*, FLACSO San José

Rojas, M (ed) (1989) *Costa Rica, la Democracia Inconclusa*, DEI, San José

Smith, H (1999) *Networks and Spaces of Negotiation in Low-Income Housing: The Case of Costa Rica*, PhD Thesis, Centre for Environment & Human Settlements, School of Planning and Housing, Edinburgh College of Art/Heriot-Watt University, Edinburgh

Touraine, A (1997) *Podremos Vivir Juntos? Iguales y Diferentes*, PPC, Madrid

Trejos, M E (1991) 'Posibilidades y limitaciones del solidarismo en la Industria', unpublished paper

Trejos, M E and Valverde, J M (1995) *Las Organizaciones del Magisterio Frente al Ajuste*, Cuaderno de Ciencias Sociales No. 80, FLACSO, San José

Trejos, M E (1997) *Relaciones Laborales y Reestructuración del Estado en Costa Rica*, EUNA, Heredia

United Nations (1987) *Global Report on Human Settlements 1986*, Oxford University Press, Oxford

Valverde, J M (1983) 'Vivienda Digna o Tugurio Institucional', *Aportes*, no 16, San José

Valverde, J M (1996) *Informe de Investigación Etapa I (Versión final). Participación Comunal/Autogestión Comunitaria y Gobierno Facilitador: El Caso de Costa Rica*, PROFAC, San José

Valverde, J M (1998) 'Descentralización y Política Social' in UNICEF (ed) *Política Social y Descentralización en Costa Rica*, UNICEF, San José

Valverde, J M, Donato, E and Rivera, R (1989) 'Costa Rica: Movimientos Sociales y Populares y Democracia' in Rojas, M (ed) *Costa Rica, la Democracia Inconclusa*, DEI, San José

Valverde, J M, Trejos, ME and Mora, M (1993) *Integración o Disolución Sociocultural: El Nuevo Rostro de la Política Social*, Editorial Porvenir, San José

Vega, J L (1987) 'Aspectos Organizativos y Estratégicos del Desarrollo Comunal en Costa Rica', mimeo, San José

CHAPTER 9

Barker, B J, Carter, C, Leroux, V and Robertson, H (1992) *Illustrated History of South Africa: The Real Story*, Readers Digest Association, Cape Town

Bolnick, J (1993) 'The People's Dialogue on Land and Shelter: Community-Driven Networking in South Africa's Informal Settlements', *Environment & Urbanization*, vol 5, no 1, pp91–110

Bolnick, J (1996) 'uTshani Buyakhuluma (The grass speaks): People's Dialogue and the South African Homeless People's Federation (1994-96)', *Environment & Urbanization*, vol 8, no 2, pp153–170

Cole, J (1987) *Crossroads: The Politics of Reform and Repression 1976–1986*, Ravan Press, Johannesburg

Isaacs, AH (1989) 'Crossroads: The Rise and Fall of a Squatter Movement in Cape Town, South Africa' in Schuurman, F and Naersen, T (eds) *Urban Social Movements in the Third World*, Routledge, London

Jenkins, P (1994) 'State-Managed Housing Stock in Cape Town – a discussion paper', Community and Urban Services Support Project, unpublished

Jenkins, P (1997) 'Policies and Praxis for Housing the Urban Poor in the New South Africa – A Case of Old Wine in New Bottles or New Wine in Old Bottles?', *Conference Proceedings, 14th Inter-Schools Conference on Development*, School of

Planning and Housing, Edinburgh College of Art/Heriot-Watt University, Edinburgh

Jenkins, P (1999a) 'The Role of Civil Society in Housing Policy Development: Some Lessons from Southern Africa', *Third World Planning Review*, vol 21, no 2

Jenkins, P (1999b) 'Difficulties Encountered in Community Involvement in Housing Delivery under the New South African Housing Policy', *Habitat International*, vol 23, no 4, pp431–446

Marais, H (1998) *South Africa – Limits to Change: The Political Economy of Transition*, Zed Books, London

Mayekiso, M (1996) *Township Politics: Civic Struggles for a New South Africa*, Monthly Review Press, New York

Nzimande B and Sikhosana M (1995) 'Civil Society: A Theoretical Survey and Critique of some South African Conceptions' in Sachikonye, LM (ed) *Democracy, Civil Society and the State: Social Movements in Southern Africa*, SAPES Trust, Zimbabwe

Parnell, S and Hart, H (1999) 'Self-help Housing as a Flexible Instrument of State Control in Twentieth Century South Africa', *Housing Studies*, vol 14, no 3, pp367–386

Posel, D (1999) 'Does Size Matter? The Apartheid State's Power of Penetration' in Judin, H and Vladislavic, I (eds) *blank...architecture, apartheid and after*, NAi, Rotterdam

Seekings, J (1998) 'No Home for Revolutionaries: The Structures and Activities of the South African National Civics Organisation in Metropolitan Cape Town, 1996–97' *Urban Forum*, vol 9, no 1, pp1–36

Silk, A (1981) *A Shanty Town in South Africa*, Ravan Press, Johannesburg

Swilling M (1999) 'Rival Futures: Struggle Visions, Post-Apartheid Choices' in Judin, H and Vladislavic, I (eds) *blank...architecture, apartheid and after*, NAi, Rotterdam

Wilkinson, P (1998) 'Housing Policy in South Africa', *Habitat International*, vol 22, no 3, pp215–229

CHAPTER 10

Bramley, G (1997) 'Housing Policy: A Case of Terminal Decline?', *Policy & Politics*, vol 25, no 1, pp387–407

Bramley, G (1998) 'Housing Surpluses and Housing Need' in Lowe, S, Spencer, S and Keenan, P (eds) *Housing Abandonment in Britain: Studies in the Causes and Effects of Low Demand Housing*, Centre for Housing Policy, University of York, York

Carr, G (1998) Transcript of interview on 14 December 1998 with Geoff Carr of Carr and Hulme, Estate Agents, 7 Station Road, Swinton

City of Salford (1998) *Unitary Development Plan: Draft Issues Paper: UDP Review 2001–2016*, City of Salford, Salford

Hague, C (1990) 'The Development and Politics of Tenant Participation in British Council Housing', *Housing Studies*, vol 5, pp242–256

Lowe, S, Spencer, S and Keenan, P (eds) (1998) *Housing Abandonment in Britain: Studies in the Causes and Effects of Low Demand Housing*, Centre for Housing Policy, University of York, York

Malpass, P (1990) *Reshaping Housing Policy*, Routledge, London

Mitchell, M (1998) Transcript of interview on 30 November 1998 with Maggie Mitchell, Assistant Director (Housing Management), Salford City Council Housing Department

Molloy, J (1998) Transcript of interview on 1 December 1998 with John Molloy,

Principal Officer (Rehousing), Salford City Council Housing Department

Osborne, R (1998) Transcript of interview on 1 December 1998 with Bob Osborne, Assistant Director (Strategy), Salford City Council Housing Department

Pawson, H, Kearns, A, Keoghan, M, Malcolm, J and Morgan, J (1997) *Managing Voids and Difficult to Let Property*, Housing Corporation, London

Power, A and Mumford, K (1999) *The Slow Death of Great Cities? Urban Abandonment or Urban Renaissance?* York Publishing Services for the Joseph Rowntree Foundation, York

Robson, R (1988) *Those Inner Cities: Reconciling the Social and Economic Aims of Urban Policy*, Oxford University Press, Oxford

Salford Partnership (1998a) *City of Salford Economic Development Strategy and Action Plan 1998/99*, Salford City Council, Salford

Salford Partnership (1998b) *Building Sustainable Communities: A Regeneration Strategy for Salford*, Salford City Council, Salford

Scottish Development Department (1977) *Scottish Housing: A Consultative Document*, Cmd 6852, HMSO, Edinburgh

Scottish Housing Advisory Committee (1970) *Council House Communities*, HMSO, Edinburgh

Townsend, J (1998) Transcript of interview on 30 November 1998 with J Townsend, Deputy Director, Salford City Council Housing Dept

CHAPTER 11

Canel (1997) 'New Social Movement Theory and Resource Mobilisation Theory: The Need for Integration' in Kaufman, M and Dilla, H (eds) *Community Power and Grassroots Democracy: The Transformation of Social Life*, Zed Books, London and New Jersey

Castells, M (1983) *The City and the Grassroots: A Cross-Cultural Theory of Urban Social Movements*, Edward Arnold, London

Dalton, G (ed) (1971) *Primitive Archaic and Modern Economies: Essays of Karl Polanyi*, Beacon Press, Boston

McCarney, P L (1996) 'Considerations on the Notion of "Governance" – New Directions for Cities in the Developing World' in McCarney, P L (ed) *Cities and Governance: New Directions in Latin America, Asia and Africa*, University of Toronto, Toronto

McCarney, P, Halfani, M and Rodriguez, A (1995) 'Towards an Understanding of Governance' in Stren, R and Bell, J K (eds) *Urban Research in the Developing World, vol 4: Perspectives on the City*, University of Toronto, Toronto

Saschikonye, L (1995) 'Democracy, Civil Society and Social Movements: An Analytical Framework', in Sachikonye, L (ed) *Democracy, Civil Society and the State: Social Movements in Southern Africa*, Harare, SAPES Books

Schuurman, F J (1989) 'Urban Social Movements: Between Regressive Utopia and Socialist Panacea', in Schuurman, F J and van Naerssen, T (eds) *Urban Social Movements in the Third World*, Routledge, London and New York

Simon, D (1992) *Cities, Capital and Development: African Cities in the World Economy*, Belhaven, London

CHAPTER 12

Cabinet Office (2000) *A National Strategy for Neighbourhood Renewal: A Framework for Consultation*, HMSO, London

Carley, M (1999) 'Neighbourhoods – Building Blocks of National Sustainability', *Town & Country Planning*, vol 68, no 2, February, pp58–60

Carley, M and Christie, I (2000, revised edition) *Managing Sustainable Development*, Earthscan, London

Carley, M, Chapman, M, Hastings, A, Kirk, K and Young, R (2000) *Urban Regeneration Through Partnership*, The Policy Press, Bristol

Chambers, R (1994) 'The Origins and Practice of Participatory Rural Appraisal', *World Development*, vol 22, no 7, pp953–969

Freire, P (1972) *Pedagogy of the Oppressed*, Penguin Books, Harmondsworth, Middlesex

Freire, P (1974) *Education: The Practice of Freedom*, Writers and Readers Publishing Cooperative, London

Green, R (1995) 'Out of the Straitjacket, Onto the Moral High Ground', *Town and Country Planning*, vol 64, no 7, July

Hamdi, N and Goethert, R (1997) *Action Planning for Cities: A Guide to Community Practice*, John Wiley & Sons, London

Healey, P (1979) 'Networking as a Normative Principle with Particular Reference to Local Government and Land Use Planning', *Local Government Studies*, vol 5, no1, pp55–68

Healey, P (1997) *Collaborative Planning: Shaping Places in Fragmented Societies*, Macmillan, London and Basingstoke

Mitlin, D and Thompson, J (1995) 'Participatory Approaches in Urban Areas: Strengthening Civil Society or Reinforcing the Status Quo?', *Environment and Urbanization*, vol 7, no 1, pp231–250

Rydin, Y (1999) 'Public Participation in Planning' in Cullingworth, J B (ed) *British Planning: 50 Years of Urban and Regional Policy*, Athlone Press, London

Srinivasan, L (1990) *Tools for Community Participation: A Manual for Training Trainers in Participatory Techniques*, PROWWESS/UNDP–World Bank Sanitation Programme, Washington

Stoker, G (1995) 'Regime Theory and Urban Politics' in Judge, D, Stoker, G and Wolman, H (eds) *Theories of Urban Politics*, SAGE, London, Thousand Oaks and New Delhi

Turner, J F C (1996) 'Tools for Building Community: An Examination of 13 Hypotheses', *Habitat International*, vol 20, no 3, pp339–347

Turner, J F C and Fitcher, R (1972) *Freedom to Build: Dweller Control of the Housing Process*, Macmillan, London and Basingstoke

Wates, N (2000) *The Community Planning Handbook*, Earthscan, London

Wilcox, D (1994) *The Guide to Effective Participation*, Partnership Books, Brighton

INDEX

*Information in notes is indexed in the form 201*n1(ch2), *ie note 1 on page 201, in the section referring to Chapter 2*

ENVIRONMENTAL PROBLEMS IN AN URBANIZING WORLD

Finding Solutions for Cities in Africa, Asia and Latin America

Jorge E Hardoy, Diana Mitlin and David Satterthwaite

This is an updated and much expanded version of the classic *Environmental Problems in Third World Cities*, describing the scale, nature and causes of environmental problems, and who bears the costs. It covers environmental impacts at all levels, from the household to the region, surveying issues such as rural–urban division, sanitation, pollution and institutional factors such as Local Agenda 21 and international finance. Stressing the centrality of sustainability to future urban development the authors present a new environmental agenda for cities, highlighting in particular the many innovative ways in which environmental problems are being addressed by low income communities themselves and the national and international framework needed to support local action.

£15.95   paperback   ISBN 1 85383 719 9   forthcoming 2001
£40.00   hardback   ISBN 1 85383 720 2

MUNICIPALITIES AND COMMUNITY PARTICIPATION

A Sourcebook for Capacity Building

Janelle Plummer

'A rich source of case studies and analysis'
Foreword by **David Satterthwaite**

Poor urban communities are increasingly involved in the delivery of services and infrastructure. The state has largely withdrawn leaving municipal authorities in charge of urban development policy, but often without the organizational or resource capacity to cope. This sourcebook presents a comprehensive account of the capacities needed for community participation to work. It sets out the options, stages and forms of participation involved in delivering services to urban communities. It also lays out the management structures, systems, skills and attitudes needed.

£20.00   paperback   1 85383 744 X

CITIES IN A GLOBALIZING WORLD

Global Report on Human Settlements 2001

United Nations Centre for Human Settlements (Habitat)

This major and influential report is successor to the Global Report 1996. It is the most reliable and comprehensive assessment of the world's cities and shelter conditions and is an essential tool and reference for academics, researchers, planners, public authorities and civil society organizations around the world. The 2001 report highlights the impacts of globalization and the influence of market forces on urban and housing policies. It studies the increased isolation and marginalization of the urban and rural poor and other vulnerable social groups and documents current housing and urban conditions, including access to basic services, proposing policies and initiatives for improved quality of life across all sectors of urban society.

£20.00   paperback   ISBN 1 85383 806 3   forthcoming 2001
£55.00   hardback   ISBN 1 85383 805 5

THE COMMUNITY PLANNING HANDBOOK

How People can Shape their Cities, Towns and Villages in Any Part of the World

Nick Wates

'In the global, cyberspace age, government and business need communities as much as communities need them. Nick Wates' timely book is essential reading for ordinary people and professionals who believe that the opportunities being thrown up by this new balance are there for the taking'
Mark Hepworth, Director, The Local Futures Group, London, UK

Growing numbers of residents are getting involved with professionals in shaping their local environment. *The Community Planning Handbook* is the essential starting point for all those involved – planners and local authorities, architects and other practitioners, community workers, students and local residents – with an accessible how-to-do-it style, best practice information on effective methods, and international scope and relevance. The glossary, bibliography and contact details provide quick access to further information and support.

£14.95   paperback   ISBN 1 85383 654 0

Orders to EARTHSCAN
FREEPOST 1, 120 PENTONVILLE ROAD, LONDON N1 9JR
Fax: +44 (0)20 7278 1142
email: earthinfo@earthscan.co.uk
www.earthscan.co.uk
